TERMINAL CHOICES

TERMINAL CHOICES

Euthanasia, Suicide,
and the
Right to Die

by

Robert N. Wennberg

William B. Eerdmans Publishing Company
Grand Rapids, Michigan

The Paternoster Press, Exeter UK

In memory of my father,
Paul G. Wennberg
(1902-1977),
who died well

Copyright © 1989 by Wm. B. Eerdmans Publishing Co.
255 Jefferson Ave. S.E., Grand Rapids, Mich. 49503
All rights reserved

Printed in the United States of America for
Wm. B. Eerdmans Publishing Co.
and
The Paternoster Press Ltd
3 Mount Radford Crescent, Exeter UK   EX2 4JW

Library of Congress Cataloging-in-Publication Data

Wennberg, Robert N.
   Terminal choices: euthanasia, suicide, and the right to die / by
Robert N. Wennberg.
    p.   cm.
   Includes bibliographical references.
   ISBN 0-8028-0454-3
   1. Euthanasia—Religious aspects—Christianity.   2. Suicide—
Religious aspects—Christianity. 3. Right to die—Religious
aspects—Christianity. I. Title.
R726W46   1989
179'.7—dc20   89-39127
                                                    CIP

British Library Cataloguing in Publication Data

Wennberg, Robert N.
   Terminal choices: euthanasia, suicide, and the right to die.
   1. Voluntary euthanasia
   I. Title.
   174'.24

   ISBN 0-85364-508-6

CONTENTS

PREFACE

This book is an attempt to deal with the basic issues that surround the euthanasia debate. The subject is important, controversial, and complex, calling for sensitivity to the realities of death and dying, a clear understanding of one's Christian faith and its implications for this significant dimension of human existence, conceptual and analytical skills to deftly make the requisite distinctions along the way, and logical rigor to enable one to draw the appropriate conclusions. Of course, in the light of such requirements, I must confess in advance my failure, but not without the hope that some progress has been made and some insights offered.

The euthanasia issue is certainly worthy of our best reflections, reflections from which we can derive considerable profit. For whether we are reflecting on the possibility of mercy killing as a legal, moral, and personal option, the use of painkilling drugs that incidentally accelerate dying, or the decision to terminate life-extending treatment, we are reflecting on issues that will confront most of us at one time or another, in one role or another. We are also dealing with perplexing and fascinating issues (even if we are not personally caught up in the maelstrom of actual decision-making), issues that force us deeply into the very heart of our Christian faith as few issues do. How should we as Christians seek to die, and how do we prepare ourselves for that final witness to our faith? What moral constraints should guide us in shaping our own deaths and in offering (hazarding to give) advice to others? What does it mean to trust the providence of God in our act of dying? Is there a dimension to dying that is "hands off," to be left to God alone and *not* to be shaped according to human judgment? Is suicide always wrong, never so much as to be contemplated by the conscientious Christian? What are the limits to the suffering we must endure to preserve and protect our lives? These and numerous other questions quickly come to the fore and force us to grapple with fundamental dimensions of faith and Christian perspective.

Here we need to acknowledge that to do God's will is not always to reach a firm conclusion about what should be done and then doing it; sometimes it is to recognize the contrary pulls, show sensitivity to the full range of competing values, and then hazard a judgment. The conscientious and well-informed Christian is not always the one with all the answers. To be too firm in one's convictions about what ought to be done is possibly the result of not taking into account or feeling the full force of *all* the competing considerations to which one ought to be sensitive. Typically a fanatic is one who is mono-valued, who recognizes only a single value or a small spectrum of values; for such an individual, decisions and advice come easily, and those who disagree are obviously mistaken. By contrast, for the more open-minded individual for whom the range of recognized and often competing values grows, matters often become more complicated, and decisions are then no longer as easy as one once thought. To be sure, upon reflecting deeply on euthanasia, one may still conclude that there are issues on which one needs to take a stand and to which an activist commitment is appropriate. But such a conclusion must be preceded by reflection and moral struggle.

I should add that one feature of this book is perhaps distinctive: I've written it from the perspective of the patient, not from the perspective of the physician or health-care professional. Basically I'm not asking "What should the physician do?" but rather "What should the patient do or have done?" The former question isn't ignored and for obvious reasons cannot be; nevertheless, the focus is on the second question. Indeed, the attention that I give to suicide reflects this orientation, because mercy killing is, from the patient's perspective, suicide. It's interesting that even many of those who firmly believe in patient autonomy write from the physician's point of view, providing the patient little assistance in giving instruction *to* the physician. The central moral agent in this book, then, is the patient, not the physician.

In recent years I have learned (and continue to learn) a great deal as a member of the Ethics Committee of the Cottage Hospital, Santa Barbara, California. I have found my colleagues on that committee, both those within and those without the health-care community, to be rich sources of wisdom and insight. They have helped me learn to temper my principles in the context of the complicated and messy reality of hospital life. In that real-life context, it seems, decisions are never easy, and the "moral professional" has no edge over his colleagues in making the "right" decision or in reaching the "correct" conclusion.

My thanks must extend to many people who helped make this book possible. Lois Gundry deciphered my indecipherable scribblings and transformed them into readable print; Siri Wennberg provided needed assistance with the index; Ned Divelbiss, with his knowledge and persistence, secured through interlibrary loan all books and articles requested; Shirley Mullen, a historian, taught me that analytic philosophers need not fear the search for wisdom; my colleagues in philosophy—Stan Obitts, Jim Mannoia, and Mark Mcleod—by their professional examples called me to greater analytic rigor; Mary Hietbrink, an excellent editor, helped me move closer to the goal of being clear and accurate; and my wife, Eleanore, provided me with what everyone needs: someone who believes in them.

CHAPTER ONE

Euthanasia: An Introduction

Historical Comments

"As long as we respect human dignity and regard kindly acts as being at least virtuous," Marvin Kohl has commented, "beneficent euthanasia, or mercy killing, will be practiced and remain a moral activity. For . . . other things being equal, our first duty is to help most where help is most needed."[1] Kohl[2] is typical of growing numbers of competent and thoughtful individuals who not only believe voluntary euthanasia to be a moral activity but have in recent years been calling for its legalization. To be sure, advocacy of euthanasia is not an exclusively modern development, for it was widely endorsed in the ancient world, being approved in cases of incurable disease by such respected ancients as Pythagoras, Plato, Sophocles, Epictetus, and Cicero.[3]

1. "Beneficent Euthanasia," *The Humanist* 34 (July / Aug. 1974): 9.
2. Kohl is also the author of *The Morality of Killing* (New York: Humanities Press, 1974). Kohl's book and several others—Eike-Henner Kluge's *Practice of Death* (New Haven: Yale University Press, 1975), Philip E. Devine's *Ethics of Homicide* (Ithaca, N.Y.: Cornell University Press, 1978), and Jonathan Glover's *Causing Death and Saving Lives* (New York: Penguin Books, 1977)—are among the best book-length philosophical explorations of euthanasia and other killing-related issues.
3. Raanan Gillon, "Suicide and Voluntary Euthanasia: Historical Perspective," in *Euthanasia and the Right to Death,* ed. A. B. Downing (Los Angeles: Nash Publishing, 1969), pp. 173-92.

Seneca (4 B.C.–A.D. 65), the Stoic philosopher, endorsed euthanasia with these oft-quoted eloquent words:

> Against all the injuries of life I have the refuge of death. If I can choose between a death of torture and one that is simple and easy, why should I not select the latter? As I choose the ship in which I sail and the house which I shall inhabit, so I will choose the death by which I leave life. In no matter more than in death should we act according to our desire. . . . Why should I endure the agonies of disease . . . when I can emancipate myself from all my torments?[4]

But until recent times advocates of euthanasia within the Christian tradition have been few in number. A major reason for this phenomenon is the widespread conviction that euthanasia is prohibited by the Sixth Commandment and thus not an option that the Christian may seriously consider. In short, mercy killing is murder, and murder is not a moral option. Undergirding the authority of the Sixth Commandment is the theological conviction that only God has the right to give and take life, the act of mercy killing being viewed as an illicit exercise of what is solely a divine prerogative. However, one advocate of euthanasia, the clergyman Leslie Weatherhead, has met this conviction with a provocative counter: "'Death,' we are told, 'should be left to God.' We do not leave birth to God. We space births. We prevent births. We arrange births. Man should learn to become the lord of death as well as the master of birth."[5] Other twentieth-century advocates of euthanasia in the Protestant and Anglican traditions include Hastings Rashdall,[6] W. R. Inge,[7] Jerry Wilson,[8] and Joseph Fletcher.[9] Roman

---

4. *Laws* IX:843.

5. Weatherhead, *The Christian Agnostic* (New York: Abingdon Press, 1965), p. 269.

6. Rashdall, *The Theory of Good and Evil*, 2nd ed. (Oxford: Oxford University Press, 1924), p. 209.

7. Inge, *Christian Ethics and Modern Problems* (New York: G. P. Putnam's Sons, 1930), pp. 393-98.

8. Wilson, *Death by Decision* (Philadelphia: Westminster Press, 1975).

9. Fletcher, *Morals and Medicine* (Boston: Beacon Press, 1954), pp. 172-210.

Catholics have joined their number and include Charles Curran[10] and Daniel Maguire.[11] These are all individuals who have identified themselves with the Christian community. But even if we were to add to their number the many more that could be listed here, it is still true that the case for euthanasia has found its most zealous advocates among those of a secular persuasion, who in turn have enjoyed varying degrees of support from members of the more (theologically) liberal wing of Protestantism. Orthodox believers—Jewish, Roman Catholic, and Protestant—have, on the other hand, tended to be among its more persistent critics. It is also true that the sympathy for euthanasia that existed in the ancient world was largely extinguished as a result of the teaching of the Christian church. As Joseph V. Sullivan has noted, "The tradition of the West has been Christian for nearly two thousand years and . . . never has this tradition sanctioned the direct killing of the innocent (apart from the divine command)."[12]

This history notwithstanding, it still may be that euthanasia is compatible with Christian belief. Since the fundamental appeal on behalf of euthanasia is an appeal to mercy and compassion, the Christian community should at least seriously consider euthanasia as a legal and moral possibility. Of course, taking euthanasia seriously is consistent—in the final analysis—with rejecting it as a *legitimate* expression of mercy and compassion.

Posing the Problem

The word "euthanasia" comes from a Greek word meaning "easy or good death"; it has come to signify the act or practice of taking the life of a person who is hopelessly ill and doing so

10. Curran, *Politics, Medicine, and Christian Ethics: A Dialogue with Paul Ramsey* (Philadelphia: Fortress Press, 1973), pp. 152-63.

11. Maguire, *Death by Choice* (New York: Schocken Books, 1975).

12. Sullivan, "The Immorality of Euthanasia," in *Beneficent Euthanasia*, ed. Marvin Kohl (Buffalo, N.Y.: Prometheus Books, 1975), p. 19.

for reasons of mercy. "Euthanasia" was first used in this sense in 1869 by British intellectual historian W. E. H. Lecky.[13] The problem for which euthanasia is offered as a solution is essentially this: today and in the foreseeable future at least some people will be dying painful and prolonged deaths from incurable diseases, or they will pass the final stages of their life in an irreversible coma, existing in what is often described as a vegetative state. And it must be underscored—if we are to appreciate the dimensions of the problem—that "dying is still very often," as one physician put it, "an ugly business." This physician, Leonard Colebrook, a former chairman of the Euthanasia Society of Great Britain and no doubt a man with a cause to plead, has illustrated his point by describing the plight of cancer patients:

> In addition to pain, many of the unhappy victims of cancer have to endure the mental misery of the presence of a foul fungating growth; of slow starvation owing to difficulty swallowing; of painful and very frequent micturition [urination]; of obstruction of the bowels; of incontinence; and of the utter prostration that makes each day and night a "death in life" as the famous physician, the late Sir William Osler, described it.[14]

To this we might add the words of Professor Guido Moricca, director of the Department of Anesthesiology and Resuscitation at the Institute Regina Elena for Cancer Research in Rome, Italy:

> Patients with advanced cancer and widespread metastases often have pain in multiple sites that is diffuse, not clearly localized, and eventually progresses to become the main symptom of the disease. . . . Unfortunately, these types of pain are difficult to control. This is due not only to the variety of the quality and sites of pain, but to the progressive nature of the disease. Moreover, often more intense pain in one region masks

13. See "euthanasia" in the Oxford English Dictionary.
14. Colebrook, quoted by A. B. Downing in "Euthanasia: The Human Context," in *Euthanasia and the Right to Death*, p. 18.

lesser pain elsewhere. Consequently, it is necessary to run after the pain which, blocked in one area, is then perceived in another region.[15]

Further, Raanan Gillon's summary of Dr. Exton-Smith's study of 220 terminally ill patients in a London geriatric hospital confronts us with the full extent of the problem: "For it is not only pain which can make the end of life miserable, as Exton-Smith's study clearly demonstrates; breathlessness, with its attendant sense of suffocation, nausea and vomiting, the inability to swallow or talk, urinary and faecal incontinence, are all symptoms which medicine cannot properly control."[16] Richard Sarjeant's litany of suffering can be joined with Gillon's: "The suffering from the terminal stages of incurable disease is not confined to pain; it may include incontinence, uncontrollable vomiting, inability to move because of fractures in the limbs and spine, and dementia from secondary deposits in the brain."[17] This, then, is the problem. The remedy being offered is euthanasia for those who desire it.

These remarks are only meant to draw attention to the kind of suffering that can on occasion accompany a dying person's last days. They are not meant to suggest that dying is always or is even for the most part accompanied by prolonged and unbearable suffering. Nor are the preceding remarks meant to deny the impressive measures that the medical profession can take to control the pain and alleviate the suffering of the dying. Indeed, Henry Miller, a physician and formerly the vice-chancellor of the University of Newcastle, may be right when he claims, "There are few fatal illnesses in which the last weeks or months cannot be made tolerable by the generous use of

15. Moricca, in *Recent Advances on Pain: Pathophysiology and Clinical Aspects*, ed. John J. Bonica et al. (Springfield, Ill.: Charles C. Thomas, 1974), p. 313.

16. Gillon, "Suicide and Voluntary Euthanasia: Historical Perspective," p. 188. For the original study, see A. N. Exton-Smith, "Terminal Illness in the Aged," *Lancet*, 5 Aug. 1961, pp. 305-8.

17. Sarjeant, *The Spectrum of Pain* (London: Rupert Hart Davis, 1969), p. 148.

drugs."[18] Thus it may be that the candidates for euthanasia will be relatively few. That is, there may be few people who will face an agonizing death that cannot be relieved by drugs and fewer still who request euthanasia even when they knowingly face such an unpleasant prospect.[19] But the frequency of such requests—and there will always be some—is not directly relevant to the question of whether such requests ought to be granted.[20]

After reflecting on the pain and suffering that can accompany a prolonged dying, some in the Christian community will agree with Leslie Weatherhead when he writes,

> I sincerely believe that those who come after us will wonder why on earth we kept a human being alive against his own will, when all dignity, beauty and meaning of life had vanished; when any gain to anyone was clearly impossible. . . . I for one would be willing to give a patient the Holy Communion and stay with him while a doctor, whose responsibility I should share, allowed him to lay down his useless body and pass in dignity into the next phase of being.[21]

18. Miller, in *Morals and Medicine*, ed. Archie Clow (London: British Broadcasting Company, 1970), p. 14.

19. Dr. Leonard Colebrook of the Euthanasia Society of Great Britain estimated that in Britain one in every one hundred patients with terminal cancer would elect euthanasia if it were legally available (reported by Downing in *Euthanasia and the Right to Death*, p. 19). This would be a small minority; nevertheless, in the United States this would translate into 4,500 persons choosing to hasten their dying by positive means out of the some 450,000 who die annually from cancer. It is difficult to say how reliable this estimate is. A study of 418 attending staff physicians at two hospitals in Seattle yielded the following results: 38 percent had heard patients request negative euthanasia (treatment termination), and 12 percent had heard patients request positive euthanasia (taking positive steps to end life). Interestingly enough, 31 percent of the physicians questioned favored changes permitting positive euthanasia (Brown, Bulger, Laws, and Thompson, "The Preservation of Life," *Journal of the American Medical Association*, 5 Jan. 1970, pp. 76-81).

20. It may have relevance for the debate over the legalization of euthanasia, however, because if there are substantial risks attaching to the legalization of euthanasia, then to the extent that the demand for euthanasia is slight, it might not be worth running those risks.

21. Weatherhead, *The Christian Agnostic*, p. 187.

We too may find ourselves attracted to voluntary euthanasia in situations where the illness is terminal, suffering is intense, death is imminent, and there is no relief consonant with rational existence.

Yet we may continue to have reservations, reservations that are understandable and—in the final analysis, I believe—right. For religious believers—and Christian believers in particular—the conviction that we would be interlopers poaching on God's domain is not a conviction that passes quickly, even when we witness suffering that could be ended swiftly and mercifully by active means. But Charles Curran, a Roman Catholic moral theologian, seeks to put just such fears to rest when he comments, "Precisely because the dying process has now begun, man's positive intervention is not an arrogant usurping of the role of God but rather in keeping with the process which is now encompassing the person."[22] So, according to Curran, mercy killing ("positive intervention") is not "an arrogant usurping of the role of God" because the patient is already *dying*—that is, a process has enveloped the patient which will lead to an inevitable and imminent death. Further, the dying is not brought about by human intervention because that is already a fact of the situation and is not the patient's own doing; mercy killing in these circumstances will simply serve to bring to a close a process that is unalterably present and whose inescapable terminus is death. Can that be so bad when the patient is facing intractable pain and suffering? This is what needs exploring.

Options and Alternatives

A basic distinction is made between two kinds of euthanasia, passive and active. Active euthanasia is identical with mercy killing and, roughly speaking, involves taking direct action to end a life—for example, intentionally giving a person a lethal

22. Curran, *Politics, Medicine, and Christian Ethics*, pp. 161-62.

dose of a drug to end a painful dying.[23] This is what most people think of when they use the term "euthanasia"—the deliberate taking of a life for reasons of mercy. Passive euthanasia, I shall initially suggest, is allowing a patient to die when he or she could be kept alive by the appropriate medical procedures.[24]

23. In the most exhaustive discussion of the conceptual boundaries of euthanasia, Tom L. Beauchamp and Arnold I. Davidson have arrived at the following definition: "In summary, we have argued . . . that the death of a human being, A, is an instance of euthanasia if and only if (1) A's death is intended by at least one other human being, B, where B is either the cause of death or a causally relevant feature of the event resulting in death (whether by action or by omission); (2) there is either sufficient current evidence for B to believe that A is acutely suffering or irreversibly comatose, or there is sufficient current evidence related to A's present condition such that one or more known causal laws supports B's belief that A will be in a condition of acute suffering or irreversible comatoseness; (3) (a) B's primary reason for intending A's death is cessation of A's (actual or predicted future) suffering or irreversible comatoseness, where B does not intend A's death for a different primary reason, though there may be other relevant reasons, and (b) there is sufficient current evidence for either A or B that causal means to A's death will not produce any more suffering than would be produced for A if B were not to intervene; (4) the causal means to the event of A's death are chosen by A or B to be as painless as possible, unless either A or B has an overriding reason for a more painful causal means, where the reason for choosing the latter causal means does not conflict with the evidence in 3b; (5) A is a nonfetal organism" (Beauchamp and Davidson, "The Definition of Euthanasia," *The Journal of Medicine and Philosophy* 4 [1979]: 304).

Although this definition is carefully thought through, disagreements arise over certain features of it. According to this definition, for example, *auto*-euthanasia or self-administered euthanasia would be a contradiction in terms (that may well be correct); additionally, euthanasia for the permanently comatose is a sensible notion (others deny this on the grounds that the comatose are not suffering and to end their lives could not therefore be an act of mercy, but Beauchamp and Davidson reply that euthanasia can still benefit the comatose— i.e., by ending a condition of indignity and honoring the previously expressed wishes of the patient); further, the illness promoting the mercy killing need not be terminal or believed to be terminal (others have thought that the illness must be terminal, but Beauchamp and Davidson judge this to be an arbitrary stipulation inconsistent with actual usage). There are other disagreements besides these, but to settle them doesn't help us solve the moral and legal problems involved, which remain exactly the same no matter how precisely we define the term "euthanasia."

24. How precisely to define passive euthanasia is, as we shall subsequently see, problematic, but for our initial purposes this broad definition will suffice. Ultimately, however, I'll introduce a more restricted understanding of the term.

Euthanasia, whether passive (letting die) or active (mercy killing), can be (a) voluntary—that is, *with* the fully informed consent of the patient, (b) involuntary—that is, *against* the will or wishes of the patient, or (c) non-voluntary—that is, *without* the consent of the patient, in circumstances where the patient isn't able either to give or to withhold consent (for example, where the patient is in an irreversible comatose state and has failed to give any prior indication about what his or her wishes might be). Unless otherwise indicated, in this discussion "euthanasia" will be used to refer to *voluntary* euthanasia. Involuntary euthanasia, of course, can only be condemned in the most emphatic of terms: it would be murder and would be so considered by all parties in the current debate.

There are four basic positions that can be taken on the issue of euthanasia:

(1) *Both passive and active euthanasia are (always) morally wrong.* According to this view, refusing life-extending treatment as well as hastening death by positive means would be judged morally unacceptable. In each case, it could be argued, the patient would be shortening life, and this is wrong. To be sure, in the one instance the patient does so by saying "no" to treatment and in the other by accepting a lethal dose of a drug, but in each instance the patient is doing the same evil thing: abbreviating his or her life.

(2) *Both passive and active euthanasia might be morally permissible.* As with the previous position, so with this one: the refusal of life-extending treatment and the hastening of death by positive means share the same moral status. According to this view, however, both these options are morally *acceptable*—if not always, at least sometimes. This view argues that both of these procedures can achieve the same good end—namely, the shortening of an excessively agonizing dying—and this good is sufficient to justify the use of either means, passive or active.

(3) *Passive euthanasia is (on occasion) morally permissible, but active euthanasia is always wrong.* Central to this view is the belief that refusing life-extending treatment (passive euthanasia) and taking positive means to shorten one's life (active euthanasia)

9

do not share the same moral status. On the contrary, it is argued, the first procedure is letting oneself die, whereas the second is killing oneself, a difference that is crucial. Although there may be occasions when one can let oneself die by refusing medical treatment in order to cease prolonging an excessively painful death, there are no occasions when one can rightfully kill oneself or rightfully kill another in order to bring an agonizing death to an end. According to this view, killing is not a legitimate expression of mercy, nor is what amounts to suicide justified by the fact that it shortens an agonizing death. But refusing medical treatment, the argument continues, is not intrinsically objectionable in the same way, and in certain circumstances it may be a morally justified course of action to follow.

(4) *Active euthanasia is morally preferable to passive euthanasia.* This may at first seem like a curious position, asserting, as it does, that killing a patient is preferable to letting him or her die, but reasons can be given for such a preference, because active euthanasia involves the employment of means that normally secure a more speedy death than that achieved by passive euthanasia, which involves waiting for the patient to die. In this vein James Rachels has commented,

> If one simply withholds treatment, it may take the patient longer to die, and so he may suffer more than he would if more direct actions were taken and a lethal injection given. This fact provides strong reason for thinking that, once the vital decision not to prolong his agony has been made, active euthanasia is actually preferable to passive euthanasia, rather than the reverse. To say otherwise is to endorse the option that leads to more suffering rather than less, and is contrary to the humanitarian impulse that prompts the decision not to prolong his life in the first place.[25]

These, then, are the alternatives in the euthanasia debate. It is the third alternative (passive euthanasia is morally permissible, but active euthanasia is not) that strikes many as a sane

25. Rachels, "Active and Passive Euthanasia," *The New England Journal of Medicine,* 9 Jan. 1975, p. 78.

middle ground between the more extreme positions represented by the first (both passive and active euthanasia are morally wrong) and the second (both passive and active euthanasia might on occasion be morally permissible). But the acceptance of passive euthanasia and the rejection of active euthanasia is a position with serious theoretical tensions that emerge most powerfully upon protracted reflection. Indeed, this position has come under serious attack in the professional literature, though it is not without able defenders.

Legalizing Euthanasia

The legalization of euthanasia is a separate issue from the question of its morality, and determining the *moral* status of euthanasia does not automatically settle the issue of its legalization. For most of us do not believe that all morally objectionable acts should be *prohibited* by law or that all acts that are intrinsically unobjectionable should be *permitted* by law. There simply does not exist—nor do we believe that there should exist—a simple equivalency between sin and crime: all crimes shouldn't be seen as sins, nor should all sins be seen as crimes. Thus, if euthanasia in whatever form is a sin, it doesn't follow that it should be made into a crime.

It has been argued, however, that a society may legitimately use the law to shape its *basic* institutions and practices to accord with its *deepest* convictions about right and wrong.[26] Accordingly, a society may choose (as ours has done) to recognize only heterosexual, monogamous marriages while refusing to grant similar recognition to homosexual or polygamous unions, and would claim to do so solely for moral reasons, thereby expressing values ultimately rooted in the Judeo-Christian tradi-

26. Much of the contemporary discussion of the relationship between law and morality is a reaction to the provocative work of Lord Patrick Devlin entitled *The Enforcement of Morals* (New York: Oxford University Press, 1965). Devlin argues that the law can play a legitimate role in enforcing morals. Critics of Devlin are numerous.

tion. An Islamic society with different beliefs about the nature of marriage would understandably and legitimately structure matters differently. Thus a society has a right to be guided by its own moral lights when it comes to shaping, by use of the law, its basic institutions and practices. In a similar fashion, it could be argued that a society which is opposed to mercy killing on moral principle may legally prohibit the practice solely because it violates moral beliefs deeply ingrained in that society. For to legalize and regulate euthanasia (if legalized, euthanasia must also be regulated) would involve a recognition of, an involvement with, and a sanctioning of an activity that, we might suppose (and this could be contested), would offend the moral sensibilities of society, and this, it would be argued, is too much to ask of any society. However, much of the debate over the wisdom of legalizing euthanasia moves in a different direction, centering instead on the possibility of gross abuse. Thus it is frequently argued that once euthanasia is legalized, we will have opened the door to tragic consequences: we will become cavalier in our attitude toward life, euthanasia will become less and less voluntary, troublesome categories of patients will be eliminated for the convenience of society, physicians will be encouraged to have a defeatist attitude in the face of death, and so forth. It is this line of argument—and not the former—that I shall subsequently examine when discussing the legalization of euthanasia.

Public Opinion

There are indications that a sizable portion of the American public—indeed, a majority—favor the legalization of voluntary mercy killing. In a 1986 Roper poll commissioned by the Hemlock Society, this question was asked: "When a person has a painful and distressing terminal disease, do you think doctors should or should not be allowed by law to end the patient's life if there is no hope of recovery and the patient requests it?" The results of the poll were as follows:

Should be allowed by law	62%
Should not be allowed by law	27%
Don't know/no answer	11%

In a 1987 California poll by Mervin Field,[27] this question was asked: "Should an incurably ill patient have the right to ask for and get life-ending medication?" (Interestingly, the question doesn't indicate that the incurably ill patient is also *terminally ill*, although I surmise that most people would have interpreted the question in that way.) The results of this poll were very similar to those of the Roper poll:

Should have the right	64%
Should not have the right	27%
Undecided	9%

Here too the results favored legalized mercy killing by a sizable margin.

In a more detailed analysis of attitudes toward active euthanasia based on a general social survey conducted by the National Opinion Research Center in 1977, some interesting correlations were discovered.[28] In this survey the crucial question was this: "When a person has a disease that cannot be cured, do you think doctors should be allowed by law to end the patient's life by some means if the patient and his family request it?" (This question, like that of the Field poll, does not indicate that the patient's condition is terminal, although the respondents may well have assumed—falsely—that a disease which is incurable is also terminal.) The respondents answered this question in the following ways:

27. The results of the Roper and Mervin Field polls were widely reported in the newspapers. I got this data from an informational letter from Americans Against Human Suffering, an advocacy group for legalized euthanasia in California.

28. See David E. Jorgenson and Ron C. Neubecker, "Euthanasia: A National Survey of Attitudes toward Voluntary Termination of Life," *Omega* 11 (1980-81): 281-91.

Yes	59%
No	36%
Don't know	4%
No answer	1%

These results are similar to those of the Roper and Field polls. Not surprisingly, it was discovered that the religiously serious were more likely to have anti-euthanasia sympathies. A breakdown of the respondents' "religious profiles" yielded the following information:

Church Attendance	(No)	(Yes)
Low	20.1	79.9
Medium	26.9	73.1
High	47.2	52.8

Religiosity	(No)	(Yes)
Weak	23.5	76.5
Strong	50.5	49.5

Thus individuals who regularly attend church and/or are more religiously oriented are more likely to be opposed to legalized mercy killing—but even among these groups there is a high rate of acceptance of legalized mercy killing.

What we don't know, of course, is whether these opinions would hold up after exposure to a serious (and, it would be hoped, not blatantly manipulative) educational campaign by pro- and anti-euthanasia forces. Indeed, one's opinions and one's *considered* opinions are often quite different. We should also remember that the questions in the surveys cited were positively framed, focusing only on features of the situation that would dispose one to give a favorable response—"no hope of recovery," "incurably ill," "a disease that cannot be cured," and so on. But, had the questions been posed negatively, the results might have been quite different. Suppose, for example, that people had been asked this question: "Does the possibility of gross abuse justify a continued legal ban on physician-administered euthanasia for those terminally ill patients who might request it?" Here one might reasonably anticipate a greater negative response because this question introduces negative considerations into the picture.

Treatment Refusal

In many ways the morality of treatment refusal is the most fascinating dimension of the euthanasia discussion. I didn't always think so, but I've come to believe that it is via a discussion of treatment refusal (that we will enter into in Chapter Five)— especially the various kinds of treatment refusals, which provide us with some of the greatest insights into the case for active euthanasia. For "conservative" and "moderate" moralists the most agonizing theoretical issues will emerge at this point, especially should we choose to endorse a full range of treatment refusals while at the same time drawing back from endorsing active euthanasia or mercy killing. The crux of the debate may be right here. At this point I am only hinting at what is to come.

CHAPTER TWO

Suicide: What Is It?

Introduction

To take seriously the issues surrounding the morality of voluntary euthanasia brings one inevitably to the topic of suicide. If euthanasia were involuntary (that is, *against* the will and wishes of the patient), then the relevant category would be homicide. But since our focus is on *voluntary* euthanasia, where the patient chooses to carry out euthanasia through the agency of another, we rightly surmise that suicide is the appropriate and applicable moral category. Certainly many who protest the moral legitimacy of voluntary euthanasia do so by charging that it is "suicide"; many who wonder whether euthanasia would be morally permissible for them ask, "Would I be committing suicide?"; and those who would be carrying out the will of the patient by performing an act of euthanasia (doctors, nurses, family, friends) may wonder whether they are "assisting a suicide" and ponder the morality of their action in those terms. Moreover, advocates of legalized voluntary euthanasia frequently speak of the right to death by suicide and insist that we cannot categorically rule out all acts of suicide as morally objectionable, especially in cases of those suffering greatly from terminal illnesses, death being the only form of release available. Even a church in New York, in sympathetically but cautiously approaching the question of euthanasia, has declared, "A last resort in the gravest of situations, suicide may be an act of . . . Christian conscience."[1] So the issue of voluntary euthanasia is inextricably linked with issues surrounding the morality and legality of suicide.

Addressing the issue of suicide is an important first step in beginning to grasp the moral and legal standing that we ought to assign to euthanasia. However, we shouldn't expect to find a perfectly satisfactory and logically tight definition of suicide that can be coupled with the appropriate moral formula (total prohibition, say) to neatly solve all our problems. What we will actually find is not only that definitions of suicide vary greatly, but also that with virtually any reasonable definition, there will be puzzling cases that defy easy classification. Simply put, there are vagaries associated with the concept of suicide that can be dispelled only by stipulation. Indeed, to wrestle with the problem of defining "suicide" will teach us a lesson in linguistic humility, but it will also serve to introduce a range of distinctions that are essential to a careful probing of the morality of euthanasia.

We should note that "suicide" is not a neutrally descriptive term like "cat," "car," or "flower." Rather, it carries with it a strong negative connotation, especially when it is part of the phrase "commit suicide." For one typically does not *commit* X where X is either something approved or something of neutral standing (cf. "commit murder," "commit a felony," "commit a crime," "commit adultery," "commit a sin," "commit treason," "commit a *faux pas*," etc.). Interestingly, however, the term "suicide" was introduced into the English language in 1651 by Walter Charleton in order to make available a more neutral and less judgmental term for acts of self-killing which until then had been described as "destroying oneself," "murdering oneself," and "slaughtering oneself"—all phrases that convey firm disapproval.[2] Charleton made his contribution to the English lan-

---

1. Pastoral letter on euthanasia and suicide from the Presbytery of New York City, 9 Mar. 1976, p. 3.

2. What I have to say about the history of the term "suicide"—and much more—can be found in David Daube's "Linguistics of Suicide," *Philosophy and Public Affairs* 1 (1971-72): 387-437. Then, of course, there's the *Oxford English Dictionary*.

guage with this sentence: "To vindicate one's self from extreme and otherwise inevitable calamity by *sui-cide* is not (certainly) a crime." This hyphenated word did not exist in the Latin but was an invention achieved by linking two Latin words, "sui" (self) and "cide" (kill). John Donne (1572–1631), a sympathizer with suicide on select occasions, introduced the term "self-homicide" in his *Biathanatos* for the same reason—to provide us with a milder and more neutral word for the deed. However, it was Charleton's "suicide" and not Donne's "self-homicide" that ultimately carried the day, in time becoming the word commonly used in English to designate acts of self-killing. In contrast, in Germany "selbstmorde" (self-murder) is still the everyday word for self-killing, "suizid" (suicide) being a word belonging to a technical, clinical vocabulary.

However, "suicide" is no longer the antiseptically neutral term that it was when Charleton first introduced it, for with the passage of time society's attitudes toward self-killing began to attach themselves to this word. Yet "suicide" is not a straightforward term of moral reproach like "murder," at least in part because we judge many acts of suicide to be outside the category of moral acts, viewing them instead as expressions of unsound minds. Thus the term "suicide" has overtones of both pathology and moral disapproval. Nevertheless, I propose to treat "suicide" like "homicide" (a killing of one human being by another) and not like "murder" (the *wrongful* killing of one human being by another). That is, if we come across an act of self-killing that we approve, I won't for *that* reason forego using the term "suicide." I will simply use the term to refer to acts of self-killing (in a way analogous to the way in which we use "homicide," a term that leaves open the possibility of justified instances of one person's killing another—e.g., killing in self-defense); I will *not* use "suicide" to refer only to *immoral* acts of self-killing (in a way analogous to the way in which we use "murder"). So when I determine that an act is a suicide, I am not to be understood as automatically condemning it, nor should I be interpreted as granting a moral reprieve should I conclude that a particular act is not a suicide. Furthermore, when I struggle to determine

18

whether a particular borderline case qualifies as a suicide, I am not engaging in a struggle to settle the issue of its moral acceptability—that will come later. Such linguistic openness is in fact quite consistent with our having a moral presumption against suicide, as most of us have against homicide—which is, after all, only rarely justified.

In beginning our search for an adequate definition of suicide, we must assume that we are *already* able, with a measure of accuracy, to recognize individual cases of suicide, for how else can we test proposed definitions and characterizations except by reference to already recognizable instances? Nevertheless, we should expect to gain from our definition an improved ability to recognize instances of suicide. We can at the outset suggest that suicide is "an intentional act of self-killing." This does not, in the final analysis, miss the mark by much, but it requires elaboration and interpretation as well as some qualification along the way. Ultimately I will frame matters in a slightly different way.

Suicide through the Agency of Another

In order for an act to be a suicide, it isn't necessary that one die "by one's own hand." Suicide doesn't require self-inflicted death after the pattern of a bullet to the brain from a gun fired by the victim or a self-administered dose of a poison. For one might persuade someone else to do the killing, and although one then dies "at the hand of another," one is nevertheless a suicide. Take the case of the man who wants to die for reasons of despair and depression but doesn't want to deny his family their insurance benefits. He secretly hires an underworld figure to kill him, thereby successfully disguising his involvement with his own demise. Is this not a suicide? It would seem so. It appears, then, that just as one can commit a *homicide* or murder through the agency of another, so one can commit *suicide* through the agency of another. Therefore, it cannot be argued that euthanasia is *not* suicide on the grounds that the doctor or nurse, acting at the behest of the patient, is the one who actually unplugs the life-support system or administers the lethal drug overdose. For if a patient's unplugging his own life-support system is suicide in a certain set of circumstances, then so is his having someone else do it for him; if a patient's self-administering a lethal dose of morphine is suicide, then so is his having another administer it at his request. The point is that the use of secondary agents to achieve one's own death is quite consistent with the concept of suicide.

Passive and Active Suicide

Suicide can be achieved by failing to act (passive suicide) as well as by acting (active suicide). To grasp this, reflect on a simple example. A woman who is in a state of depression is accidentally given a drink containing a lethal dose of poison. Unaware of its contents, she consumes the drink. Upon being informed of what has happened, she is provided with a safe and effective antidote—but she refuses to take the antidote and subsequently dies. If we assume that she refused the antidote because she wanted to die, I think we would conclude that she committed suicide. Thus we seem justified in concluding that suicide can be carried out passively as well as actively. It would follow that a death brought about by treatment refusal could not be ruled out as suicide solely on the grounds that it was achieved by passive means, for it might be an instance of passive suicide (though for other reasons, of course, it might not be suicide at all). The poisoned woman who refuses the antidote is refusing medical treatment and in that regard does exactly the same thing as the individual who chooses passive euthanasia. Thus the choice of a passive mode (treatment refusal) rather than an active mode (administration of a lethal drug) does not *by itself* serve to distinguish suicide from non-suicide.

Suicide and Natural Causes

Often we think of suicide as involving positive human intervention in contrast to a death by natural causes. We tend to assume that a death by natural causes can't be a suicide. But that isn't always so. Consider the example of the despairing and depressed diabetic in his mid-forties who is otherwise in good health. He stops taking his insulin injections in order to end his life. Since he lives alone and has no regular visitors, no one discovers him immediately when he passes into a diabetic coma, and he dies.

This man died of natural causes, but all the same we judge that he died a suicide. Thus one can commit suicide by (1) passively acquiescing to (2) a natural death, the presence of *both* features being consistent with suicide.

Suicide in the Face of an Inevitable Death

One can also commit suicide in the face of an imminent and inevitable death. In other words, an act of taking one's life is not precluded from being an act of suicide because one is going to die shortly anyway. This point is amply underscored by a historical example: a Nazi war criminal (e.g., Hermann Goering), under sentence of death, takes a cyanide capsule and kills himself just before the sentence can be carried out by the Allied authorities. We don't hesitate to label this a suicide. In the specific case of Hermann Goering, we usually find his death described something like this: "Two hours before his scheduled hanging, he committed suicide by swallowing a poison capsule."[3] One could hardly conceive of a more imminent and inevitable death. So if we concur that Goering committed suicide, we must also conclude that taking one's life against the backdrop of an inevitable and imminent death does not by itself rule out suicide.

3. *Columbia Encyclopedia,* 3rd ed., s.v. "Goering, Hermann Wilhelm."

Suicide and Intention

A suicide is someone who *intends* to die, either as a means (e.g., I will kill myself in order to relieve my family of the burden of caring for me) or as an end (e.g., I will kill myself as an ultimate act of existential freedom). Here we move to the heart of the matter. And although this claim raises a number of complications, it is nevertheless a claim that is crucial in understanding the nature of suicide and ultimately coming to moral terms with certain central aspects of the euthanasia debate.

To begin, we must recognize that certain definitions of suicide have been offered which depart from the claim that the individual must intend his or her own death. Emile Durkheim, for example, in his classic sociological study of suicide, defines the term so broadly that it includes "all cases of death resulting directly or indirectly from a positive or negative act of the victim himself which he knows will produce this result."[4] This means, very simply, that if I perform any act which I *know* will result in my death—even if I don't intend my death—then, according to Durkheim's understanding, I have committed suicide. Now intentions are notoriously elusive: not only are we often uncertain about the intentions of others, but we often are perplexed about our own intentions. It was for this reason that Durkheim proposed a definition of suicide that made no reference to intention. For research purposes it simplified matters if one did not have to determine whether or not the victim *intended* his or her death. Nevertheless, such a use of the term "suicide" departs radically from common usage. Think of a soldier, bayonet fixed, who charges the enemy, knowing that he will be killed—we do not normally think of him as a suicide. Nor do we normally classify as a suicide the person who is willing to be killed rather than renounce her religious or political beliefs. But this is exactly what Durkheim's definition entails.

4. Durkheim, *Suicide: A Study in Sociology,* trans. John A. Spaulding and George Simpson (New York: Free University Press, 1951), p. 44. This landmark study was originally published in 1897.

To arrive at a definition that, unlike Durkheim's, is more in keeping with common usage, we need to distinguish between (a) *foreseen but unintended consequences* of an act and (b) *intended consequences* of an act. If one's death is foreseen—that is, is an expected or anticipated consequence of what one is doing—but nevertheless is unintended, then one is *not*, according to common usage, a suicide. By contrast, one *is* a suicide if one desires to die (usually as a means to some end) and acts on that desire by taking appropriate measures. And by "intends one's death" I do mean the simultaneous presence of both of these features: desiring one's death and acting on *that* desire.

In this context, "to desire death" does not carry with it overtones of relishing the prospect of death or eagerly embracing death—although in some suicides that may actually be the case. For one can also desire death in the sense that one accepts it as being *less undesirable* than the alternatives that one faces—for example, continued life marked by much suffering may be viewed as less desirable than death. Thus I can *want* to die in order to bring my suffering to an end without *delighting* in the prospect of death. In the same way, I can *desire* or *want* to have an operation that will remedy a condition that seriously impairs the quality of my life, but because of the considerable pain and suffering accompanying the operation, I may embrace it less than enthusiastically, experiencing some measure of trepidation and hesitancy. Nevertheless, I do desire to have the operation: I want it as a means of improving the quality of my life.

It is for this reason that the soldier who charges the enemy knowing that he most likely will die is not a suicide. In charging the enemy he is not acting out a desire to die, is not choosing this act as a means to his death, but rather is accepting a foreseen yet unwelcome consequence of what he is doing. In this connection, E. W. Kluge helpfully distinguishes between a "suicide proper" and a "suicidal act." A suicide proper, he rightly insists, must fulfill *all* of the following three conditions: "(1) the action must, with reasonable certainty, lead to the death of the person engaging in it; (2) it must be known to the actor that his death would be a virtual certainty were he to engage in that act;

(3) the actor must engage in that action for the express purpose of bringing about his own death."[5] By contrast, a suicidal act need fulfill only one or both of the first two conditions. And it is the third condition that captures what I am also referring to when I speak of "intending" one's death. Following Kluge, then, I would say that the soldier is engaging in a suicidal act, but his death would not be a suicide because he is not fulfilling the third condition—he is not undertaking his mission for the express purpose of ending his life. Durkheim, on the other hand, sets aside the third condition and characterizes as a suicide any act that fulfills only the first two conditions.

According to Durkheim's definition, not only is the soldier a suicide, but so also is the Christian believer in A.D. 275 who is confronted by the Roman authorities with the following choice: renounce your faith or be fed to the lions. Although terrified by the prospect of such a death, the believer refuses to renounce her faith and so is fed to the lions. Since she performed an act (refusing to renounce her faith) that she *knew* would result in her death (being fed to the lions), she is, according to Durkheim, a suicide. The Christian community, of course, has another term for her: "martyr." But the reason she is not a suicide—according to the definition I am proposing—is unrelated to the high regard in which she would be held by the Christian community; she is not a suicide solely because her decision to affirm her faith in such difficult circumstances was not one she made *in order* to bring about her death—or, to use Kluge's terminology, she did not make her decision for "the express purpose" of bringing about her death. In other words, although she expected her death, she did not intend it. Had she killed herself in order to avoid rape or slavery—not an uncommon phenomenon among early Christians—*then* she would have been a suicide because her death would have been the intended means of avoiding the perceived ignominy of rape or slavery. Had she been a member of the Jewish community at

5. Kluge, *The Practice of Death* (New Haven: Yale University Press, 1975), p. 103.

24

Masada—where 960 men, women, and children took their lives rather than be captured by the Romans—she also would have been a suicide. In these cases death was intended. But our martyr is not a suicide because she did not intend her death either as a means or as an end.

The early Christian martyr died for her religious convictions in a political context, but it is also possible to die for one's religious convictions in a medical context. Consider the example of the Jehovah's Witness injured in a car accident who refuses, as a matter of religious principle, the blood transfusions required to save her life. She dies as a result of her act of refusal.[6] Again, this is *not* a suicide because the woman did not intend her death: she refused the transfusions not to cause her death but to honor what she sincerely believed to be a divine prohibition against "partaking" of human blood.[7] Had she survived without the blood transfusions, that would *not* have frustrated her ends. And it's not solely a matter of dying for religious principle; it's a matter of intention. Had this woman deliberately shot and killed herself with a pistol in order to avoid having blood transfusions forced upon her, she would have been a suicide despite her religious motivation, because in that case she would have shot herself for the express purpose of causing her death.

Another example will underscore the point. A heavy drinker and smoker, aware that she is running a high risk of shortening her life but free of any death wish, nevertheless continues to both drink and smoke heavily. When she dies, it is reliably estimated that she would have lived for another eight to ten years had she curtailed her smoking and drinking. This woman—although she shortened her life by a number of years and although we may judge that she lived her life irrespon-

6. In emergency contexts such as this, the request of a Jehovah's Witness would often be ignored.

7. Unlike the Christian Scientist, who would reject *all* medical treatment on religious principle, the Jehovah's Witness finds objectionable only medical assistance that involves what is judged to be a violation of the teachings of the books of Leviticus (cf. 3:17; 7:26, 27; 17:14) and Deuteronomy (cf. 12:16, 23; 15:23), which prohibit "eating" the blood of animals and birds.

sibly—is not a suicide because she did not intend her death: she did not smoke and drink *for the express purpose* of shortening her life. She no more intended her death than she intended the hangovers that she regularly experienced after a night of alcoholic excess. Both the hangovers and the death were *foreseen but unintended* consequences of her excessive alcohol and tobacco consumption. Therefore, hers is not a death by suicide.

Neither are the deaths of the following individuals suicides:

> A man suffering from a severe medical condition that seriously impairs the quality of his life (viz., he is bedridden and in constant pain, although not terminal) may elect to have a high-risk operation. The probabilities are that he will not survive the surgery; nevertheless, should the operation prove successful, it would completely remedy his condition. He chooses to have the operation but dies as a result.
>
> A patient in the latter stages of terminal illness is given, at her request, increasingly large doses of morphine in order to adequately control her acute pain. The ever-larger doses of morphine threaten to accelerate her death. And, in fact, her decision to take the doses does serve to shorten her life.

These are not suicides because neither individual chose death either as a means or as an end. In both cases the individuals involved were willing to accept the risk of death but weren't seeking it: in the first instance, the patient chose to undergo the operation in the hope of restoring the quality of his life, not in order to terminate his life; in the second instance, the patient requested ever-larger doses of morphine in order to control her pain, not to terminate her life. Both of these individuals judged the *risk* of death to be worth the possible gain, but neither intended their deaths.

Death as Unintended but Nevertheless Welcome

As we have seen, a suicide requires that one intend one's own death; therefore, should one's death be only an expected but unintended side effect, that fact precludes it from being a suicide. However, expected side effects or anticipated consequences need not be *undesired* in order for them to be *unintended*. Not at all. Certainly it is easier to identify consequences as unintended when they are also undesired or unwanted, but these two things do not always go hand in hand. For one can have a certain desire and act in a way that will bring about what is desired and yet not be acting on that desire.

Consider the case of Professor Robertson, a scrupulously honest and fair-minded teacher who awards A's to four of the five students in her honors seminar. Although a woman with rigorous academic standards who never awards high grades unless they are merited, she nevertheless is warmly disposed toward her students and is always gladdened by the pleasure that they experience when they receive high grades.[8] Here we have a situation in which the foreseen consequences (student happiness) are viewed positively. Nevertheless, we would *not* say that the professor, who knew very well that the awarding of A's would please her students and who positively desired that outcome, *intended* to make her students happy by awarding them A's. To say this would be to impugn the professor's professional integrity. What enabled her to couple integrity with warmheartedness was that in awarding A's Professor Robertson was not in fact acting on her desire that her students receive pleasure from their grades but was acting on a desire to reward her students in accord with the quality of their performance; the pleasure that the students received was for her simply a welcome side effect. The professor did not award the A's for "the express purpose" of giving her students pleasure. Therefore, one can have a desire, act in a way that one *knows* will bring about what one desires, and yet all the same not be acting on that desire.

Death too can be a *welcome* side effect without being intended and therefore without transforming what one is doing

---

8. The idea for this case is taken from Norvin Richards, "Double Effect and Moral Character," *Mind* 93 (1984): 382.

into suicide. Consider our third-century Christian martyr who faced death rather than renounce her faith. Suppose she had a strong, unwavering desire to die and be ushered into the presence of the God she had faithfully served all her life. That still would not render her death a suicide so long as the death she desired was merely an unintended side effect of her refusal to renounce her faith—that is, so long as she did not act on her desire to die, did not confess her faith in order to bring about her death.

There are medical contexts, too, in which death is desired and welcomed but nevertheless not intended. It may be that the generous use of morphine required to satisfactorily control the pain accompanying a terminal illness also accelerates the rate of one's dying—an acceleration that one positively welcomes. However, one need not select this course of treatment for *that* reason; one may select it for the control of pain that it secures. That is, one acts on the desire to control pain, not on the desire to end one's life. The side effect, although welcome, is nevertheless an *unintended* side effect. If, on the other hand, the morphine dosage is higher than the dose required to control the pain and is high enough to cause death, then the drug is being used for the express purpose of bringing about one's death, and in such circumstances death ceases to be a mere side effect. This, simply put, is a suicide.

Altruistic Suicides

It is sometimes claimed that a self-killing must be self-interested or prompted by self-regarding motives in order to be a suicide.[9] But to preclude calling a self-killing "suicide" because it is altruistically motivated appears to be an arbitrary restriction. We can steal, lie, and even murder for the benefit of some third party or

9. That is the claim, for example, of this definition of suicide—"the direct and deliberate taking of one's life for any self-regarding motive" ("Suicide," in *Dictionary of Christian Ethics,* ed. John Macquarrie [Philadelphia: Westminster Press, 1967], p. 335).

parties. Why, then, can we not commit suicide for the benefit of others? Altruistic acts of stealing, lying, murdering, and committing suicide may be relatively rare and unexpected, but all the same we need not withdraw the terms "steal" or "lie" or "murder" or "suicide" to describe them. Because such acts run counter to our normal expectations, an added word of explanation is usually called for (e.g., "She stole, we must remember, *in order to feed her family*") lest we mislead. The point is this: to speak of an "altruistic suicide" is not a contradiction. Indeed, a suicide can be prompted by a wide range of motives, including those we would judge to be high-minded and noble. Thus the character of one's motives does not serve to distinguish suicide from other self-killings. An act of self-killing is not transformed into a non-suicide by the admirable motives that prompt it. Take the case of the Allied aviator captured during World War II. Knowledgeable about imminent Allied invasion plans, he swallows a cyanide capsule, knowing that otherwise he will be brainwashed and tortured into divulging this crucial information. He dies before his Nazi captors can extract this information from him, and many lives are thus saved. This is, I suggest, a heroic act—but it is also a suicide. For the aviator intentionally ended his own life and did so to avoid being exploited as a source of information by his Nazi captors; he willed his death as a means to the end he desired to achieve. Thereby he fulfilled all the essential characteristics of a suicide.

A self-killing, then, does not cease to be suicide because we view the motivation prompting it in a favorable light. A second case furthers the point. Richard Arthur is suffering a lengthy terminal illness that is draining his financial resources and reducing the size of the estate that he will leave to his wife. Since she will be dependent upon that estate as her means of support, Arthur decides to end his life by shooting himself in the head, thereby preventing further depletion of his estate and protecting his wife's future security. The motivation prompting Arthur to end his life is certainly noble. We may or may not judge him to be justified in terminating his life, but all the same we do not exclude this as a case of suicide simply because we respect his motives. Had Arthur been prompted by a desire to avoid the pain and suffering of his terminal illness, his death would have been a self-interested suicide. As it was, his was an *altruistic* suicide—but a suicide all the same.

Suicide and Treatment Refusal

At the outset of this discussion we need to acknowledge that the relationship between suicide and treatment refusal is conceptually problematic. I'm going to propose that rejecting life-extending treatment should not be called suicide when one is irreversibly dying, even though one intends death; nevertheless, such a proposal is not beyond legitimate dispute. In this area as much as anywhere, the vagaries of the concept of suicide come to the fore. This is obvious when we look at three different cases of treatment refusal and consider three different ways that the connection between suicide and treatment refusal can be drawn.

The first case of treatment refusal is one that will almost universally be viewed as a non-suicide even though the treatment refusal is life-shortening:

> Joan Smith is hospitalized toward the end of what has been a lengthy terminal illness. She is confronted with the option of accepting a new course of treatment that holds out the firm prospect of extending her life by a couple of weeks. This treatment will, however, involve painful surgery with burdensome post-operative effects. In other words, this treatment will extend Smith's dying but also make that dying more burdensome than it otherwise would be. Smith rejects the treatment because she doesn't want her few remaining days to be occupied with the suffering caused by such surgery.

This is not a suicide, even though Smith's refusal of treatment shortens her life by a few weeks. There is simply no requisite intent: Smith rejects treatment not in order to die sooner but in order to die less painfully. If it should turn out that by refusing treatment Smith doesn't actually shorten her life, her purposes wouldn't be thwarted, because she rejects surgery not to die sooner rather than later but to die free from the burdens of surgery. Smith is not a suicide, just as the patient who accepts large doses of morphine in order to control pain is not a suicide, even though those large doses accelerate the patient's dying. In neither case is death or the shortening of life the intent: the surgery is rejected to avoid the accompanying pain and discomfort, and the morphine is taken to eliminate pain. In both cases shortening life is a foreseen but unintended side-effect of what the individual does. Therefore, neither is a suicide.

However, consider a second case, one that is a bit more problematic:

> Anne Robinson is hospitalized toward the end of what has been a lengthy and agonizing terminal illness. Her suffering continues unabated in the form of pain and nausea. Robinson is confronted with the option of accepting a new course of treatment that holds out the firm prospect of extending her life by a few weeks. This treatment (unlike Smith's) is painless and inexpensive, but it will extend an already agonizing dying. Not wishing to prolong her agony, Robinson refuses the treatment.

Has Robinson committed suicide? In this case, unlike in Smith's case, the intent requirement *is* fulfilled, because Robinson refuses treatment solely because it is life-prolonging, not because it is painful (it is in fact painless). In other words, she rejects the treatment not because it makes her dying worse but because it makes it longer. To be sure, both Smith and Robinson are concerned with pain and wish to avoid it by refusing treatment, but there is this difference: Robinson refuses treatment in order to shorten her life and thereby reduce her pain (shortening her life is the intended means for reducing her suffering), whereas Smith rejects treatment because it directly brings suffering with it, not because it is life-prolonging. Robinson, then, refuses treatment for the express purpose of dying sooner rather than later. Some have thought this distinction to be crucial, and others have not—and here we introduce two differing opinions of Robinson's refusal of treatment:

31

(1) Some claim Robinson's death *is* a suicide because whenever one intentionally, by active or passive means, brings about one's death, one has committed suicide. Robinson has the power to die sooner or later, and she exercises her power by intentionally choosing the former. Her death, therefore, is a suicide. To be sure, Robinson is dying and her death is imminent, but one can, we should recall, commit suicide under these conditions. To be sure, Robinson dies a natural death, but a natural death can be a suicide. To be sure, Robinson uses passive means, but one can commit suicide passively as well as actively. It would be argued, therefore, that there is no basis on which to exclude Robinson as a suicide. Smith is not a suicide because she does not intend her death, but Robinson does intend her death and therefore is a suicide.

(2) Others claim Robinson's death is *not* a suicide because in order to commit suicide one must create one's own dying (or refuse to eliminate a reversible dying condition not of one's own making). Indeed, we should note that Robinson's case would not strike most people as a suicide: she is dying, she will be dead shortly no matter what she does, and she simply acquiesces to an irreversible dying condition not of her own making. Significantly, Robinson does not *create* her own dying, although she *shapes* her dying, abbreviating its length by refusing treatment. In this regard, contrast Robinson with a dying cancer patient who takes a lethal drug overdose. This individual has introduced a separate pre-emptive fatal condition with its own dying distinct from that produced by the terminal cancer. Robinson, although she intends her death ("death" being understood as the terminus of a dying condition), does not create her own dying. Here we need to emphasize that dying modes can be sufficiently distinct so that one mode (dying of cancer) can be superseded by another (dying by drug overdose or gunshot). When such replacement is effected—actively or passively—in order to shorten one's life, we have a case of suicide. But when one seeks to shorten life merely by refusing to retard the progress of an inescapable dying condition—even though one actually intends one's death—we do not have a case of suicide. Robinson is not a suicide, then, because she

neither (a) created her own dying nor (b) refused to eliminate a reversible dying condition.

If we accept this last suggestion, then we must acknowledge that our third example of treatment refusal *is* a suicide. The subject, Phil Jones, has cancer, and is suffering a difficult and painful dying. A diabetic, he decides to stop his insulin injections. Consequently, he passes into a diabetic coma and dies. In one regard Jones does the same thing as the person who ingests a cyanide capsule: he intentionally creates a pre-emptive fatal condition that takes his life before he can die of cancer. Jones is not merely shaping an irreversible dying like Robinson; he is, by an act of will, introducing a second dying condition that supersedes the primary dying condition that threatens his life. However, *if* it doesn't seem that Jones has committed suicide (and many would say that it doesn't), then we need to draw the connection between suicide and treatment refusal in yet a third way in order to exclude Jones as a suicide. To do so, we can simply stipulate that treatment refusal is never an act of suicide when one is irreversibly dying and death is imminent. According to this construal, none of the preceding cases (Smith, Robinson, or Jones) is a suicide because each individual is inescapably dying and will be dead shortly in any event. So, as long as one is irreversibly dying, the refusal of life-extending treatment is not suicide.

Thus we have three ways of connecting suicide with a dying patient's refusal of life-extending treatment. Let's take a systematic look at what has been suggested:

(1) *To intentionally shorten one's life by treatment refusal is always suicide.*

(a) Thus, whenever one refuses treatment for the express purpose of dying sooner rather than later and succeeds in doing so, we have a suicide.

(b) Thus, whenever the life-extending treatment is painless, convenient, and inexpensive, its rejection constitutes suicide because the only reason for rejection is to shorten one's life (religious considerations aside—e.g., the Jehovah's Witness who rejects blood transfusions for religious reasons).

(c) Thus Smith is not a suicide because she doesn't intend her death but intends only to avoid the suffering that the operation would cause her. Robinson and Jones, however, are both suicides because they do what they do for the express purpose of dying sooner rather than later.

(2) *To intentionally shorten one's life by treatment refusal is suicide only when one thereby "creates" one's own dying.*

(a) Thus not all intentional shortening of life is suicide (as the previous view claims); only the intentional shortening of one's life that is achieved by creating one's own dying is suicide.

(b) Thus one can take advantage of an inescapable dying condition, allowing it to run its course unimpeded, without committing suicide.

(c) Thus Smith and Robinson are not suicides because they don't create their own dying, but Jones is a suicide because his rejection of insulin creates a dying condition that takes his life.

(3) *To intentionally shorten one's life by rejecting life-extending treatment is* not *suicide so long as one is irreversibly dying.*

(a) Thus one can intentionally shorten one's life by rejecting treatment without committing suicide as long as one is already irreversibly dying.

(b) Thus one can even intentionally create a pre-emptive dying condition (e.g., reject insulin) without committing suicide as long as one is already irreversibly dying.

(c) Thus Smith, Robinson, and Jones are not suicides because all are irreversibly dying.

(d) However, killing oneself with cyanide capsules, a drug overdose, or a gunshot to the head is suicide even when one is dying because those acts are not merely treatment refusals.

I believe that all three of these interpretations are defensible. This shouldn't take us completely by surprise, since we had no guarantee to begin with that the concept of suicide is a logically precise notion which, when faithfully unpacked, will have unambiguous implications for every possible situation. If it is the case that the notion of suicide is somewhat ambiguous (as our explorations have just indicated), then we would be wise *not* to use the term "suicide" in areas in which its application is uncertain (e.g., treatment refusal), lest the judgmental overtones of the term incline us to prejudge moral issues that need instead to be given careful and open-minded consideration. In other words, if it is not clear or obvious that treatment refusal by an irreversibly dying patient is suicide, then we shouldn't call it suicide. That is, we should favor the third position outlined.

Of course, we can *say* that we should be open to the possibility that treatment refusals that are suicides might also be morally permissible, but that is easier said than done. Granted, I have indicated that the term "suicide" is to be understood as a morally neutral term like "homicide" and not a judgmental term like "murder," but declarations like this will not change the fact that "suicide" is for many of us a prejudicial term and that we must struggle to maintain an open mind toward acts which are so described. It is better, then, that a term such as "suicide" which brings with it such emotive content be used only when we are certain that we have an instance of suicide and that the application of the term is beyond serious question. Therefore, when we subsequently discuss treatment refusal by the irreversibly dying, our discussion of its moral permissibility will proceed free from any reference to suicide.

Terminally Ill but Not Dying

I have just suggested that when one is irreversibly dying, one can reject life-extending treatment without one's refusal being characterizable as a suicide. But what shall we say about the case of Tom Albertson? He is diagnosed as having a terminal condition. With appropriate medical treatment he can live for two years; without treatment he will be dead within a month. Depressed over the prospect of facing death for two years, Albertson refuses the proposed treatment and dies in three weeks.

I am strongly inclined to think that Albertson *did* commit suicide. But haven't I just suggested that an irreversibly dying patient who rejects treatment is *not* a suicide? Doesn't it follow that Albertson is not a suicide, since he fulfills these conditions? I would suggest that although Albertson's condition is terminal, he is not dying. For one can have, I suggest, a fatal or terminal condition without necessarily being in a dying state, because dying is only the final phase of a terminal condition. The notion of "dying," although not a concept with precise parameters, does carry with it the implication that death is imminent. Dying cannot go on for months or years—for days or (a few) weeks, perhaps, but not months or years. When one is dying, the biological organism is breaking down in certain radical ways such that death will occur shortly. Thus Albertson, although he has a terminal condition, is not yet dying, and by his treatment refusal he intentionally brings about his own dying in a context where death is not imminent.[10]

Summary

In sum, suicide is intentionally bringing about one's death by passive or active means—except when one is irreversibly dying,

10. Tom L. Beauchamp shows he is in fundamental agreement with my position when he concludes, "An act is *not* a suicide if the person who dies suffers from a terminal disease or from a mortal injury which, by refusal of treatment, he or she passively allows to cause his or her death—even if the person intends to die" ("Suicide," in *Matters of Life and Death,* 2nd ed., ed. Tom Regan [New York: Random House, 1986], pp. 84-85). The difference between Beauchamp's position and mine is that Beauchamp believes that all those suffering from mortal injuries or terminal illnesses who refuse treatment are non-suicides. By contrast, I assert that it is only for those individuals who are dying and for whom death is imminent that treatment refusals which intend death are not suicides. According to my thinking, then, a kind of time restriction is operative here. Beauchamp feels that this time restriction cannot be precisely formulated—how close must death be in order for treatment refusal to be non-suicide? Indeed, precise formulas do not exist, but this only means that in addition to cases which are clearly suicides we will have cases that are unclear, that we will be uncertain about whether they are suicides because we will be uncertain about whether death is imminent enough for the act of treatment refusal to be non-suicide.

in which case treatment refusal should not be called suicide. This analysis does not attempt to deal with all the difficult issues surrounding the concept of suicide, but it does attempt to deal with those issues that would be relevant to our understanding of suicide in the context of the euthanasia debate. Let's briefly review the principal points of our analysis:

(1) A person who commits suicide is a person who *acts on the desire to die*—that is, he or she pursues a course of action for the express purpose of ending his or her life. This is what it means to say that the person who commits suicide *intends* to die. Accordingly, the woman who shortens her life by smoking and drinking heavily, the Jehovah's Witness who refuses blood transfusions and dies, the martyr who faces death rather than renounce her faith—none of these are suicides. The reason? None of these individuals acted on the desire to die; none performed their respective acts (smoking and drinking, refusing blood transfusions, confessing her faith) for the express purpose of ending their lives. This is true also of the person who takes increasingly large doses of morphine for the purpose of pain control, knowing that she is risking death in doing so. Here, too, the individual acts not on the desire to die but rather only on the desire to control pain. However, should this individual knowingly increase the dose of morphine beyond the point required to control pain and to the point that the dosage is likely to cause death, then she is acting on the desire to die, and should death ensue, it would be a suicide.

(2) One does not act on a desire to die when one brings about one's dying as a mere side effect; this remains so even when one desires death. That is, one can both desire to die and perform an act that one knows will bring about one's death but not be acting on *that* desire because one is in fact acting on *another* desire altogether. Thus the patient taking morphine does not commit suicide by performing an act she knows will bring about her death because she is acting on the desire to control pain—not acting on the desire (although it is present) to die.

(3) The relationship between suicide and treatment refusal

37

is, as we saw, conceptually uncertain. It is arguable that the rejection of life-extending treatment by an irreversibly *dying* patient *should not be called suicide* even though the patient acts on the desire to die (a) by allowing a dying condition (that one did not create, could not prevent, and cannot remove) to run its course rather than temporarily impeding its progress by appropriate treatment or (b) even by rejecting treatment that serves to create a pre-emptive dying condition. By contrast, when one uses active means—that is, engages in a direct assault on bodily life (e.g., a drug overdose, a gunshot to the head, etc.)—that is a suicide, even though one is dying. On this point some may not be fully convinced. Why, they ask, is the irreversibly dying patient's shortening of his or her life judged *not to be* a suicide when intentionally effected by means of treatment refusal (of whatever kind) but judged *to be* a suicide when effected by a gunshot or an overdose? Thus far I have offered only two considerations in support of this assertion: (a) it basically corresponds with our pre-reflective intuition about which individual cases are or are not characterizable as suicide, and (b) the term "suicide," because of its moral overtones, ought to be used sparingly—that is, only when its use is incontrovertible. (We will deal with this issue more thoroughly in Chapter Five, when we reflect on the morality of treatment refusal.)

The definition of suicide that I have proposed attempts to do justice to common usage; it is, in the main, a descriptive definition, not a stipulative one. It attempts to include all and only those cases that most of us would recognize to be cases of suicide; it does not reflect a conscious attempt to serve a moral agenda by intentionally including only acts judged to be evil, wrong, or morally problematic in special ways, although that may to a considerable extent turn out to be the case. And is that the case? That is the question we will turn to as we move beyond linguistic distinctions to moral ones, as we inquire into the moral status of suicide.

38

CHAPTER THREE

The Morality of Suicide

Introduction

In discussing the *morality* of suicide, I am assuming that not all suicides are expressions of mental illness. Indeed, if they were, then it would be no more appropriate to speak of the morality of suicide than it would be to speak of the morality of schizophrenia. It is a piece of dogmatism, however, to insist that all suicides are irrational acts, only expressions of a psychiatric disorder. For other societies and other cultures have virtually institutionalized certain forms of suicide. Take, for example, the widespread acceptance of suicide in the ancient Greco-Roman world. Consider, too, *suttee* in India (a Hindu custom whereby a widow voluntarily submits to cremation on the funeral pyre of her husband as an act of devotion) and *hari-kari* in Japan (suicidal disembowelment as an alternative to final defeat by one's enemy or an act carried out in lieu of the death penalty). Whatever we may think of such acts, they do not constitute institutionalized insanity. True, in our own culture, which tends to frown on suicide, it may be more likely that a suicide's action will be prompted by a mental disorder. Still, there is no reason to believe that this is always so, for the person committing suicide may simply be someone who disagrees with the attitude toward suicide that prevails in his society, or it may be that he failed to be true to his own belief that suicide is wrong. The person with diagnosed bone cancer, for example, who decides to end his life may act wrongly but not necessarily irrationally or insanely. Again, this is not to deny that many suicides are the result of unsound minds or serious emotional disturbances, or to suggest that moral categories of right, wrong, permissible, and so forth do not apply. But suicides are not always attributable to mental or emotional illness, and our present concern is with those suicides that are non-pathological and to which moral categories *do* apply.

We will conduct this exploration of the morality of suicide by interacting with some of the historically important contributors to this topic. What follows, therefore, is not simply a historical survey; rather, it is an attempt to provide moral focus and reach substantive conclusions. Consequently, the emphasis will be not on fine points of historical interpretation but on the use to which we can put these significant contributors in clarifying our own thinking and in reaching our own conclusions about the moral status of suicide. All of them have something to teach us, even if the lesson is a negative one.

Greco-Roman Attitudes: A Spirit of Toleration

The Christian attitude toward suicide and euthanasia is commonly presented as a reaction to and a radical departure from the permissive attitudes toward these practices that prevailed in the Greco-Roman world. The Christian church, at least from the time of Augustine onward, was firm, uncompromising, and absolutist in rejecting both suicide and euthanasia. Indeed, those who today call for a revision of current attitudes toward these practices (e.g., various right-to-die organizations) often see themselves as advocating a return to this ancient and more permissive moral perspective. And, unquestionably, suicide and euthanasia enjoyed widespread acceptance in the classical world, especially among the upper classes.[1]

---

1. For one interesting discussion, see Danielle Gourevitch, "Suicide among the Sick in Classical Antiquity," *Bulletin of the History of Medicine* 43 (1969): 501-18.

Not all who lived and thought in the world of ancient Greece and Rome shared the prevailing view, however. The Pythagoreans,[2] for example, emphatically rejected all suicide for religious reasons. They believed that earthly existence, with its pain and possibly agonizing death, was God's punishment for past sins: he had placed fallen souls in human bodies for the purpose of serving out their allotted period of penal servitude. To commit suicide, therefore, was to refuse to accept one's just punishment; it was both morally wrong and an offense to God, who alone was to determine the length of one's sentence.

Many scholars argue that the Pythagoreans may have been influential in the formation of the Hippocratic oath (associated with Hippocrates, the famous ancient physician and contemporary of Socrates).[3] For both the Pythagoreans and the Hippocratic tradition rejected a range of practices that were widely accepted in their own culture. In a crucial passage the Hippocratic oath declares, "I will neither give a deadly drug to anybody if asked for it, nor will I make a suggestion to this effect. Similarly, I will not give to a woman an abortive remedy. In purity and holiness I will guard my life and my art." Here is a dual rejection of the widespread practices of euthanasia and abortion. This rejection was not widely shared, however. Paul Carrick, who refers to the Hippocratic oath as an "esoteric document," comments, "If, in addition, it does represent some sort of reform movement in Greek medical practice, then it is plausible to infer that its adherents constituted a relatively small group of physicians."[4] Yet, ironically, this "esoteric" oath has gained considerable prominence in modern times, becom-

2. Pythagoras (ca. 580–ca. 500 B.C.), the founder of the school that bears his name, was a pre-Socratic philosopher. Although the Pythagorean movement was pre-Christian, Pythagoreanism did experience a brief revival during the beginning of the Christian era. See "Pythagoras and Pythagoreanism" in vol. 7 of *The Encyclopedia of Philosophy,* ed. Paul Edwards (New York: Macmillan/Free Press, 1967), p. 39.

3. Ludwig Edelstein, "Hippocrates," in *The Oxford Classical Dictionary,* 2nd ed. (Oxford: Clarendon Press, 1970), pp. 518-19.

4. Carrick, *Medical Ethics in Antiquity* (Dordrecht: D. Reidel, 1984), p. 96.

ing the oath commonly taken by physicians when they enter medical practice.[5]

Two other significant figures who dissented from the prevailing attitude toward suicide in the ancient world were Plato and Aristotle, his pupil. Plato took a negative attitude toward suicide in general, although he was sympathetic toward euthanasia in cases of agonizing and debilitating illness.[6] Aristotle opposed suicide even more strongly, disagreeing with Plato's endorsement of euthanasia on the grounds that to quit life in the face of suffering is an act of cowardice.[7] Plato's basic argument against suicide was a *religious* one: we are the property of the gods and are not to desert our post before we are relieved.[8] Aristotle offered a *secular* argument, contending that the suicide unjustly deprives society of one of its productive members.[9] Both of these arguments are echoed in the Christian tradition: Augustine repeated Plato's argument, and Aquinas appropriated Aristotle's.

More representative of the Greco-Roman period than either Plato or Aristotle are the Stoic philosophers, who exhibited a sympathy for suicide and euthanasia that was more characteristic of the predominant attitudes of their day. The Stoic philosopher Seneca (4 B.C.–A.D. 65), for example, eloquently endorsed euthanasia:

> Against all the injuries of life I have the refuge of death. If I can choose between a death of torture and one that is simple and easy, why should I not select the latter? As I choose the ship in which I sail and the house which I shall inhabit, so I will choose the death by which I leave life. In no matter more than in death should we

---

5. Physicians today swear to an abridged version of the Hippocratic oath which is more ambiguous when it comes to such practices as abortion and euthanasia. Thus it is sworn: ". . . and will give no drug, perform no operation, for a criminal purpose, even if solicited, far less suggest it" (*The Columbia Encyclopedia*, s.v. "Hippocrates").

6. *Laws* XI: 873 C.

7. *Nicomachean Ethics*, 1116a 12-15.

8. *Phaedo*, 62 b-c.

9. *Nicomachean Ethics*, 111, 1115 b7.

act according to our desire. . . . Why should I endure the agonies of disease . . . when I can emancipate myself from all my torments?[10]

Many see Seneca's position as the very antithesis of what is acceptable for a person with Christian values. Arthur Dyck, a prominent contributor to the current debate, puts matters very much in these terms when he comments, "The Stoic heritage declares that my life and my selfhood are my own to dispose of as I see fit. The Jewish and Christian heritages declare that my life and my selfhood are not mine to dispose of as I see fit."[11] So the contemporary discussion of suicide, Dyck argues, confronts us with a choice of moral perspectives: Stoic vs. Christian. Thus the choices that confront us today were framed long ago, and they consist in deciding who has sovereignty over the individual life: God or the individual.

But Dyck's assertions invite criticism. Although aspects of Seneca's position may appear to support Dyck's claim that Stoicism teaches that persons can dispose of their lives as they see fit,[12] we may question whether this is a fair characterization of Stoicism once we take into account the Stoics' strong emphasis on duty to God and the importance of making oneself worthy of one's Creator. In fact, the suggestion that we can dispose of our lives as we see fit, not as God sees fit, would really have no place in Stoic thinking. Indeed, if we can commit suicide in the face of terminal illness or under other circumstances, this is only because doing so accords with God's will. One student of Stoicism has characterized their position in this way: "It is a man's duty to bear the pains that God sends him: only if deprived of life's necessities does he know that God is sounding the recall."[13]

10. *Laws* IX: 843.
11. Dyck, "An Alternative to the Ethic of Euthanasia," *To Live and to Die: When, Why, & How,* ed. Robert H. Williams (New York: Springer-Verlag, 1973), p. 109.
12. Seneca's talking about choosing one's death as one would choose a house to inhabit or a ship in which to travel seems to indicate that one can feel free to end one's life on a whim. Yet, to illustrate what he has in mind, Seneca mentions death in order to avoid torture and death in order to avoid the agonies of disease.
13. F. H. Sandbach, *The Stoics* (New York: W. W. Norton, 1975), p. 51.

In fact, it may be a man's duty to depart life by suicide even though he is happy, or it may be his duty to remain in life, eschewing suicide, even though he is wretched.[14]

Paul Carrick[15] points out that Stoics usually judged suicide to be warranted on just five conditions:

(1) if one would thereby perform a real service to others
(2) if one would thereby avoid committing an unlawful deed
(3) if one were impoverished
(4) if one were chronically ill
(5) if one were losing one's rational faculties

These conditions clearly arise out of an attitude toward suicide that is far more permissive than that found in the Christian tradition. Nevertheless, even here there are limits to the grounds that the Stoics recognized as justifying suicide. Further, if one interprets the existence of any one of the justifying conditions as a call from God to depart this life, as the Stoics did, then one has, in essence, religious grounds for committing suicide. Endorsing euthanasia, therefore, does not require that I also endorse the ethic that my life is my own to do with as I please, not as God pleases. Indeed, as religious advocates of euthanasia—Stoic or Christian—maintain (even if they do so mistakenly), euthanasia involves ending life in a manner compatible with God's will and in response to his call. Thus a rejection of the ethic that my life is my own to dispose of as I see fit does not also require a rejection of euthanasia, because euthanasia might or might not be a disposal of life just as God sees fit—that has to be argued on a case-by-case basis. The point is, however, that we can no more rule out euthanasia than we can rule out killing in self-defense by appeal to the religious ethic that life is to be disposed of as God sees fit, because the crucial question is, "How does God see fit to have us dispose of our lives?" To be sure, part of Dyck's argument must be acknowledged: many who advocate the practice and legaliza-

14. Sandbach, *The Stoics*, pp. 48-52.
15. Carrick, *Medical Ethics in Antiquity*, p. 146.

tion of euthanasia do judge that they may dispose of their lives as they see fit. But my point is that to come down on the other side of this divide, concluding that life is to be disposed of only as God wills, does not settle the issue of euthanasia until we become clear on how God in fact wants us to dispose of our lives.

The Bible: A Curious Silence

Karl Barth noted that it is a "remarkable fact that in the Bible suicide is nowhere explicitly forbidden." He went on to comment, "This is a painful fact to all who have tried to understand and apply the Bible moralistically."[16] Indeed, nowhere is there a direct prohibition of suicide, nor is the issue of suicide even broached. We may wonder why this is so. Dietrich Bonhoeffer sought to explain this silence in the following way:

> The reason for this is not that the Bible sanctions suicide, but that instead of prohibiting it, it desires to call the despairing to repentance and to mercy. A man who is on the brink of suicide no longer has ears for commands or prohibitions; all he can hear now is God's merciful summons to faith, to deliverance and to conversion. A man who is desperate cannot be saved by a law that appeals to his own strength; such a law will only drive him to even more hopeless despair. One who despairs of life can be helped only by the saving deed of another, the offer of new life which is to be lived not by his own strength but by the grace of God. A man who can no longer live is not helped by any command that he should live, but only by a new spirit.[17]

Bonhoeffer's comments may constitute good pastoral advice for dealing with suicidal individuals—it is better to provide help and offer hope than to moralize and issue commands—but we may question whether this is what prompted the biblical

16. Barth, *Church Dogmatics*, vol. 3: *The Doctrine of Creation*, Pt. 4, trans. A. T. Mackay et al., ed. G. W. Bromiley and T. F. Torrance (Edinburgh: T. & T. Clark, 1961), p. 408.

17. Bonhoeffer, *Ethics* (New York: Macmillan, 1965), pp. 169-70.

writers to remain silent on a topic that otherwise supposedly they would have addressed. Actually, Bonhoeffer himself discussed suicide (moralized about it, if you will) and passed a negative moral judgment on it at that, but he didn't feel that *his* moralizing was incompatible with the insight that making moral pronouncements is not the way to help those who, in the dark night of despair, are contemplating suicide. Further, the purpose of a moral discussion of suicide is not only to help those on the brink of suicide but also to shape moral attitudes *before* that point is reached, as well as to help the rest of us morally assess those who do commit or attempt to commit suicide. Moreover, one can question whether moralizing is never appropriate when dealing with persons contemplating suicide. Certainly a would-be suicide who retained some sense of duty would not be beyond the reach of all moral reason, nor would a person wavering over the morality of a contemplated suicide. Surely we could argue with a Seneca who was contemplating suicide; surely we could appeal to his Stoic convictions.

Perhaps a better explanation for the biblical silence is that suicide was not a serious problem in Jewish life, and thus the need for any moralizing was precluded. Accordingly, there may be merit and point to this observation found in the *Encyclopedia of Religion and Ethics:* "The ancient Hebrews were, on the whole . . . joyously fond of life and not given to tampering with the natural instinct of self-preservation."[18] Or perhaps—better—the Jewish belief that life is a gift from God to be lived out under providentially ordained conditions was so strong that it produced a society in which suicide was never seriously considered as a moral possibility and therefore did not require an explicit moral prohibition. In any case, the biblical silence need not be interpreted as approval or even indifference; indeed, both the Jewish and Christian traditions, as they have subsequently reflected on their sacred texts, have in fact repudiated suicide, finding it incompatible with their theological beliefs.

18. G. Margoliouth, "Suicide (Jewish)," in vol. 12 of *Encyclopedia of Religion and Ethics,* ed. James Hastings (New York: Charles Scribner's Sons, 1966), p. 38.

There are four cases of suicide recorded in the Old Testament: Abimelech (Judg. 9:50-56), Saul and his armor-bearer (1 Sam. 31:1-6; 2 Sam. 1:1-15; 1 Chron. 10:1-13), Zimri (1 Kings 16:18-19), and Ahithophel (2 Sam. 17:23). Abimelech, mortally wounded by a woman during a battle, had his armor-bearer kill him to save himself from the ignominy of having it said that he was killed by a woman; Saul, badly wounded in battle, intentionally fell on his own sword to avoid being killed and made sport of by his enemies (Saul's armor-bearer also killed himself); Zimri, defeated in battle, killed himself by sequestering himself in the king's house and setting it on fire; Ahithophel hanged himself after Absalom and the elders of Israel rejected his counsel to pursue and kill David. The case of Samson (Judg. 16:23-31) is less certain. His death may or may not be a suicide, depending on the interpretation given certain particulars surrounding his death. If, by bringing down the temple upon the Philistines, Samson intended their deaths while only foreseeing—even if hoping for—his own, then Samson did not commit suicide.

However, it needs to be pointed out that in each case of suicide recorded in Scripture, death represents a tragic end to a life that did not (at least in its latter stages) meet with God's approval. This is true of the several accounts of suicide in the Old Testament, and it is also true of the one account of suicide in the New Testament, the well-known case of Judas (Matt. 27:3-10; but cf. Acts 1:18-19). Finally, there is the case of Paul preventing his jailer's suicide (Acts 16:25-29): the jailer, mistakenly believing that Paul, Silas, and the other prisoners under his care had escaped, was about to kill himself when Paul intervened, informing him that all prisoners were present and accounted for.

Karl Barth judges the three great suicides of the Bible to be Saul, Ahithophel, and Judas. He sees each of these deaths as the culmination of a decision to usurp God's sovereignty. Saul desired to be a king after the fashion of the Gentiles, the sovereignty of the king replacing that of Jehovah. Ahithophel turned his back on God's elect (David) and sided with the rebel Absalom. Judas held back from a wholehearted commitment to Jesus and by his act of betrayal wished to assert his own control

over events. This pattern leads Barth to declare, "Those who refuse God's grace and try to exist as their own lords and masters
are on the way at the end of which they can only fall on their
own swords like Saul or hang themselves like Ahithophel and
Judas."[19] Thus, although the acts of suicide recorded in Scripture are not explicitly condemned, it would be a mistake to view
this silence as tacit approval or indifference, especially in light
of the fact that each of these suicides was the culmination of a
life that had—as presented in Scripture—turned away from
God. The dark shadow that hung over the last days of these men
also hangs over the manner in which they ended their lives.
Nevertheless, it would also be a mistake to use these accounts
to draw far-reaching conclusions about the moral character of
suicide and euthanasia. To successfully reach such conclusions
requires systematic moral and theological reflection.

The Jewish Tradition: A Hard Line with a Surprising Exception

In summarizing the attitude toward suicide found in the Talmud
(the recognized authority for Orthodox Jews), one commentator
has said, "The time of death is determined by God, and none
dare anticipate His decree. Suicide was regarded with the ut-
most abhorrence and denounced as a heinous sin. . . . Where
self-harm ends in suicide all teachers agree that it is forbidden."[20] This abhorrence was expressed and a statement was in
effect issued to the larger community through the refusal to give
the person who committed suicide full burial honors: no
memorial address was to be offered, and no rending of garments
as an act of mourning was to occur.[21] Indeed, respect for God's

19. Barth, *Church Dogmatics*, vol. 3: *The Doctrine of Creation*, Pt. 4, p. 409.
20. A. Cohen, *Everyman's Talmud* (New York: E. P. Dutton, 1932), p. 75.
21. For a full discussion of this and other suicide-related matters, see Fred
Rosner's "Suicide in Biblical, Talmudic and Rabbinic Writings," *Tradition: A Journal of Orthodox Thought* 2 (1970): 25-40. Rosner points out, however, that burial
rites were to be given to several kinds of suicides: children (who, it was judged,

sovereign lordship over life and death was so strong that one of the tractates of the Talmud (Avodah Zorrah 18a) honors a rabbi who was burned alive by the Romans; when his disciples encouraged him to hold his mouth open so that the flames would consume him more quickly, he refused, saying, "Let Him who gave me my soul take it away, but no one should injure oneself."[22] The martyr thus refused to accelerate his own dying, leaving the exact time of his death to the flames and therefore, he judged, to God.

In defending its attitude toward suicide, the Jewish tradition used many of the same arguments later found in the Christian tradition. Thus Josephus (ca. 37 A.D.–ca. 100), the first Jewish commentator to emphatically repudiate suicide, offered a familiar range of arguments: suicide is contrary to our natural instinct to preserve our lives; it is to treat God's gift of life with contempt; since God gave us life, only he has the right to end it; those who commit suicide will suffer in Hades.[23] One modern rabbi contends that suicide is the moral equivalent of murder, since whether an individual kills himself or another, he ends the life of one who belongs to God and thereby (in both cases) denies the divine ownership of life; further, the person who commits suicide forever removes all possibility of repentance.[24] Both of these arguments are also found in Augustine.

Yet, despite this abhorrence of suicide, there is in the Jewish tradition a veneration of certain acts of mass suicide that the Jewish community views as acts of martyrdom. There is, of course, the famous incident at Masada, where 960 men, women, and children killed themselves when it became clear that the

---

had not yet reached the age of accountability), those acting under extreme emotional and physical stress, those of unsound mind, and those who killed themselves to atone for past sins.

22. *The Babylonian Talmud,* Nezikin, vol. 4 (London: Soncino Press, 1935), pp. 92-93.

23. Josephus, *The Jewish War,* trans. G. A. Williamson (Harmondsworth, Eng.: Penguin Books, 1959), pp. 209-10. All of these arguments are echoed in the Christian tradition.

24. See Rosner, "Suicide in Biblical, Talmudic and Rabbinic Writings," p. 37.

Roman assault on their fortress-sanctuary was about to succeed. Eleazar, the leader of the resisting Jews, convinced the group to enter into a suicide pact with these words: "My loyal followers, long ago we resolved to serve neither the Romans nor anyone else but only God, who alone is the true and righteous Lord of Men: now the time has come that bids us prove our determination by our own deeds."[25] Thus the 960 faithful were convinced to end their lives. However, they are not condemned but rather *honored* in the Jewish tradition.

Further, in the Talmud (Gittin 57b) there is an account of 400 boys and girls who are carried off for "immoral purposes." They discern what is about to happen to them, and in an act of faithfulness to God they end their lives by throwing themselves into the sea and drowning. "If we drown in the sea," they reason, "we shall attain the life of the future world."[26] This account of children committing group suicide has a painful counterpart in our era in the incident of the ninety-three maidens. Margaret Pabst Battin recounts it in *Ethical Issues in Suicide:*

> During the Second World War, the directress of an orthodox Jewish girls' school in a Nazi-occupied city came to understand that her girls, ranging in age from twelve to eighteen, had been kept from extermination in order to provide sexual services for the Gestapo. When the Gestapo announced its intention to avail themselves of these services—ordering the directress to see that the girls were washed and prepared for defloration by "pure Aryan youth"—she called an assembly and distributed poisons to each of the students, teachers and herself. The ninety-three maidens, as they have come to be called, swallowed the poison, recited a final prayer, and died undefiled.[27]

And yet another incident can be recalled: at York in 1190, 500 Jews committed suicide rather than submit to Christian persecutors who threatened them with forced baptism, slavery, and

---

25. So reported by Josephus in *The Jewish War*, p. 385.

26. *The Babylonian Talmud*, Seder Nashim, vol. 4, p. 266.

27. Battin, *Ethical Issues in Suicide* (Englewood Cliffs, N.J.: Prentice-Hall, 1982), p. 166.

death. Nor was the incident at York an isolated one, as *The Jewish Encyclopedia* notes: "Many similar incidences are to be found in the history of the Jews in England, France, and Germany."[28] Indeed, during the medieval period, suicide among Jews was so prevalent as a way to avoid forced conversion or to prevent one's children from being taken away and raised as Christians that the Jewish prayer book included a benediction to be recited before killing oneself and one's children.[29]

These suicides were not justified in terms of self-interest because they were not committed in order to avoid pain or suffering; they were expressions of the Jewish doctrine of *Kiddush ha-shem* ("sanctification of the divine name"), a doctrine based on Leviticus 22:31-32: "So you shall keep my commandments and do them: I am the Lord. And you shall not profane my holy name, but I will be *hallowed* among the people of Israel; I am the Lord who sancti[fies] you" (italics mine). This is the doctrine which says that the Jewish believer is to do everything in his or her power—including taking his or her own life if circumstances require—to glorify the name of God. Anything that would bring discredit to the faith of Israel is to be avoided at all costs. One is never to become a vehicle—even if an unwilling one—through whom the God of Israel is profaned and ridiculed. Rather than be used in this way, one will choose self-destruction and thereby glorify God. Indeed, in the incidents that we have recounted—those of Masada, the 400 boys and girls of the Talmud, the ninety-three maidens of Nazi Germany, and the Jewish community at York—the acts of suicide would be widely viewed in the Jewish community as acts glorifying the name of God. By ending one's life rather than submitting to slavery, forced conversion, or some other degradation of one's Jewish person, one declares that one lives by a higher loyalty and thereby sanctifies the name of God. In ending one's life in these circumstances, one affirms in death the values and the commit-

28. *The Jewish Encyclopedia,* vol. 11, ed. Isidore Singer (New York: Funk & Wagnalls, 1925), p. 581.

29. *Encyclopedia Judaica,* vol. 10, ed. Cecil Roth and Geoffrey Wigoder (New York: Macmillan, 1971), p. 984.

ment to God by which one lived. In such circumstances suicide is not a repudiation of those values but an affirmation of them.[30]

It is for this reason that the Jewish tradition, in contrast to the Christian tradition, looks favorably upon the death of Saul, who kills himself rather than be captured and made sport of by the enemies of Israel. From the Jewish perspective, Saul's self-inflicted death falls under the doctrine of *Kiddush ha-shem* and is a good end to a life that in other respects had gone astray. According to such an interpretation, Saul's falling on his own sword is not an expression of despair or a self-interested act and therefore is viewed as an acceptable way to end his life. Suicide as an expression of *Kiddush ha-shem* is, then, consistent with the rabbi's refusal to hold his mouth open in order to accelerate his own death, because for him to have done so would have been a solely self-interested act. Thus, although there is in Judaism this doctrine of *Kiddush ha-shem*, which has no counterpart in Christianity, Judaism nevertheless does not seek to justify self-interested suicide or euthanasia.[31]

30. In Sholem Asch's fictional account of the ninety-three maidens, the directress of the school addresses those under her charge with these words: "*Kiddush Hashem* is one of the holiest commands laid down for us in the Torah. We must now think of it as the highest duty imposed upon us by God, in order that we may fulfill the holiest of his commandments. This we have learned from the earliest of our martyrs, from all those who were murdered for their faith throughout the entire length of Jewish History. God has enjoined us to love him with all our hearts and our souls. *Kiddush Hashem* gives us the opportunity to serve God with our souls. As the rabbis have ordered, we have the right to make use of self-destruction in order that we may not be utilized for evil. This was the belief of our fathers. When they, too, were in danger of being forced into sin or being forced, God forbid, to accept another faith, they slaughtered their wives and children with their own hands before themselves. From this we learn that in times when we are in danger of sin, when we are in danger of weakening, God forbid, then we have a right to destroy ourselves. Death by our own hand is considered by the God of the Universe as a sanctification of His Name. Therefore, we shall take this solution in our situation, and we shall prepare ourselves to come before the seat of glory in purity and holiness" ("A Child Leads the Way," *Tales of My People* [Freeport, N.Y.: Books for Libraries Press, 1948], pp. 196-97).

31. The rabbinic tradition often appealed to one central text in rejecting suicide—Genesis 9:5: "*And for your lifeblood I will surely demand an accounting* [italics mine]. I will demand an accounting from every animal. And from each

Augustine: Suicide Is Worse Than Murder

It was the condemnation of suicide by Augustine (A.D. 354–430) that was the single most important factor in setting the face of the Christian church firmly against acts of self-killing. Whether Augustine was simply making explicit what was already inferentially present in the biblical writings or whether he, with his stern condemnation, was moving beyond the biblical witness, the fact remains that it was his *City of God* which for the first time forcefully brought suicide as a moral issue to the attention of the Christian community and established the subsequent prevailing attitude toward it—that suicide is self-murder and deserving of the same strong condemnation that we normally reserve for murder itself. Indeed, according to Augustine, to intentionally cause one's own death by falling on one's sword is every bit as objectionable and wicked as causing death by thrusting that same sword into an innocent second party.

In rejecting suicide, Augustine was addressing both the pagan and the Christian worlds. For by demonstrating the immorality of suicide, he could defend the Christian preference for Job—who suffered long and much but clung to life and trusted God—over Cato the Younger, the highly respected and principled opponent of Julius Caesar who took his own life when the latter came to power.[32] In reviling the Christian church for its preference for Job as a spiritual model, the pagan community failed to comprehend that suicide was, as Augustine judged it, the moral equivalent of murder. Once that was recognized, however, the Christian preference stood confirmed: better by far to be a Job than a Cato. But even more important was the much-needed word that Augustine directed to the Christian commu-

---

man, too, I will demand an accounting for the life of his fellow man" (NIV). That there is a direct prohibition of suicide to be found in this verse is most doubtful. Indeed, a scrutiny of major commentaries discloses that this is not even an interpretation felt plausible enough to require a refutation.

32. Augustine, *The City of God*, trans. Marcus Dods (New York: Modern Library, 1950), Bk. 1:24. Hereafter parenthetical citations in the text will indicate appropriate book and section numbers of the work.

nity, in which certain groups, such as the Donatists (a schismatic group that had broken with the main body of Christians in North Africa), eagerly courted martyrdom, often engineering their own deaths by baiting their potential persecutors into killing them. "Whatever the number of Christian martyrs, one fact at any rate is certain," says Henry Romilly Fedden, author of a sociohistorical study of suicide: "a very large percentage of them gave up their lives voluntarily, going out deliberately to procure their own self-destruction. It was hardly an unusual thing to journey, as did St. Anthony, in the persecutions of Diocletian, a full 200 miles with no object in view but to secure one's own death."[33] This was not the heroic and principled self-sacrifice traditionally associated with martyrdom but was instead a suicidal squandering of human life. By closing the door on suicide with an emphatic and absolute prohibition, Augustine sought not only to put an end to such "martyrdoms" but also to end the practice of Christian women killing themselves rather than face the prospect of being raped by their persecutors (Bk. 1:18). In this regard Augustine reasoned that the soul is the seat of virtue, and sexual violation of the body does not compromise one's virtue, for where there is no consent, there is no sin; thus the soul remains pure. Even should the woman anticipate being led into sin by the emergence of "lust," suicide is not the proper response to such a prospect. To kill oneself in order to avoid committing adultery involves a flawed strategy: it is to commit a greater sin (self-murder) in order to avoid a lesser one (adultery); it is to render certain a present sin in order to avoid an uncertain future sin (Bk. 1:25).

Furthermore, suicide is not only "a detestable and damnable wickedness" (Bk. 1:25) in the same moral category with murder; it is in one respect actually worse than murder because, according to Augustine, it leaves no room for a "healing penitence" (Bk. 1:17). Murderers can at least repent and restore their relationship with God, but for suicides this possi-

---

33. Fedden, *Suicide: A Social and Historical Study* (London: Peter Davies, 1938), p. 118.

bility is precluded, so they enter eternity in an unforgiven condition.

However, even granting the wickedness of suicide and the tragedy of concluding life in such a disappointing fashion, Christians need not accept Augustine's judgment that suicide is a "damnable" sin in the literal sense of "damning one forever." For certain complex instances call his judgment into question. What about the heart-attack victim who dies while brutalizing his wife or in the midst of an adulterous liaison? Does his failure to repent in this life forever remove the possibility of forgiveness in the next? And must we never pass from this life with unconfessed and unrepented sin lest we never find forgiveness and reconciliation with God in the next? This would be an awkward conclusion to reach, for, as Bonhoeffer observed, "*Many* Christians have died sudden deaths without having repented of all their sins. This is setting too much store by the last moment of life."[34] Or perhaps J. Davis McCaughey's words are even closer to the truth: "Suicides are not alone in dying in an unrepentant state: others—*perhaps most of us*—will die with unrepented sins."[35]

Crucial to the points that Augustine sought to make was his characterization of suicide as self-murder. His search for a biblical basis from which to condemn suicide as self-murder finally brought him to this pivotal text: "You shall not kill" (Exod. 20:13; Deut. 5:17). This commandment, Augustine noted, is not qualified in any way—as is, for example, the Ninth Commandment: "You shall not bear false witness *against your neighbor*" (Exod. 20:16; Deut. 5:20). Despite this qualification, it would still be wrong to bear false witness against *yourself,* Augustine contended. Therefore, he concluded, how much more evident it is that killing oneself violates a commandment where that qualification is not even present, for we are not told "You shall not kill *your neighbor*" but simply told "You shall not kill." To be sure,

34. Bonhoeffer, *Ethics,* p. 169.
35. McCaughey, "Suicide: Some Theological Considerations," *Theology* 70 (1967): 67, italics added.

Augustine pointed out, "plants" and "irrational animals" do not fall within the purview of this commandment, and killing them is no violation of it. Rather, the scope of this prohibition includes all and only innocent human beings. "The commandment is, 'thou shalt not kill man'; therefore neither another nor yourself, for he who kills himself still kills nothing else than man" (Bk. 1:20). With these words we have the heart of Augustine's biblical case against suicide: it is a transgression of the Sixth Commandment. The operative logic here is simple and straightforward:

You shall not kill man.
I am a man.
Therefore, I shall not kill myself.

Because the command simply prohibits the killing of human beings, it prohibits both homicide *and* suicide, for each is an act of killing a human being.

We may, however, have doubts about the success of Augustine's efforts at proscribing suicide by direct appeal to the Sixth Commandment. Interpreters of Scripture may disagree over whether the Hebrew word in the Sixth Commandment is best translated "kill" or "murder," but they invariably agree that the Sixth Commandment is directed at certain acts of homicide, and they find no intent to proscribe suicide. Of course, this is not to say that the biblical tradition finds suicide morally unobjectionable but only that the Sixth Commandment is not concerned with suicide. For the Sixth Commandment is, after all, part of a series of commands that deal with duty to *one's neighbor*—honor your father and your mother, you shall not kill, you shall not commit adultery, you shall not bear false witness, you shall not covet (Exod. 20:12-17; Deut. 5:17-21). Just as the first four commands center on our duty to God, so the next six declare our duty *to neighbor*. Therefore, *The Interpreter's Bible* is correct when it concludes that the Sixth Commandment has "no direct bearing . . . on suicide."[36] What

36. "Genesis," in vol. 1 of *The Interpreter's Bible*, ed. George Arthur Buttrick et al. (New York: Cokesbury-Abingdon Press, 1952), p. 986.

we are being told in the Sixth Commandment is not to kill our neighbor.

Some Substantive Reflections

The construal of the Sixth Commandment as a direct prohibition of suicide cannot be sustained; nevertheless, the Sixth Commandment might have *indirect* application to suicide. For the moral basis of the Sixth Commandment may provide a basis from which we can morally assess acts of self-killing, because it may be that what makes killing others wrong also makes killing oneself wrong. Accordingly, we need to ask ourselves this question: What is it that makes killing another human being wrong, and does that feature also attach to intentional acts of self-killing? Of course, it might be that suicide is wrong for reasons *other than* those that make unjustified homicide wrong; but, according to the interpretation suggested by Augustine, homicide and suicide are wrong for the *same* reason. With this in mind, let us briefly explore some of the factors that suggest themselves as rendering intentional and willful acts of homicide wrong and see if they also apply to suicide.

First, what naturally comes to most contemporary minds when searching for an explanation of why killing other innocent individuals is wrong is that it is a violation of a right to life. If you kill me, and if you are to be condemned for killing me, then it is because you have violated my right to life. However, it strikes most people as conceptually odd to suggest that my committing suicide would be wrong because I thereby would violate my own right to life. What is odd is the suggestion that an individual can be both the one whose right is violated and the one who does the violating.[37] Usually we think of rights as protective moral coverings that shield our interests from being

37. Such oddities do have analogies elsewhere, however. In self-deception, for example, I am both the deceived and the deceiver—which, of course, is a puzzling psychological phenomenon.

overridden *by others*. Accordingly, we invoke our rights to protect those interests, or we can waive our rights if we so choose. Thus, if you steal my money, you violate my right to that money; but if I foolishly—even wrongly—squander my money or give it away, I do not thereby violate my own right to it, since by giving it away I have relinquished or waived my right to it. Now it may be that the right to life, being a basic human right, cannot be waived or renounced; nevertheless, it remains odd to suggest that suicide is wrong because persons thereby violate their own right to life. This is not obviously a sensible notion.

Moreover, the biblical writings do *not* condemn murder on the grounds that it is a violation of the victims' right to life. Killing might be a serious threat to community life, and it might well be a violation of God's sovereignty over life, but it is not a violation of a right to life—at least this terminology is not used. Indeed, talk about rights was not even introduced into the Western tradition until William of Occam (d. ca. 1349).[38] Of course, the concept might be present even where the terminology is not. Nevertheless, we ought to be suspicious of the notion that talk of a right to life is the best way to capture the Christian vision of the wrongness of killing, since what we find in the biblical witness is a strong emphasis upon God as the sovereign Lord of life and death, so that killing would be viewed as a violation of *his right* to that life rather than a violation of *our right* to it. Problematically, an individual right to life might bring with it the discretionary authority for the individual to waive that right and thereby cancel the obligation that others have not to kill. Accordingly, if I waive my right to life, then the individual who is the recipient of my waiver can kill me without violating my right to life and therefore without doing what makes the killing of the innocent such a serious wrong. This would seem to place in

38. See Kurt Baier, "When Does the Right to Life Begin?" in *Human Rights*, ed. J. Roland Pennock and John W. Chapman (New York: New York University Press, 1981), p. 202.

human hands a sovereignty that from a Christian perspective rightfully belongs to God. But, even if talk of a right to life could be given a Christian home and even if a right to life is not a right that can be waived, it is not a notion that transfers neatly to suicide, for it remains perplexing how one can violate one's own right to life by an act of self-killing.

Second, killing others might be viewed as wrong because it is the ultimate act of harm, and surely we have an obligation not to harm the innocent. Certainly we do seem to view killing as the most serious form of harm that we can inflict. When we punish people, therefore, we take ourselves to be inflicting harm on them, and in this regard the death penalty is usually considered the most severe penalty that we can impose, and hence the most severe form of harm. Moreover, when a person is confronted with a choice such as "Lose your leg or lose your life to cancer," invariably it is judged better to lose one's leg than to lose one's life, better to incur a lesser harm than a much greater one. In such instances death is viewed as a form of harm, and to kill is to harm the person killed. But we may wonder why, in the context of Christian theology, death should be viewed this way, or why it should be viewed as harm in the context of *any* world-and-life view that affirms individual immortality. According to such a view, death is, after all, the transfer of the individual from one sphere of conscious existence to another; and if the subsequent form of existence is no worse than the previous one (questions of damnation aside), then we have not inflicted any harm by our act of killing—at least not the catastrophic harm that we typically think death brings. If, on the other hand, death is annihilation of the self, the permanent obliteration of conscious existence, then it is perhaps understandable that we should fear death and view it as the worst possible evil that we can inflict on another human being.[39] But I am supposing that

39. We should note that not everyone would agree that death is a form of harm, for there is a long tradition, going back at least to the Greek philosopher Epicurus (341–270 B.C.), that argues that the fear of death is irrational, since in

annihilation of the self is not consistent with the Christian vision of life after death, a vision which includes belief in individual postmortem survival. So whatever the harm that is involved in killing another human being, it does not—if Christian theological claims are true—consist in denying the victim a future conscious state.

No doubt a strong and confident belief in an afterlife does not come easily even for the sincere Christian believer, despite the hopefully deepening conviction that nothing "will be able to separate us from the love of God in Christ Jesus our Lord" (Rom. 8:39). Christians too fear death. The testimony of our senses seems so overwhelming: men and women enter their graves and apparently are no more. And perhaps all members of the Christian community will, in the face of death, know the dual presence of hope and fear, belief and unbelief. This natural fear of death may be understood theologically as a product of the Fall (i.e., it is a mark of our separation from God) and/or a divinely ordained means to insure that we not treat cheaply the life that God has given us, for were there no fear of death, we would most likely not take many of the measures required to preserve and protect our lives. Indeed, upon suspecting that we have a potentially fatal illness, we rush to the physician more from a primitive fear of death than from such a high principle as "Bodily life is a trust from God and must be faithfully preserved." Such principles function more as justifications *after* the fact than as motivations before it. Thus in any life-threatening situations it is fear, possibly even terror, that impels us to

order to be harmed one must exist, but when one dies one passes out of existence, and thus there is no longer a subject that can be either harmed or benefited. We will no more be harmed by the fact that we shall not exist a hundred years from now than we were harmed by the fact that we did not exist a hundred years ago. Epicurus sought to make the point this way: "So death, the most terrifying of ills, is nothing to us, since so long as we exist, death is not with us, but when death comes, then we do not exist. It does not then concern either the living or the dead, since for the former it is not, and the latter are no more" ("The Letter of Epicurus to Menoeceus," in *Great Traditions in Ethics: An Introduction,* 4th ed., ed. Ethel Albert et al. [New York: D. Van Nostrand, 1980], p. 72).

action. Unquestionably, such fear has survival value, for it keeps us from taking many foolish, life-threatening risks that otherwise we might very well take, and it often prompts us to act quickly and decisively to preserve our lives when the occasion so requires. If we operated with absolutely no fear of death, we would likely squander our lives, our ethical principles not being sufficient by themselves to prompt the required life-preserving behavior.

Of course, even if persons are immortal and even if there is relatively benign postmortem existence awaiting us, there would still be various forms of harm typically associated with killing: none of them, however, would be sufficient to fully account for the seriousness of taking human life. First, there can and often is physical pain associated with being killed. Needless to say, to be shot, stabbed, or beaten to death hurts and frightens as well as robs one of earthly existence, but dying can also be sudden and painless, the person killed being completely unaware of what has happened (e.g., a person killed while sleeping). However, the evil of an act of murder would not be diminished because the victim was caught unawares. Second, killing can hurt those who are linked by bonds of love, friendship, and dependency to the person who is killed. But that is not what is centrally wrong with murder, for even if the murder victim was a friendless transient or an isolated hermit who had no family and whose death would cause no such harm, the central wrong associated with murder nevertheless would remain. Third, it is true that killing incites fear and threatens the security of the larger community. Certainly life would be most unpleasant if one lived with the constant threat that one might be murdered at any moment. Nevertheless, there could be secret killings (that is, undetected murders) which, because they were never discovered, caused no fear in the community, but they would still be wrong, and wrong for all the basic reasons that make murder a serious wrong. Thus none of these harms—individually or collectively—adequately account for the evil of killing other human beings. And if the Christian vision of life after death is correct, then it may be difficult to see how the *full* moral seriousness of murder can be accounted for in terms of the harm inflicted on the victim.[40]

However, it has been argued by the Christian philosopher Brian Sayers[41] that even for Christians, with their prospect of heaven, death involves loss—not utter loss, to be sure, but loss all the same—and therefore it is understandable why Christians typically do not confront death with equanimity. This is not a failure of faith but a realistic recognition that death involves loss. For just as it costs the Christian something when he or she dies to self and to sin, so it costs the Christian something when he or she dies physically. There is, then, something in physical death (not just in dying) to be genuinely feared; Christians, too, suffer loss, even though they will also enjoy enormous gain. However, we are assured that suffering significant loss is consistent with the enormous gain that heaven brings. And what loss do Christians suffer? Sayers says only that "death may still deprive a believer of many enjoyable and significant activities."[42] The one specific that he mentions (in a footnote, which no doubt indicates that he means only to be suggestive) is sexual activity, which Jesus informs us will not occur in heaven (Mark 12:18-27).[43]

In recognizing that death is genuinely an enemy (even though in some sense a conquered enemy), Sayers is seeking to capture something that is too often neglected in Christian discussions of death; nevertheless, we may wonder whether the loss that Christians suffer can be captured by specifying earthly activities that have no heavenly counterpart and which at death are

---

40. It has been argued that the concept of heaven and the concept of murder are incompatible. Thus R. E. Ewin has commented, "If *everybody really* believed that when we die we go to heaven—all those grapes, on a hot day there are half a dozen comely angels to fan us, . . . and there is no tax on beer—if everybody really believed that, then, whether or not their beliefs were true, we probably would not have a concept of murder at all" ("What Is Wrong with Killing People?" *Philosophical Quarterly* 22 [1972]: 130).

41. Sayers, "Death as a Loss," *Faith and Philosophy* 4 (Apr. 1987): 149-59.

42. Sayers, "Death as a Loss," p. 157.

43. Sayers, "Death as a Loss," p. 159n.23.

forever put aside. More significant than sexual activity, perhaps, is marriage itself, but what other activities fall into this category? Matters are complicated by the fact that our vision of heaven is none too clear, so that here as much as anywhere we see through a glass darkly. Therefore, we seem to have raised issues for debate and pondering rather than for terror, fear, or regret.

When attempting to think of death as loss, perhaps we would do better to think of projects and tasks left unfulfilled, of relationships severed or never consummated, and so on. When a young man or woman is killed in his or her prime, we all sense the tragedy involved in such a death. And certainly there is a need for deep Christian reflection on the twin realities that seem so incompatible: (1) such deaths are genuinely tragic, and (2) death is the gateway into the fullness of God's kingdom. My concern, however, is with what it is that makes killing other human beings wrong. Even granting that death involves loss, is it imposing that loss that makes killing wrong? One problem with this suggestion has been pointed out by Philip Devine, the author of *The Ethics of Homicide:* "If one gauges the harm done by killing in terms of what the person killed loses by being killed, then not all killings would be equally damaging to their victims. In particular it would be in general worse to kill young people than old ones. . . . Against this kind of argument must be set the egalitarian intuition that all people are essentially equal, and that one homicide is therefore just as bad as any other."[44]

But what about suicide? Is it wrong solely because one is harming oneself by ending one's life? If this is what makes killing oneself wrong, then when the point is reached where one's own interests are best served by death—that is, when killing is no longer harm—one can in good conscience proceed to kill oneself. Thus the morality of suicide becomes exclusively a matter of prudential calculation, and one's life becomes one's own to be lived or not according to how one's interests are best served. This, of course, is ethical egoism, a moral theory that is

44. Devine, *The Ethics of Homicide* (Ithaca, N.Y.: Cornell University Press, 1978), pp. 22-23.

at radical odds with biblical teachings and the Christian tradition. Such an egoistic cost-benefit analysis of suicide simply omits one's obligation to God and to neighbor. According to that obligation, my life is not my own, which is to say that whatever weight my own interests are to be assigned, they are by no means the only relevant consideration and perhaps not even the primary consideration in determining the rightness and wrongness of suicide.

Although not all grounds for condemning killing have been surveyed, I wish to bring matters to a head by suggesting and endorsing the following account. To kill another person is to fail to respect that person as an autonomous moral agent who has been called into being by God. For, according to the biblical witness, human beings are made in the image of God, and therefore we are rational, self-determining agents whose earthly existence is the divinely appointed occasion to seek God (cf. Acts 17:26-27), to determine ultimate loyalties and to live them out— to participate, in other words, in a process that has as its outcome our destiny as moral and spiritual beings. Since to kill a person is to frustrate that opportunity, killing is wrong for some of the same reasons that it is wrong to use either force or non-rational manipulative means to impose a value system on others: it prevents the realization of the divine intention for those lives, the living out of freely chosen life purposes. Of course, killing is morally worse than brainwashing or the forceful imposition of values because it constitutes the ultimate invasion into the life of another: it involves a permanent end of all temporal opportunity to live out life purposes and thus participate in a process initiated by God himself. To respect the lives of persons is to respect the divine calling that each person has, for each individual is a participant in a drama, the outcome of which is his or her moral and spiritual destiny. Accordingly, it is wrong to kill innocent persons because it is an unjust interruption of the divinely conferred occasion to pursue life purposes.

This account is not undercut by the reality of postmortem existence; it in fact requires that reality. For it is this life, this existence that is the divinely ordained sphere for choice, decision, the affirmation of moral and spiritual values, and the selection of life purposes, and it is these choices that find their fulfillment and culmination in the next life. As Karl Barth has stated, this life is "the one great opportunity of meeting God and rejoicing in his praise."[45] The calling of each person is to be respected, and thus the life of each person is to be prized, preserved, and protected. To murder is, as we generally believe, the worst assault possible on the meaning and significance of human life, and is rightfully construed as the worst of moral crimes. Further, this account is not framed in terms of a right to life that can be waived as the individual deems fit. Therefore, my granting another person permission to kill me would not alter the morally objectionable character of an act of killing, for it would continue to be a breach of a duty to honor a life that has been granted by God for the purpose of shaping a spiritual existence and doing so in confrontation with the vicissitudes of life. And it would seem plain from this line of argument that those factors which render acts of homicide objectionable also apply to willful acts of suicide and render them objectionable as well. For to kill oneself is to opt out of life's enterprise and to contravene the divine intention for human existence. It is to do with one's own life what one does when one kills another: it is to terminate a process sovereignly ordained by God for the creation of sons and daughters of God and the reclamation of a separated humanity. Suicide is wrong, then, for the same reason that homicide is (usually) wrong. In this regard, Augustine was correct.

Aquinas: A Triple Indictment

Thomas Aquinas (1225–1274) is as uncompromising in his criticism of suicide as was Augustine.[46] In fact, Aquinas borrows from Augustine (as well as from Aristotle) in pressing his at-

---

45. Barth, *Church Dogmatics*, vol. 3: *The Doctrine of Creation*, Pt. 4, p. 336.
46. Aquinas's assessment of suicide is to be found in *Summa Theologica*, Part II-II, Q. 64, Art. 5.

tack. Although his criticism does not have the same intense character as Augustine's, this is partly due to the different historical contexts in which these two theologians wrote. Aquinas was not confronted with the urgent practical problem that confronted Augustine, which was a Christian community enamored with suicidal martyrdom and surrounded by a large pagan community with a permissive attitude toward suicide. Accordingly, Aquinas exhibits a more detached manner in his threefold moral criticism of suicide: he claims that one who commits suicide fails in one's duty (a) to oneself, (b) to one's community, and (c) to one's God. Let us look at each of these in turn.

The First Indictment: A Failure in One's Duty to Oneself

Suicide is wrong, according to Aquinas's initial argument, because it is a breach of charity. Charity is a duty we have toward ourselves because to act otherwise is "contrary to the inclination of nature" whereby we naturally love ourselves and seek to preserve ourselves in existence. Just as homosexuality would be judged, according to Aquinas's natural-law tradition, to be "unnatural"—that is, contrary to human nature (in some sense)—so Aquinas judges suicide to be "unnatural." To kill oneself is to perform a hateful, self-destructive deed that is contrary to the requirements of natural law and therefore wrong. Here notice that Aquinas appears to be assuming that suicide is invariably an act of self-harm and therefore cannot be an expression of charity toward oneself. We, on the other hand, may not be fully convinced of this, at least in those cases of suicide-euthanasia in which the patient is dying a lengthy and painful death. On the contrary, to kill oneself in such circumstances might reasonably be construed as an act that *benefits*—not harms. (We will explore this issue more thoroughly in the next chapter.)

Notice that in failing in this duty to exercise charity to oneself, one is failing in a duty *to oneself*. Aquinas is not alone in construing suicide as a breach of duty to oneself: among others,

Alan Donagan, author of *The Theory of Morality*, also classifies the duty not to kill oneself (at will) as a duty that human beings have to themselves, though for Donagan suicide is a failure to respect oneself as a rational creature.[47] It is true that if the suicide *believes* that self-killing is self-extinction, then the suicide's attitude toward the value of his or her rational capacities may be morally deficient, and there would then be a failure to respect oneself as a rational creature. But in passing we may at least ponder how it is that suicide can be a failure to respect one's rational capacities if in fact there is an afterlife, in which case death does not extinguish those rational capacities and suicide would not be the fundamental assault on the self that it would be in a world where death involves the permanent extinction of personal consciousness.

Further, the claim that we have duties *to ourselves*, a claim made by both Aquinas and Donagan, is in dispute. For it has often been argued that we can have duties to God and to other human beings but not to ourselves. Certainly I have a duty, say, to care for *my* health, to use but one example, but this is a duty I have either *to God* (to care for the life he has entrusted to me) or *to others* (to be healthy so that I can make my contribution to my community and family, and not become an unnecessary burden). Although this duty concerns *my* health, it is nevertheless not a duty that I have *to* myself. So should we consider my failure to care for my health solely as it relates to me, then I will be said to have acted *foolishly* but not immorally—mine would be a prudential failure, not a moral one. For I act immorally only as those to whom I have duties are taken into account, and I have no duties to myself.

And why can't I have a duty to myself? Because, it is often argued, the concept of having a duty to oneself is incoherent; it breaks down logically. We can, for instance, forgive those who have failed in their duties to us, but it makes no *moral* sense to say that we forgive *ourselves* for having failed in our duty to ourselves. To be sure, we sometimes say, "If I did such-and-such, I

47. Donagan, *The Theory of Morality* (Chicago: University of Chicago Press, 1977), pp. 76-81.

could never forgive myself," but this is a manner of speaking, a way of communicating that the deed would be seriously wrong and that we would judge ourselves most harshly should we do it. It does not imply—as it would if taken literally—that we sometimes actually do forgive ourselves, absolving ourselves of guilt or restoring a broken relationship with ourselves. Further, we can—often at least—release others from duties that they have to us (e.g., we can release someone from a promise that they have made to us), but if we have duties to ourselves and if we can release ourselves from those duties at will, then we in effect have no duties to ourselves, because a duty from which we can release ourselves at will is simply not a duty. Now neither of these observations shows conclusively that we can't have a duty to ourselves, for possibly the logic of duties to self is different from the logic of duties to others. Nevertheless, I confess to a certain unease over the notion that we have such duties, that we can, in other words, be morally beholden to ourselves, which is not to be confused with the notion that we have duties which *concern* ourselves but which actually are duties to God or to neighbor, to whom we can be morally beholden.

The Second Indictment: A Failure in One's Duty to One's Community

Aquinas's second argument against suicide is one that he borrows from Aristotle: to commit suicide is to rob the community of one of its contributing members. That this consideration does not *by itself* fully capture the objectionable character of suicide should be clear; if it did, it would follow that suicide would be morally no worse than deciding to live a hermit's existence, for this too denies the community of one of its members. For, after all, some people do become hermits, and we tend to view them more as eccentrics than as evildoers. Is suicide, we may wonder, no worse than this? Possibly we are being too easy on hermits and should view them in a more critical light, seeing them as shirking the valuable and required contribution to society that they could and should make. Nevertheless, it is difficult to morally equate the hermit and the suicide, even after making allowance for the fact that the suicide's decision is irrevocable, while the hermit's is not. However, whatever we may finally think of this as a general objection to suicide, it is not applicable to those contemplated cases of suicide-euthanasia in which the individual is in the latter stages of a terminal illness and therefore not in a position to make a contribution to society—indeed, may actually be a drain on its resources.[48]

The Third Indictment: A Failure in One's Duty to One's God

The third of Aquinas's arguments against suicide is that suicide is a violation of the sovereignty of God and therefore a failure in our duty to our Creator. His reasoning is that I belong to God because I have been created by him, life is God's gift to me, and thus for me to kill myself is to make a decision that is only God's to make. "For it belongs to God alone to pronounce sentence of death and life, according to Deut. XXII,39," declares Aquinas: "'I will kill and I will make to live!'"[49]

In this argument Aquinas may be trading on the following two principles:

(1) If X brings Y into existence, then Y belongs to X (that is, the created belongs to the creator).

(2) If Y belongs to X, then only X is to decree when Y's death occurs (that is, only the creator is to decree when the death of the created is to occur).

---

48. In focusing on the negative consequences of suicide, we would do better to specify the immediate family, rather than the larger community, as the social unit that is most adversely—indeed, devastatingly—affected and to whom the ultimate injustice is done. For one of the real tragedies associated with suicide is the negative impact of such an act upon family members, who by a violent act have been deprived of a loved one to whom they were attached by close bonds of affection, and who consequently experience extreme emotional distress, anger, and intense feelings of guilt and rejection. The resulting emotional scars and psychological problems may last a lifetime. Studies of suicides and surviving family members amply bear this out.

49. *Summa Theologica*, Part II-II, Q.64, Art. 5.

We may, however, legitimately question both of these principles. For we would not be tempted to grant to parents—who do, after all, bring their children into existence—a right to determine when their offspring are to die, even should we believe that there is no God and parents are the sole creators of their children. Nor, for that matter, would we be tempted to give to an evil being, should he be our creator, a comparable sovereignty over life and death.

Although these two principles are rightly suspect, we need not assume that the argument Aquinas offers us trades on them, and even if it does trade on them, we can make the appropriate corrections. For what is crucial is not, I suggest, that God *creates* us and that therefore we are to be subject to his sovereignty, but that *God* creates us. It is not that life is a gift from *someone,* but that it is a gift from *God,* whose purposes for those he has created are just and righteous and good. Indeed, as Plato put it, "One should not escape from a good master" (*Phaedo,* 62e). Thus we are beholden to God to live our lives within the parameters that he has established because those parameters are consistent with his character as a perfectly good being. We can, therefore, substitute for the preceding two principles the following two:

(1) If *God* brings Y into existence, then Y belongs to God.
(2) If Y belongs to *God,* then God and not Y or anyone else is to decree when Y's death occurs.

Thus as Christians we most certainly should affirm that a person's death ought to occur only when God decrees that it occur. This affirmation, however, only raises a crucial question: How exactly does God decree an individual's death or pronounce the sentence of death? We cannot accept the proposition that only *natural deaths* are decreed by God. For if we believe that there are morally justified killings of one individual by another (e.g., killing in the waging of a just war, killing in self-defense, or possibly killing by judicial execution), then we do *not* believe that natural deaths (e.g., from incurable cancer or from a bolt of lightning) are the only way that God pronounces his sentence. So when I kill another person, say, in legitimate self-defense, I have not violated God's sovereignty over life and death, since such a killing falls *within* the parameters established by God (here I assume the falsity of pacifism). Thus it appears that in certain circumstances we can kill other persons without violating the sovereignty of God; we cannot, however, kill others *at will,* for then we do usurp that sovereignty. When I murder another, therefore, *I* pronounce the sentence of death and that is wrong, but when I kill in justified self-defense, *God* pronounces the sentence of death. In each case the individual who is killed dies by my hand; the difference is that the one act of killing (murder) takes me outside the moral parameters established by God, whereas the other (self-defense) does not. If the killing is within those parameters, then the divine decree about how and when a person is to die is not violated; indeed, such killings must be viewed in some sense as expressions of the divine decree. It is false, then, to say that only natural deaths are decreed by God. This, of course, is what pacifists believe, but since most Christians are not pacifists, it cannot be what the rest of us believe. What we believe is that there are morally justified killings, and because they are morally justified, we must also affirm that they are decreed by God and are not violations of his sovereignty. But are there morally justified suicides and therefore self-killings decreed by God? We have already had occasion to note that there is a strong moral presumption against suicide because suicide (like homicide) involves the interruption of the divinely conferred occasion to pursue life purposes, shape a moral and spiritual destiny, gain friendship with God, and to do so in the context provided by God—a world not free of pain and suffering, of natural illness and disease, and so on. To opt out of life via suicide runs the grave moral risk of rejecting the divine purpose for human life.

Additional Substantive Reflections

If there are morally justified acts of suicide, it follows that, because they would be morally justified, they would also be decreed (in some sense) by God and thus not be violations of divine sovereignty. Here it is tempting to suggest that cases of justified suicide parallel cases of justified homicide, suicide being justified in exactly those circumstances where homicide is justified—which would be a narrowly circumscribed set of cases, to be sure. Let us look, then, at some specific cases and see if circumstances that justify homicide might also serve to justify suicide.

First, if I can justifiably kill enemy combatants while waging a just war, can't I justifiably kill myself while waging that same war? Recall the case of the captured Allied pilot: he swallows a lethal cyanide capsule to prevent his Nazi captors from extracting crucial information from him about imminent Allied invasion plans. This, I concluded, was a suicide, although a heroic suicide—one that I now suggest is morally justified, no wrong attaching to it. Thus, even as in waging a just war there are occasions on which we can justifiably kill others and justi- fiably place our own lives at high risk (as in combat), there may also be occasions (rare, no doubt) on which we can deliberately take our own lives. These would be circumstances in which we could, by killing ourselves, avoid being used in significant ways to further the ends of unjust forces.[50] This is exactly what the Allied pilot does.

As a second category of justified suicide, consider self-ad- ministered judicial execution. Here the most famous case is that of Socrates drinking the hemlock and by so doing carrying out the sentence of the state. Although this is perhaps a borderline case, opinion being divided over whether or not it is a suicide, it is nevertheless a self-killing in some sense and one to which no wrong attaches, we might reasonably suppose.

The third category, self-defense, seems to apply only to

50. Consider the following: "Rabbi S. Goren, the chief rabbi of the Israel Defense Army, expressed the view that a soldier taken prisoner was entitled and even obliged to commit suicide if he feared that he might not be able to withstand torture, or that under it he might reveal military secrets. He was, however, sub- jected to considerable criticism for this view" ("Suicide," *Encyclopedia Judaica*, vol. 15, ed. Cecil Roth and Geoffrey Wigoder [New York: Macmillan, 1971], p. 490).

homicide—I can kill *another* to save my life from unjustified lethal attack, but I cannot kill *myself* to save my life from a lethal threat posed by me. The latter suggestion is certainly incoherent. However, consider that killing in self-defense may simply be a subcategory of killing in defense of innocent life in general. For when I justifiably defend myself against lethal assault, I act in defense of the innocent, though in this case I myself am the innocent who is being defended. But it is not inconceivable that I might end my life in order to protect *other* innocent life from being killed by me while I am in a future state of insanity (which I anticipate). Alan Donagan presents Kant's example of just such a suicide: "A man who had been bitten by a mad dog already felt hydrophobia, and he explained, in a letter he left, that since so far as he knew the disease was incurable, he killed himself lest he harm others as well in his madness, the onset of which he already felt."[51] Indeed, if things were as the man thought, and he would *kill* others should he continue to live, then a self-killing would not be morally wrong, since the man would take his own life in order to protect other innocent life.

All of these examples of justified suicide represent rather curious and strained situations, far removed from the lives of most of us. So, although these three categories of suicide might be justified, they do not provide any ground for believing suicide to be morally permissible in the course of normal human existence.

Conclusion and Prospectus

We saw that there is no direct prohibition of suicide in the Bible. However, this silence provides no basis for concluding that the biblical sources approve suicide or judge it to be morally unobjectionable, for there is at least one other possible explanation for this silence: suicide was not a sufficiently common practice among the Jewish and early Christian communities to merit at-

51. Donagan, *The Theory of Morality,* p. 78.

tention. Furthermore, the suicides recorded in Scripture occur in the lives of individuals who at the time of their deaths were at odds with God's purposes, and their mode of death (i.e., suicide) is inferentially implicated in the divine disfavor. Finally, both the Jewish and the Christian traditions, as they have reflected on their biblical origins, have emphatically rejected suicide. It would be difficult to believe that both those traditions have radically misconstrued the basic thrust of the biblical witness.

In the section about Augustine I proposed that an immoral self-killing is wrong for the same reason that an immoral homicide is wrong: it is an unjust interruption of a divinely conferred occasion to pursue life purposes and to shape an ultimate spiritual destiny. More specifically, life is the opportunity God gives us to come to know him and participate in a process of personal, moral, and spiritual transformation. To kill without divine warrant is to challenge the divine intention for creating life. I argued that killing is not wrong—or at least is not primarily wrong— because it is a violation of a right to life or because it is an act of ultimate harm, offering reasons for rejecting both of these accounts. I did assume the falsity of pacifism and assumed as well that there are justified acts of *homicide*: killing in self-defense, killing in a just war, and possibly certain acts of judicial execution. These would be acts of killing in defense of the innocent and therefore would not be "unjust interruptions." Because there are justified acts of killing, it is not the case that only unavoidable *natural deaths* are decreed by God. Thus the divine sovereignty over life and death is not exercised exclusively through the natural order but can be exercised through human agents who kill with moral justification.

I suggested that there might be acts of justified suicide paralleling those acts of justified homicide. Admittedly, they would be rare occurrences (sufficiently rare as to border on the theoretical)—rarer, one would rightly suppose, than justified homicides, which themselves are not a common occurrence for most of us. However, what we have not yet specifically explored is whether there are cases of justified *egoistic* suicide, or what I shall subsequently label "surcease suicide"—suicide for the purpose of avoiding *great* personal harm and suffering. That we cannot kill ourselves *at will* is established by the considerations already offered: life is a gift from God that has been granted to us that we might choose life purposes and affirm ultimate loyalties within the context of an earthly existence that brings to all of us (in varying degrees) problems, pain, and suffering. But can the pain and suffering become sufficiently great that we are relieved of our normal obligation to preserve and protect our lives? Can circumstances conspire to make it impossible for us to choose or fulfill life purposes even on the most limited scale, so that we are released from this strong and important obligation?

CHAPTER FOUR

Surcease Suicide and Voluntary Active Euthanasia

Introduction

"Surcease suicide" is suicide committed for the purpose of avoiding grave personal harm; such suicides are self-interested and are carried out in the belief that one will be better off as a consequence. Voluntary active euthanasia is, from the standpoint of the patient, an instance of surcease suicide: the patient commits suicide through the agency of a physician, a nurse, or whomever, and does so for his or her own benefit. In most discussions of euthanasia, the focus is on the moral propriety of physicians and family members cooperating with the terminal patient who is requesting euthanasia. In contrast, by framing matters in terms of suicide, we shift the focus to the patient and the moral legitimacy of his or her request for euthanasia. I am assuming that we do have a strong obligation to preserve and protect our lives, to treat with the highest respect the gift of life that God has granted us, and to face suffering and pain with courage and faith in God's good purposes for our lives. Nevertheless, we may want to know whether or not the human situation can ever become sufficiently burdensome, suffering sufficiently intense, and one's prospects sufficiently bleak so that one is relieved of this obligation and one can in good conscience end one's life. To take an extreme example, can a soldier trapped in a burning tank from which there is no hope of escape legitimately end his life with a pistol shot to the head rather than die in agony in a fiery inferno? To take a less extreme example, can a terminally ill patient who is suffering considerably from bone cancer justifiably bring her own life to an end? To say "yes" in response to either of these questions is to endorse a form of what is here being referred to as "surcease suicide."

Better Off Dead?

A fundamental belief behind the notion of surcease suicide is that on occasion people will be better off dead, that people can sometimes improve their lot by ending their lives. If death were never in a person's interest, there could never be genuine acts of *surcease* suicide or acts that are appropriately called "mercy" killings. It does seem natural to suppose that the soldier trapped in the burning tank, for example, is not mistaken in holding to the belief that his interests are best served by suicide. Indeed, some may wonder whether he ought to kill himself, but do we really doubt that it is in his interest to do so? In fact, it is the perception that suicide is in the soldier's interest that raises the moral problem for us—moral reservations over the legitimacy of suicide now coming into conflict with our desire to legitimate the only course of conduct (suicide) that can bring an end to agonizing and apparently pointless suffering. It also seems natural to suppose that "Death came as a blessing," the consolation frequently offered to bereaved friends and relatives of a long-suffering terminal patient, is at least sometimes spoken truly, and therefore that death can at least sometimes be a blessing and a benefit. According to this view, death is not an *absolute* evil to be avoided at all costs and in all circumstances, and life is not an *absolute* good to be preserved and maintained at all costs. Thus pain and suffering can become sufficiently great so that death is transformed into a positive good, but it is no less a good—it could be argued—because it is secured by suicide rather than coming about as a result of natural causes. Therefore, if death on occasion is a good, why can we not secure that good for ourselves or help others secure that good by suicide?

Central to the case for surcease suicide, then, is the contention that suicide can bring some benefit and in certain cases considerable benefit to the person committing suicide. But is this claim beyond all serious dispute? And how relevant are postmortem expectations? In this regard, Christians typically believe in life after death, and orthodox Christians believe that both heaven and hell are postmortem realities. In contrast, others believe that death involves the permanent end to all conscious existence. And what, we may wonder, are the implications of these differing views for the claim that suicide is sometimes in a person's interest?

To begin our exploration, let us assume, contrary to traditional Christian belief, that death ends personal existence. What are the implications of such a view for the claim that suicide sometimes benefits the person who commits suicide? There may be problems here, for if an act is to be construed as benefiting an individual, is it a requirement that the individual be better off after the act than he or she was before it? If so, then who is it that is better off after suicide than before, there being no "who" to be better off, personal existence having ended with death? Indeed, we may wonder, how could one improve one's situation by passing out of existence? That is, if death is permanent oblivion, how could a person suffering greatly as a result of a terminal illness go from a less desirable to a more desirable state by means of suicide? Marvin Kohl, author of *The Morality of Killing*, puts the problem this way: "To say that 'X is benefitting by ceasing to exist' implies that X exists though ceasing to exist which is contradictory."[1] Indeed, where is this subject who is better off? Kohl's own answer to the logical problem posed by the absence of a postmortem subject is to speak instead of the benefit brought to the dying but *pre*-mortem subject. The person benefited by surcease suicide is the person who exists prior to the act of sui-

1. Kohl, *The Morality of Killing* (New York: Humanities Press, 1974), p. 82.

cide and prior to passing out of existence. Thus, he says, "just as there is nothing logically odd about saying that we can help a dying patient by making him more comfortable, there is nothing odd about saying that we can help a person by hastening the process of dying."[2]

Clearly, Kohl is correct: the individual who is benefited by death must be the individual who existed *before* death, since after death there is no person (according to the present hypothesis) who can be the subject of this benefit. Therefore, this simply amounts to the claim that a person would be better off living a shorter rather than a longer life, should the longer life have to be purchased at the cost of agonizing pain or excruciating suffering. It is the claim that under extremely difficult circumstances a person (trapped, say, in a burning tank) would be better off living the shorter life (ended slightly sooner by a pistol shot to the head) than he would be living the longer life (ended slightly later in a fiery inferno). So it seems that it does make sense— even granting the assumption that death involves the permanent end of all conscious existence—to say that an individual could be benefited by an act of suicide.

But what about those of us operating within a traditional Christian framework? Can we endorse with assurance the beneficial character of surcease suicide and the merciful character of euthanasia? For in the scriptural tradition not only is life after death affirmed, but the nature of such life is specified, even if in a rather general way, by means of much symbolic language and apocalyptic imagery. Indeed, biblical teaching affirms and orthodox Christianity endorses the view that both heaven and hell are postmortem realities. As J. S. Whale, author of *Christian Doctrine,* notes, "There is something genuinely at stake in every man's life, the climax whereof is death. Dying is inevitable, but arriving at the destination God offers is not inevitable."[3] Thus, should it be the case that suicide invariably deflects one from arriving at the destination to which Whale refers,

---

2. Kohl, *The Morality of Killing,* p. 82.
3. Whale, *Christian Doctrine* (London: Fontana Books, 1957), p. 178.

then there could, of course, be *no* suicide that benefits. Nonetheless, although I believe there is reason to *doubt* that it is in one's interest to willfully end one's life, my doubt is not the product of a belief that those who commit suicide sever their relationship with God.

We have already rejected the contention that suicide damns because it supposedly precludes all opportunity for repentance. We argued that the assumption "Only sins repented of in this life are forgiven in the next" is unworkable, condemning many, perhaps most, if not all. To what has already been said we can submit for consideration the helpful words of Karl Barth:

> The opinion that it [suicide] alone is unforgivable rests on the false view that the last will and act of man in time, because they are the last and take place as it were on the very threshold of eternity, are authoritatively and conclusively decisive for his eternal destiny and God's verdict on him. But this cannot be said of any isolated will or act of man, and therefore not even of the last. God sees and weighs the whole of human life. He judges the heart. And He judges it according to His own righteousness which is that of mercy. He thus judges the content of the last hour in the context of the whole. Even a righteous man may be in the wrong at the last. Even the most sincere believer may be hurled on his death-bed into the most profound confusion and uncertainty, even though there be no suggestion of suicide. What would become of him if there were no forgiveness at this point? Yet if there is forgiveness for him, why not for the suicide?[4]

So suicide is not to be construed as an unforgivable sin on the grounds that it is the very last act of a person and supposedly beyond the pale of forgiveness.

Nor should suicide invariably be construed as an unforgivable sin because it constitutes a definitive rejection of God and of life's meaning, a cumulative expression of one's whole

---

4. Barth, *Church Dogmatics*, vol. 3: *The Doctrine of Creation*, Pt. 4 (Edinburgh: T. & T. Clark, 1961), p. 405.

life orientation. Suicide may, in a few instances, be prompted by just such a dark religious pessimism and rebellion, but most suicides—even most non-pathological suicides, I suggest—are probably not of this kind. Even should a particular suicide be a failure to adequately care for the life that has been entrusted to the individual, it may be no worse than the failure of the heavy smoker or excessive risk-taker. In such cases of suicide, the moral failure involved can be fully recognized without having to construe it in terms that forever sever the suicides' relationship with God. To be sure, in certain cases of suicide there may be a premature submission to death, and this may constitute a lack of courage in the face of suffering or a failure to fully appreciate the value of life, but it need not be an ultimate act of religious rebellion.

Why, then, the hesitancy to endorse the beneficial character of suicide? It is not, I suggest, that *hell* awaits the suicide but that *judgment* awaits, and it awaits all of us. Therefore, with a sense of mystery and deep respect for divine sovereignty but with no conviction that those who commit suicide place themselves beyond divine grace, we can appreciate Dietrich Bonhoeffer's observation about the would-be suicide: "Even if his earthly life has become a torment for him, he must commit it intact into God's hands from which it came, and he must not try to break free by his own efforts, for in dying he falls again into the hand of God which he found too severe while he lived."[5] Indeed, whether we live or whether we die, we are in God's hands, and death does not place us beyond the control of divine sovereignty. Herein lies the real ground for doubt about the claim that by killing ourselves we can better our lot.

To affirm the reality of divine judgment, as Christian theology does, is to acknowledge that no ultimate and permanent advantage will be secured by doing evil; such advantage will be negated by divine judgment, even should that negation only take the form of the deepest of regrets over the manner in which we have disposed of God's gift of life. And surely in this context we

5. Bonhoeffer, *Ethics* (New York: Macmillan, 1955), p. 170.

can attribute more subtlety and refinement to the divine operations than hell requires. So if, in the divine economy, evil acts will not in the long run be allowed to benefit the doer, then, *should* suicide be an evil, it will *not* bring benefit and advantage. In contemplating the possibility of surcease suicide, therefore, our assurance that we will secure benefit for ourselves can be no greater than our assurance that we act in concord with God's will and thus that we are not doing what will ultimately evoke a divine negation. For Christians, then, the morality of suicide, the will of God, and the beneficial character of suicide are issues that are inextricably intertwined. Accordingly, if there is some uncertainty about the moral permissibility of a given act of suicide, then there must also be uncertainty over its beneficial character.

Suffering and Grace

It is frequently argued by those in the Christian tradition that suffering has a sanctifying value: through suffering, people can become "more mature, more experienced, more modest, more genuinely humble, more open to others—in a word, more human."[6] We must acknowledge that suffering can also be *destructive* of moral and spiritual values (and that in many— possibly most—circumstances it is the *relief* of suffering that best preserves those values); nevertheless, the Christian community would concur that suffering can prove spiritually beneficial when accompanied by an openness to God's working and to his grace. This is no less true when the suffering accompanies a terminal illness. Further, with the prospect of postmortem existence, these gains will not be lost at death but will continue to be part of the ongoing life of the individual. In *The Theory of Good and Evil*, Hastings Rashdall discerns the significance of postmortem existence for the potential value of suffering, especially suffering accompanying a terminal illness:

6. Hans Küng, *On Being a Christian* (Garden City, N.Y.: Doubleday, 1976), p. 579.

There are many cases in which I should myself be unable to re-gard as rational the prohibition of suicide without admitting the postulate of immortality. The good will is possible even in ex-tremest agony, but the good will is not all that is necessary for well-being; and it does seem possible to decide whether the con-tinuance of moral discipline is worth the prolongation of an exis-tence from which all else that gives value to life has departed without asking what are to be the fruits of this moral discipline, whether it is rational to hope for another state in which the character thus formed may have further opportunities of express-ing itself in moral activity and of producing that happiness without which all other good must be incomplete.[7]

Thus the prospect of a postmortem existence in which character development is preserved and given continued opportunity to exercise itself means that a terminal illness is not rendered un-redeemably evil because one is suffering and will die shortly.

It is this consideration that is often advanced as a reason for *discounting* the appeal to suffering when contemplating the possibility of euthanasia. Rather than providing a reason for ac-cepting euthanasia, suffering gives reason for *rejecting* it. The Roman Catholic author J. P. Kenny seems to argue in just this fashion when he comments,

The proponents of voluntary euthanasia ignore the Christian con-cept of suffering and deny, at least implicitly, its supernatural value. Christian morality freely admits that man may employ all the resources of nature to alleviate or to suppress physical pain. But it also maintains that suffering is not purely negative. Physi-cal suffering can have religious overtones and supernatural value. The positive aspect of suffering can be understood only through the light of revelation and the eyes of faith. For a Chris-tian suffering can be a means of purification and sanctification if he accepts it in a spirit of penance and with resignation to the will of God.[8]

---

7. Rashdall, *The Theory of Good and Evil*, vol. 1 (London: Oxford Univer-sity Press, 1924), p. 209.

8. Kenny, "Euthanasia," *New Catholic Encyclopedia*, vol. 5 (New York: McGraw-Hill, 1967), p. 640.

No doubt what Kenny has to say about suffering would be affirmed by all who share a Christian perspective: suffering can by the grace of God have beneficial consequences and supernatural value for the sufferer. However, none of this bears out the conclusion that euthanasia and surcease suicide are invariably forbidden (though they may be forbidden for *other* reasons), nor does it undercut the appeal to suffering made *in support of* these practices. For we do not demonstrate that a course of action is the will of God—in this case, bearing with a terminal illness to its very painful conclusion—by pointing to the suffering that will accompany it, even when we acknowledge that suffering can prove spiritually profitable. Rather, we *first* seek to show that a course of action is the will of God, which *in turn* justifies bearing with the suffering it brings in its wake. We do not, for example, reject anesthesia before undergoing painful surgery on the grounds that suffering can be of spiritual benefit. Whereas we often do take genuine consolation from the fact that the suffering we feel compelled to endure may contribute to our maturing as Christians and to our growth as spiritual beings, we never use this fact to conclude that the pain and suffering which confront us must be endured rather than dealt with in some other fashion. Indeed, we don't conclude that a course of action is obligatory because the attendant suffering will or might be spiritually profitable. Rather, our reasoning is just the reverse: we conclude that the suffering will or might be spiritually profitable because we *first* concluded that the course of action is God's will for us. What has spiritual value, then, is suffering that comes in the wake of pursuing God's will or—in purely ethical terms—doing what is right. So we may agree that it is possible for suffering to be a means of sanctification and purification; still, that general consideration does not tell us whether or not active euthanasia and surcease suicide are moral options for Christians, any more than it will tell us whether or not anesthesia is a moral option.

At this point it might be interjected that we have adequate spiritual resources to enable us to successfully face the most agonizing of situations, God's grace being sufficient for every human extremity, so that accelerating the dying process by positive means is unnecessary, and if unnecessary, then immoral. Indeed, "My grace is sufficient for you, for my power is made perfect in weakness" (2 Cor. 12:9). But once again there appears to be something wrong with this line of reasoning. For the mistake made earlier appears to be repeated here: it is incorrect to reason that, because spiritual resources sufficient to confront suffering with courage and dignity are available, we don't take personal pain and suffering into account when seeking to ascertain God's will; rather, when we attempt to determine God's will we take into account a wide range of considerations, including the pain and suffering to be endured, and should we judge a difficult course to be the will of God—as it might be, suffering and all—*then* we are to seek grace sufficient to confront our suffering with dignity, courage, and a firm sense of submission to God's will. This is the suffering that will prove spiritually profitable and for which there is grace sufficient to sustain the sufferer.

Suffering and Release from Obligations

There is another side to suffering, however, that needs to be taken into account. When suffering becomes sufficiently great, we sometimes judge ourselves to be actually relieved of obligations and duties that otherwise hold. Thus under normal circumstances I need not risk bodily harm or financial loss to keep, say, a promised appointment. Although such a promise certainly carries weight and requires effort, even inconvenience, in order to fulfill it, there are limits, and in this kind of case perhaps relatively low limits. When those limits are reached—and no precise calculus exists to determine this—I am no longer obliged to keep my promise. In some contexts, of course, a promise may bind one to a much higher set of limits—for example, one's pledge to serve one's country in the armed services. Even in these circumstances, however, there are still limits—for example, one is usually not required to go on "suicide" missions; one has the option to volunteer or not. But the point is that in a wide range of cases we recognize that heavy burdens can release us from obligations that otherwise hold. Accordingly, we may ask this question: In the case of our obligation to preserve and protect our lives, are there limits beyond which we are not obliged to go? Consider what is an extreme (and potentially misleading) case, that of the soldier trapped in a burning tank (not uncommon in tank warfare) who decides to end his life with a bullet to the head rather than die an agonizing death by fire. Is this morally permissible? An affirmative answer does not seem unreasonable, considering these features of the case: (a) the alternative to suicide is an excruciatingly painful death, (b) he is going to die momentarily anyway, (c) his suffering would serve no useful purpose—that is, he would not benefit others by suffering, and (d) because his suffering would be all-consuming, it is doubtful that he could even exercise his spiritual and rational capacities during this final phase of his life. There are no biblical proof texts that will establish this point nor any that will successfully contradict it, but it is a conclusion that seems consistent with the portrait of a compassionate God who does not demand of his creatures more than they are able to endure and no more than there seems any reasonable point to endure. This acknowledgment, however, does not do much by way of setting precedents, since it represents a judgment directed at a rare and catastrophic case. It does not, for example, tell us whether surcease suicide for the terminally ill is morally acceptable, because one would imagine that no terminal illness would bring with it quite as agonizing a death as the one in the illustrative case, especially in view of the palliative measures that the medical profession makes available to the terminally ill. But it does suggest that even the duty to refrain from ending our lives may have limits.

However, it is important to remind ourselves that there is a danger in doing ethics by relying heavily on extreme cases, and the case of the soldier who commits suicide as the only alternative to being burned alive in a tank is just such a case. By focusing on extreme cases, we can unfairly undermine confidence in the firmness of moral rules that in the context of normal human existence are in fact sound and virtually exception-less.[9] For as Charles Fried, author of *Right and Wrong*, has cogently observed, moral rules apply to a large middle ground that is bounded on the one side by the trivial and on the other by the catastrophic.[10] Between these boundaries traditional moral rules function with virtual sovereignty, but outside them these rules may lack application. Accordingly, what we want to know in essence is this: Can surcease suicide be justified *within* the boundaries suggested by Fried? That is, can one, in the course of *normal* dying, reach the point where suffering is so intense that one is permitted to end one's life?

In light of the Christian belief that life is a trust from God to be lived out in a fallen world with all its harsh realities, including suffering, any act of ending one's life even in the face of those harsh realities involves considerable moral risk. For, in appealing to suffering from a terminal condition in order to justify suicide, we appeal to a condition that is part of the world in which God has intentionally placed us to live out our lives: it is part of the world in which we have been placed to engage in soul-making; it is part of the world in which we have been placed in order to make our ultimate commitments, to determine our ultimate loyalties, and to have them tested in varying circumstances. To opt out of this world by suicide is to question God's wisdom in placing us in such a world to begin with. From a Christian perspective, this is, morally speaking, a high-risk undertaking. And since I see no way to eliminate that risk—that is, since I do not believe (short of the catastrophic case) that the person committing suicide can have confidence that he or she is acting rightly or permissibly—then it appears that our present task can only be one of searching for factors that might serve to *reduce*—but not eliminate—that risk. In this regard, we have perhaps already

9. Indeed, I would suggest that this is a fault attaching to the work of Joseph Fletcher, who, in presenting his "situation ethics," became a creative master of the extreme case, using such cases as a means of casting doubt on the trustworthy character of traditional moral rules.

10. Fried, *Right and Wrong* (Cambridge: Harvard University Press, 1978), p. 10.

identified one such factor: the presence of intractable and agonizing pain and suffering. This should come as no surprise, since it is appeal to the suffering that euthanasia-suicide can eliminate that is invariably invoked in support of it. Still, the act of suicide remains morally doubtful despite the presence of this risk-reducing factor. But are there other factors that might serve to reduce the moral risk involved in suicide?

Suicide and God's Purpose for Human Life

The Christian community does not endorse an ethic that makes the individual unlimited master over his or her life. Such a vision of human lordship is negated by the Pauline declaration that "you are not your own; you were bought with a price" (1 Cor. 6:19-20). We belong to God, who has created and redeemed us; therefore, in determining how we are to live and die, we rightly look to the divine purpose in creating and redeeming. So if there are justified suicides, they must be consistent with that purpose. The logic of such a line of thought is straightforward: if we human beings have been created and redeemed for a certain purpose, then to the extent to which that purpose can no longer be realized, to that extent life has lost its rationale, and the moral risk involved in terminating one's life is reduced. If, as previously suggested, earthly existence is the divinely appointed opportunity to come to know and love God and to participate in a process of being transformed into his likeness, a process that involves both decision-making and soul-making, then to the extent to which that purpose is frustrated by certain events, suicide becomes less objectionable and less risky.

Thus, if a person is rendered permanently comatose, it would seem that the divine purpose for that life can no longer be realized within the sphere of earthly existence. In such circumstances personal life is at an end, and there remains only a defectively functioning biological organism where once there was a person. The divine purpose for human life requires the presence of personal consciousness, which in the case of the permanently comatose person has been lost. Of course, in the most fundamental sense, such an individual is already dead, and talk of suicide perhaps makes no sense. But clearly this appears to be a case where the divine purpose in creating and redeeming can no longer be fulfilled; for where the individual is irreversibly comatose, where there is only permanent oblivion, there can be no moral and spiritual growth, no exercise of human agency, no growing closer to God and neighbor, no service or worship offered in love and gratitude—in short, nothing that invests human life with its special value. Of course, what we really want to know is this: Can a *non-comatose* individual end his or her own life either because the divine purpose for human life can no longer be realized or because the capacity to participate in that purpose has been so severely compromised? Or is it the case that as long as one possesses consciousness, one is somehow capable of participating in God's purpose for human life?

It needs underscoring that while life is a supreme value, it gains much of its value from the other values that it makes possible—for example, the love and worship of God, service to others, enjoyment of the created order, personal growth and accomplishment. In this connection Richard McCormick, a Roman Catholic moral theologian, has raised two critical questions that nicely frame the problem for us. First, from the Judeo-Christian perspective, what are the higher values that life makes possible? Second, how does the extreme suffering that may accompany, say, a terminal illness interfere with the realization of those higher values? McCormick answers his own questions in the following way:

> The first question must be answered in terms of love of God and neighbor. This sums up briefly the meaning, substance, and consummation of life from a Judeo-Christian perspective. What is or can easily be missed is that these two loves are not separable. St. John wrote: "If any man says I love God and hates his brother, he is a liar. For he who loves not his brother, whom he sees, how can he love God whom he does not see?" (1 John 4:20-21). This means that our love of neighbor is in some very real sense our love of God. The good our love wants to do Him and to which He en-

ables us, can be done only for the neighbor, as Karl Rahner has so forcefully argued. It is in others that God demands to be recognized and loved. If this is true, it means that, in Judeo-Christian perspective, the meaning, substance, and consummation of life is found in human *relationships*, and the qualities of justice, respect, concern, compassion, and support, that surround them.

Second, how is the attainment of this "higher, more important (than life) good" rendered "too difficult" by life-supports that are gravely burdensome? One who must support his life with disproportionate effort focuses the time, attention, energy, and resources of himself and others not precisely on relationships. Such concentration easily becomes overconcentration and distorts one's view of and weakens one's pursuit of the very relational goods that define our growth and flourishing. The importance of relationships gets lost in the struggle for survival. The very Judeo-Christian meaning of life is seriously jeopardized when undue and unending effort must go into its maintenance.[11]

McCormick's comments are a creative and potentially helpful attempt to deal with our current inquiry. His stress on personal relationships (with God and with neighbor) as the paramount value that life makes possible seems fundamentally correct. He then argues that our struggle for survival can become so all-consuming that it jeopardizes our ability to enter into relationships with fellow human beings, and since our relationship with God comes largely via our relationships with human beings, such preoccupation with survival in turn jeopardizes our relationship with God. However, to the extent that McCormick claims that loving and relating to God is possible only as we are loving and relating to *neighbor*, his view is too strong. For surely a man alone on a desert island can love and worship God despite a total lack of human company. And while there is an intimate connection between these loves, it does not seem to be of such a character that I can love God and relate to him only by loving and relating to neighbor. But there is no need to argue in

11. McCormick, "To Save or Let Die," in *Life or Death—Who Controls*, ed. Nancy and John Ostheimer (New York: Springer Publishing, 1976), p. 260.

quite this way. For if a patient's almost total preoccupation with the struggle for survival makes relationships with other people nearly impossible, that will also, as a matter of fact, have much the same effect on his relationship with God. And it should be stressed that a terminal patient's condition in *extreme* circumstances may be such that waking hours are dominated by pain and perhaps by nausea, vomiting, and convulsions as well, with the only relief available provided by drugs that drive him or her into unconsciousness. Laurence McCullough helpfully points out that pain and suffering can be "overwhelming" and thereby destroy the possibility of all other experience. He speaks, for example, of the "dread terror" that afflicts those suffering with cancer of the larynx: "As this disease grows progressively worse, the throat is further and further constricted until it becomes impossible to breathe. Anyone who has ever come close to drowning can recount vividly the power with which the terror of suffocation can seize and wholly occupy one."[12] Although I believe that a personal relationship with God is possible even in these extreme circumstances, I can imagine that the full character of this relationship might be jeopardized and therefore that the higher values that invest human life with its special value have indeed been jeopardized. Again, however, we should recognize that here we are talking about the presence of factors that may serve to reduce—*not eliminate*—the moral risk attaching to suicide.

Suicide and the Dying Person

So far we have identified two factors that may serve to reduce the risk involved in surcease suicide: (a) gross suffering and (b) the elimination of those values for which human beings have been created and redeemed. Here I wish to introduce a third factor: the person is dying. Two initial comments are in order before

12. McCullough, "Pain, Suffering, and Life-extending Technologies," in *Life Span*, ed. Robert M. Veatch (San Francisco: Harper & Row, 1979), p. 132.

proceeding in our discussion. First, although the term "dying" cannot be defined with precision, I wish to identify it with the *final phase* of a terminal condition. So I am not suggesting, for example, that a person who has terminal cancer is by that fact alone to be classified as dying. Indeed, someone who has terminal cancer but who has two years to live is not dying. For the notion of dying carries with it the idea that death is imminent, but death is not imminent when one has two years or even, I suggest, six months to live. To be sure, "imminent" is itself a term that defies precise definition, and its meaning is relative to the context in which it is used. Nevertheless, more appropriate to such a definition is a time span measured in *days*—not years, months, or even weeks. Second, when one is dying there is a breakdown in the physical organism such that treatment can no longer retard or perhaps only minimally retard the dying process.

How, then, does ending one's life while one is dying reduce the moral risk of such an act of life-taking? It does so by addressing the Christian concern that in ending one's life one plays God, poaching on God's domain, arrogantly assuming a right that belongs to God alone. It is with this very concern in mind that Charles Curran, a Roman Catholic moral theologian, has observed, "Precisely because the dying process has now begun, man's positive intervention is not an arrogant usurping of the role of God but rather in keeping with the process which is now encompassing the person."[13] What Curran is saying is that mercy killing or taking one's own life ("positive intervention") is not "an arrogant usurping of the role of God" because the patient is already dying—that is, the patient is already enveloped by a process that will lead to his or her inevitable and imminent death. Further, the dying is not brought about by human intervention, for that is already a fact of the situation. Under such circumstances, therefore, positive intervention will serve only to accelerate a process that is unalterably present and whose inescapable terminus is death. This, I suggest, may re-

13. Curran, *Politics, Medicine, and Christian Ethics* (Philadelphia: Fortress Press, 1973), pp. 161-62.

duce moral risk because it reduces the chance that one is "arrogantly" exercising a divine prerogative, a pressing concern within the context of Christian belief. Nevertheless, the concern that we are playing God is a legitimate one, and we need to fully appreciate its force.

Playing God

The religious person's concern that ending one's life is playing God may *seem* to be predicated on the indefensible assumption that respecting the *natural* ordering of events is respecting the *divine* ordering of events. According to this view, letting nature have its way is interpreted as letting God have his way—hence the importance of dying a natural death (which is God's doing) in contrast to taking steps to end one's life. So honoring God's sovereignty over death is a matter of letting nature have its way, God's working and nature's working being identified as one and the same. However, we do not in fact believe that leaving death and dying to nature is the same as leaving it to God and that taking death and dying out of the hands of nature is the same as taking it out of the hands of God. No such simple equation is workable. For if this were true, we could not intervene in order to *save* a person from a natural death without thereby removing matters from God's hands. If this were true, putting a pacemaker in a man's chest to keep him alive would have to be viewed as a usurpation of God's sovereignty over life—but, of course, we do not believe this.

On the contrary, we applaud the fact that death has to a considerable extent been wrestled from nature's control and has been brought under the dominion of modern medicine: illnesses are cured and death postponed, in some cases for many years; drugs are administered, and thus pain that has accompanied certain kinds of illness from time immemorial is eliminated; a physician ceases treatment and permits death to come in circumstances where he could continue to fend it off but out of mercy chooses not to. In all of this we are deciding whether or

93

not to let *nature* have its way, but we do not construe any of this as deciding whether or not to let *God* have his way. How can it be, then, that we play God when we end life but we do not play God when we extend life?

Moreover, we have good theological reasons for rejecting any simple and straightforward equating of nature's working with God's will. For biblical teaching is that *nature* as well as humanity is fallen (Gen. 3:16-19; Rom. 8:19-23), which is to say that the natural order does not perfectly express God's will any more than we human beings perfectly express his will. Accordingly, we wrestle with nature to channel it in directions that we discern to be expressive of God's will because they are helpful to humanity; thus we build dams, seed clouds, irrigate land, drain swamps, seek medical cures for diseases, and so forth—all efforts at rejecting nature's deliverances. We need not automatically assume, therefore, that a natural but lengthy and terribly painful death is to be accepted simply because it is natural. On the contrary, it might be asked, why shouldn't we seek to control the dying process (in this case shortening it) in ways we discern to be expressive of kindness and compassion, and consequently in keeping with God's will, not because the dying process is natural, but because it is shaped by mercy, love, and considerations of human well-being? Now such remarks seem to indicate that the moral risk should attach to actions that depart from love and mercy rather than actions that depart from what nature seeks to dictate. Then why this concern that a death be natural in order for it to be a death that comes to us from God? Why this fear that determining the time of one's own death is playing God?

It is true that we live our lives in a fallen world—a world in which both human beings and nature stand in need of redemption and reclamation—and therefore we should not simply equate natural events with God's unalterable will. Nevertheless, it is in precisely this world that we have been called to live our lives. It is this very world with all its fallenness—including pain, suffering, and death—that is the divinely appointed arena in which we are to make our moral choices and spiritual commitments, to gain friendship with

God, and to shape an eternal destiny. Thus the fallen character of the world, which Christians fully recognize, does not provide a reason for opting out of that world and for rejecting our divine call to live within it. To be sure, we are to build dams, seed clouds, irrigate land, drain swamps, seek medical cures for diseases, and so forth because such activities constitute part of our call to live in this present but less-than-perfect world. But when we cannot bend the natural order to serve good ends (as often we cannot) and suffering ensues (as often it does), we are to bear it with courage and patience because this still remains the world in which we have been placed by God to live our lives, a world in which recalcitrant nature often successfully resists our best efforts to direct it to good ends. So from the fact that Christians view the natural order as fallen it does not follow that we can easily justify circumventing a painful dying by means of suicide. It is in just such a fallen world that we have been placed to live and die. From a Christian perspective, what requires justification is not continuing our existence in this world but removing ourselves from it.

But why is it—to revert to our initial question—that we play God when we end life but we do not play God when we extend life? (Of course, with the ability of modern technology to keep people alive, which in certain cases serves only to artificially extend an agonizing dying, it may understandably be claimed that this too is playing God.) The reason that religious believers do not generally view extending life as playing God is that extending life is usually viewed as furthering God's purposes. In such cases we become healing instruments through whom the divine will is being executed; far from taking matters out of God's hands (that is, "playing God"), we become extensions of his hands. It is significant that such life extension serves God's very intention in creating human beings, for preserving life preserves the divinely granted opportunity to find God, affirm life purposes, grow in grace, and so forth. In contrast, when we *terminate* human life, we are likely to be in conflict with that intention, and therefore we are in danger of doing what is gravely wrong.

It is not, then, the simple-minded belief "leaving it to nature is leaving it to God" which lies behind the Christian fear that ending one's life is usurping a divine prerogative. Rather, the fear is that in ending life we may prematurely end not only a journey ordained by God but a journey whose purpose has yet to be fully achieved, there still being meaningful life to be lived even if under difficult circumstances. It is respect for that journey, ordained as it is by God and filled with eternal significance, that renders the Christian cautious about either terminating it or failing to promote its continuation. The divine prerogative is to have the journey properly respected and safeguarded by those participating in it. Indeed, because of this prerogative we operate with two basic presumptions: (1) we presume that life extension *is* God's will unless we have good reason to believe otherwise, and (2) we presume that life termination is *not* God's will unless we have good reason to believe otherwise.

When we reflect on the prospect of surcease suicide, we rightly recognize it to be at best a morally problematic course of action, and consequently we search, as I have done, for features attaching to individual cases that may reduce, though seldom eliminate, the moral risk involved in such acts. Three such features have been identified: (1) the presence of severe and intractable suffering, (2) the presence of conditions that frustrate the divine purpose in creating and redeeming individual human life, and (3) the presence of a final phase of a terminal condition—that is, one is dying.

"Where There Is Life, There Is Hope"

"Where there is life, there is hope," it is sometimes said, and it is argued that as long as there is life, there is the possibility of miraculous recovery, whether by "miraculous recovery" we mean one of those rare recoveries that completely defies present medical knowledge and prognostication but is ultimately explicable on scientific grounds, or we mean a supernatural intervention by divine agency. In either case, the objection runs, a terminally ill patient always has *that* hope, and because hope exists, it is a reckless act that would actively intervene by means of suicide or active euthanasia to terminate life when—just maybe—the patient won't die. It is not only the possibility of a miracle but also the possibility that a last-minute cure will be found which prompts the saying "Where there is life, there is hope." Here dramatic stories can be told—and, of course, should be told—to insure a complete picture of things. In this regard, consider the following account:

> In 1921 George R. Minot was found to have diabetes at the age of thirty-six. For the next two years he fought a losing battle to control his disease by diet, the only means then available. In 1923, insulin became available and Dr. Minot's life was saved. After this Minot went to work on a series of experiments that culminated in his 1927 report that large quantities of liver could bring about the regeneration of red blood cells in the bone marrow. This was an effective treatment of pernicious anemia and won for Minot the Nobel prize in 1934.[14]

Minot was a fortunate man. In some cases a person can be so ravaged by a disease that even should a "cure" be discovered, that person is beyond the point of help. But not only is it possible that a last-minute cure will be discovered; it is also possible that the diagnosis of the doctor or doctors is mistaken, that the illness is not terminal, and the suffering is only temporary. Here, too, one can provide cases every bit as dramatic as the Minot case—cases in which diagnostic errors were made and the patients did not die, despite medical prognosis to the contrary. This kind of thing does happen, and that fact should be acknowledged.

However, there does come a point in the development of an illness where we have overwhelming evidence that no diagnostic error has been made, and we have a reasonable basis for concluding that the possibility of a last-minute cure is sufficiently remote as to border on the miraculous. And here it could be noted that we are not *required* to make crucial life-and-death decisions

14. Daniel Maguire, *Death by Choice* (New York: Schocken Books, 1975), p. 147.

(indeed, any decisions with momentous implications) based on the hope of a miracle. We may feel free to choose options that keep alive the possibility of a miracle, but is that the choice that we *have* to make? Indeed, if we are under an obligation not to end our lives in order to hold out for the possibility of a miracle or last-minute cure, then it appears that we are also under an obligation to use all the techniques that modern medicine provides to keep ourselves alive in hope of that same miracle or last-minute cure—no matter the agony and pain inflicted in the process. This would hardly be a pleasant implication to have to accept. Thus it seems to me that the grave reservations that the Christian community rightly has over suicide are not grounded in the fear that it excludes the possibility of a miraculous recovery.

Suicide and Non-Terminal Illness

In 1969 the British Voluntary Euthanasia Bill was defeated in the House of Lords by a vote of 61 to 40. Spearheaded by the Euthanasia Society of Great Britain, an organization that has diligently sought the legalization of euthanasia for some fifty years, the bill stirred considerable interest and debate. But in many minds the accidental-injury provision found in Article A of the bill was especially problematic. This article, which was a declaration to be made and signed by the individual seeking euthanasia, read as follows:

> If I should at any time suffer from a serious physical illness or impairment reasonably thought in my case to be incurable and expected to cause me severe distress or render me incapable of rational existence, I request the administration of euthanasia at a time or in circumstances to be indicated or specified by me or, if it is apparent that I have become incapable of giving directions, at the discretion of the physician in charge of my case.[15]

15. A. B. Downing, *Euthanasia and the Right to Death* (Los Angeles: Nash Publishing, 1969), pp. 205-6.

Thus Article A permitted euthanasia in cases where the illness or physical impairment was incurable and of a distressing character *but not necessarily terminal.* Supporters of the bill were quick to point out the value of euthanasia in such cases: "Certainly some of the most tragic cases crying out for euthanasia arise out of accidents, and unlike terminal cases, the agony might stretch out over many years."[16]

Indeed, we may suspect that an endorsement of surcease suicide in cases in which the suffering is experienced as unbearable carries with it a logically implied endorsement of suicide in cases in which the suffering is equally intense though not associated with any terminal illness. For if it is excruciating suffering that warrants surcease suicide, what reasons can we give for restricting the range of surcease suicide to those who are terminally ill? Why, in other words, should the non-terminal nature of one's suffering exclude one from qualifying or make it more difficult for one to qualify as a fitting subject for suicide? To be sure, the person with a non-terminal illness has longer to live, and should that person choose to commit suicide, he or she would be eliminating a greater span of future existence than persons who take their lives when confronted by terminal illness. But this person is also eliminating a proportionately greater quantum of pain and suffering, and if the smaller quantum justifies the elimination of the shorter span of life, then the greater quantum might justify the elimination of the longer span.

However, suicide in the case of an individual suffering from a non-terminal illness does in practice involve a greater risk, a risk that is greatly reduced in those cases in which a person is judged by competent medical authorities to be in the latter stages of a terminal illness. For in the case of a non-terminal illness one runs a greater chance of error in evaluating the future, since there are more variables that need to be taken into account—namely, the possibility that in time one will learn to cope with the suffering, the possibility that what is now experienced

16. Mary Rose Barrington, "Voluntary Euthanasia Act, 198-?" in *Beneficent Euthanasia,* ed. Marvin Kohl (Buffalo, N.Y.: Prometheus Books, 1975), p. 212.

as unbearable will not continue to be so, the possibility that medical advances will be able to alleviate or possibly even eliminate the suffering, and so forth. Not only is there greater risk of error in assessing the future, but there is also a known future to be lived, one of considerable duration that one is rejecting, a future that holds open the possibility of something more than unendurable existence—namely, a life of personal fulfillment in which one discharges substantial obligations to family, society, and God. Indeed, this may be a special opportunity to bear witness to the sustaining grace of God. It is for this reason, I suggest, that a case of suffering associated with non-terminal illness is to be viewed differently than a case of suffering associated with terminal illness. In both circumstances suicide involves moral risk, but in the case of non-terminal suffering that risk appears much greater.

Some Special Christian Concerns

Secular champions of suicide and euthanasia are often animated by a spirit different from that animating Christians, even if in its own way that spirit is admirable. Such advocates of a right to die frequently express concern that they will be incapacitated by illness and as a result will be unable to control their own environment, rendered dependent on the care and ministrations of others; they will often acknowledge that this is what prompts them to embrace euthanasia as an attractive option. For them euthanasia represents an escape from helplessness, an escape from dependency on others. Many of them are strong and assertive individuals, masters of their own environment, and they are repelled by the possibility that illness may drive them back into a state of childlike dependency. This fear is not, of course, peculiar to the strong-willed secular humanist. To some extent we all identify with it. But without being insensitive to this fear, I wish to suggest that the possibility of dependency should not be quite so repellent to the Christian, for to accept one's dependency upon the love, the care, and the help of others is part of an ultimate sense of dependency that is meant to characterize the Christian life as a whole. From a Christian perspective, to be dependent upon the care of others is to suffer no indignity if such care is accepted in humility and love as ultimately a gift from God, upon whom we are all at every moment dependent. Dependency itself, then, is not objectionable. Granted, accepting a relationship of dependency upon others must be distinguished from the incapacity to live one's life—to carry out one's own life plan, to enter into meaningful relationships, and so on. The two things are not the same, though they are often—but not always—two sides of the same predicament. My point, however, is that Christians are not to allow a pride that finds dependency itself intolerable to prompt them to embrace suicide as a way of escape.

In addition, it must be acknowledged that many people are horrified by the suggestion that terminally ill patients who are dying may put themselves to death or be put to death at their request. Consequently, Christian believers contemplating the possibility of surcease suicide, fraught with moral danger as it is, must also take into account the impact of such an action upon the community of faith of which they are a part and which they hold dear, and upon the larger uncommitted community of which they are also a part. For such an act of life termination may be perceived as a shocking rejection of God's rightful sovereignty over life and death, as a repudiation of God as a sufficient source of strength in time of trouble, as a raging against divinely appointed suffering, and, finally, as an act of total spiritual despair. This is a relevant moral consideration which, if not to be seen as decisive, is not to be ignored either, because Christians by the manner of both their living and their dying seek to declare Christ's lordship to a world that does not always view matters with perfect spiritual vision or with adequate love and understanding. Thus suicide is a questionable vehicle for making a Christian statement about the meaning of life by the manner of one's death, in part because of how that death will be understood and possibly misunderstood by others.

The Principle of Double Effect

Since I have explored the grave moral risk involved in taking active steps to end one's life in the face of a terminal illness, it may be conjectured that I think that there is nothing that can be legitimately done that will accelerate the dying of a dying patient. But that is not the case—not the case, at least, for those who endorse what is called the principle of double effect. Administering a lethal dose of a drug for the sole purpose of terminating the life of a suffering patient would be directly killing an innocent human being and, according to a number of moral traditions, most notably the Roman Catholic, absolutely forbidden. According to this same tradition, however, there is a form of killing an innocent human being (oneself or another) that is *not* absolutely forbidden: indirect killing in situations in which death is foreseen but not intended. The position is *not* that the innocent can be killed at will as long as the killing is done indirectly, but rather that under certain carefully specified circumstances the indirect killing of the innocent might be justified. To be sure, either way the innocent are equally dead; nevertheless, the direct (intended) killing of the innocent is forbidden in all circumstances, whereas the indirect (unintended but foreseen) killing of the innocent is morally permitted in certain carefully specified circumstances.

To gain an intuitive feel for what is being argued, consider the application of this distinction in a sphere outside that of medical ethics. In warfare the lives of innocent civilians are often at risk, and military decisions must be made that involve the killing of such innocents. Suppose, to take an example from World War II, that the Allied forces are going to bomb a key munitions factory located in a major German industrial city. The munitions factory is, according to the just-war theory, a legitimate military target, and those manufacturing the munitions do not enjoy immunity from lethal attack. Those who make the bullets, like those who fire them, and unlike "innocent civilians," are legitimate targets. However, there may be those living nearby—the families of the munitions workers, say—who *do* have genuine "innocent civilian" status. Further, let us suppose that the Allied forces know that some of the bombs directed at the munitions factory will miss their target, go astray, and, regrettably, kill some of these innocent civilians. This loss of innocent life is permissible if the munitions factory is a significant military target.

Crucial to this line of reasoning is the fact that the innocent who are killed are not killed intentionally. That is, they are not killed on purpose; their deaths are only a foreseen but unintended consequence of attacking a legitimate target. In contrast, it would *not* be permissible to send commandos into this city (were that possible) to round up the families of the munitions workers and threaten to kill them—women and children—one by one until the workers ceased producing munitions. Practicalities aside, this would not be morally justified, even if *fewer* innocents were killed this way than by a bombing raid, because—again—the direct and intentional killing of the innocent is never to be sanctioned. And this seems correct on an intuitive level: it appears that the commando raid would be morally worse than the bombing raid even if fewer innocent were killed in the former than in the latter. Utilitarianism, which seeks always to achieve the best overall results, would support that action which involves the killing of the fewest innocent people. Thus, in contrast to utilitarianism, the traditional approach would preclude the direct killing of the innocent despite the overall advantages that might be secured by doing so. There are, then, certain moral restraints placed on the pursuit of good ends, and one of those restraints is that we not directly attack the innocent.

But let us return to a medical context. It was Pope Pius XII, a conservative moralist, who applied the distinction between direct and indirect killing, along with the principle of double effect, to justify the indirect killing of dying patients. He reasoned that if, in the treatment of a terminally ill patient suffering great pain, "the actual administration of drugs brings about two distinct effects, the one the relief of pain, the other the shortening of life, the action is lawful."[17] Consider in this connection an ex-

17. Pope Pius XII, *Acta Apostolicae Sedis,* 49: 146.

ample that we've used before: the administration of morphine as an effective painkiller. A problem with the use of morphine is that the patient rapidly develops a tolerance to the drug, thus requiring increasingly large doses to obtain relief. Eventually the patient reaches the point where the amount of morphine needed to kill the pain may prove fatal. It is this sort of "killing" that the Roman Catholic principle of double effect sanctions, but it would not sanction an increase in the dose of morphine beyond what was judged necessary to control the pain, because then the patient's death would be directly intended.

More specifically, according to the principle of double effect, an act that has evil effects may be morally acceptable when each of the following conditions is fulfilled:

(1) The act is not morally evil in and of itself. (Injecting morphine into a pain-ridden patient is not evil in and of itself.)

(2) This act produces two effects, one good (it controls the pain) and one evil (it shortens the patient's life).

(3) The evil effect is foreseen but not intended. (The patient's death or the shortening of the patient's life is foreseen as an unavoidable by-product of the morphine injection.)

(4) The good effect is not the result of the evil effect. (The pain relief is not achieved by killing the patient—that could be accomplished by a bullet to the head—which would be doing "evil that good might come"; rather, the morphine injection relieves the pain but at the cost of shortening the life expectancy of the patient.)

(5) There is a strong enough reason (a proportionate good) for implementing the good effect to balance allowing the unintended evil effect. (The unremitting suffering in the face of an imminent and inevitable death is a reason proportionately serious to balance the gravity of the evil effect of shortening a person's life, albeit unintentionally.)

(6) There is no other way to achieve the good effect without also causing the evil effect or even something still worse.

A protracted debate has centered on the principle of

double effect; the principle has both ardent advocates[18] and equally ardent detractors.[19] (I count myself as one who sympathizes with the principle.) But maybe more crucial than this principle for an understanding of our greater openness to the indirect shortening of life by morphine injection is the fact that the death of the patient in such circumstances is not inevitable, even though the continued administration of the morphine is accompanied by an increasing *risk* of death, possibly even a high risk. In this respect it is unlike active euthanasia, in which the lethal dose would be carefully measured to insure a certain and immediate death. Thus we view the administration of morphine to reduce suffering not really as killing but as an act of *risking death* to secure pain relief, analogous to risking death by submitting to a potentially life-saving operation. In the case of morphine, we judge the risk to be worth it, granted that the pain is severe and death is near. And if the morphine causes death, it at least does so at the point at which it is no longer possible to control the pain.

Philip Devine, himself a supporter of the principle of double effect, has argued that those who kill *indirectly* are not so likely to view themselves as "lords of life and death" as are those

18. Defenders of the principle of double effect include Elizabeth Anscombe, author of "Modern Moral Philosophy," in *Ethics*, ed. Judith Jarvis Thomson and Gerald Dworkin (New York: Harper & Row, 1968), and "War and Murder," in *War and Morality*, ed. Richard Wasserstrom (Belmont, Calif.: Wadsworth, 1970); Philip E. Devine, *The Ethics of Homicide* (Ithaca, N.Y.: Cornell University Press, 1978), pp. 106-33; Bonnie Steinbock, "The Intentional Termination of Life," in *Ethical Issues in Modern Medicine*, ed. John Arras and Robert Hunt (Palo Alto, Calif.: Mayfield Publishing, 1983), pp. 223-28. For an interesting, qualified defense, see Norvin Richards, "Double Effect and Moral Character," *Mind* 93 (1984): 381-97; R. A. Duff, "Absolute Principles and Double Effect," *Analysis* 36 (Jan. 1976): 68-80. There are, of course, numerous defenders among Roman Catholic moral theologians, but even here there are those who dissent.

19. Critics are legion, especially among philosophers with utilitarian sympathies. See Jonathan Bennett, "Whatever the Consequences," *Analysis* 26 (1966): 83-102; John Harris, *Violence and Responsibility* (London: Routledge & Kegan Paul, 1980), pp. 48-65; R. G. Frey, *Rights, Killing, and Suffering* (Oxford: Basil Blackwell, 1983), pp. 118-40: Jonathan Glover, *Causing Deaths and Saving Lives* (New York: Penguin, 1977), pp. 86-91.

who kill directly.)[20] Granted license to *indirect* killing, therefore, is less dangerous for a society than licensing *direct* killing. Indeed, as I have just suggested, the generous administration of morphine for the purpose of controlling pain is more like risking death than it is like killing, so it is less likely to be seen as setting a precedent for killing and generating the attitude that we can kill when we judge it best to do so. And should we conclude that there are substantial risks attaching to the legalization of active euthanasia, we need not have a similar concern about accepting morphine as a means of controlling pain in those cases where it carries with it the risk of hastening the death of the dying patient.

Summary and Prospectus

In this chapter we have explored the morality of surcease suicide—self-interested suicide—committed for the purpose of avoiding grave personal harm. Such suicide, as we saw, presupposes that sometimes suicide can be in a person's best interest. However, this presupposition is open to doubt on Christian theological grounds, for the doctrine of divine judgment is that no ultimate and permanent advantage comes from doing evil. This is not to assume that suicide is evil, but it is to affirm that *if* it is evil, then the supposed advantage will be the object of a divine negation. Accordingly, we can be certain that suicide benefits only if we are also certain that suicide or a particular act of suicide is not wrong, and rarely would that be the case.

I also argued that suicide involves moral risk even when it is chosen as a means of escape from severe suffering because, from a Christian perspective, God has given us life as a trust to be lived out in a fallen world with its pain and suffering, this world being the divinely ordained context in which we are to shape ourselves as moral and spiritual beings with an eye to an eternal destiny. Nevertheless, I argued that there are factors

20. Devine, *The Ethics of Homicide*, p. 131.

which perhaps serve to reduce—though not eliminate—the moral risk involved. These factors include (1) the presence of intractable and agonizing pain and suffering, (2) the presence of a condition which serves to frustrate the divine purpose for human life, and (3) the presence of a final phase of a terminal condition—that is, one is dying. Even with these conditions present, we are talking of decision-making in the context of uncertainty and moral ambiguity, and unquestionably fraught with moral danger.

I have also argued that the hastening of death by means of morphine administered to control the pain of the dying is not morally problematic in the way that direct killing is. It does not involve intentionally ending life, it does not carry with it the same social risks, it is an instance of "risking death" in order to control pain, and it even has the support of the conservative moral tradition of the Roman Catholic Church.

CHAPTER FIVE

Passive Euthanasia and the Refusal of Life-Extending Treatment

Introduction

Less controversial than active euthanasia is the debate that centers on what is called voluntary passive euthanasia, a not altogether satisfactory term but one that has nonetheless become a standard piece of terminology in the professional literature. Not only is this *term* widely used, but also the *practice* of passive euthanasia (depending, in part, on how we define the term) is widely accepted, and it is accepted by many who would find *active* euthanasia morally objectionable and would vigorously resist its legalization. This is a position held by many people: *passive* euthanasia is "letting die" and is sometimes morally justified, while *active* euthanasia is "killing" and is never justified. It is thus believed with regards to treating a terminally ill patient that, while the time may come when the physician may cease treatment and withdraw life-support systems, thereby allowing the patient to die a natural death, the time *never* comes when the physician can, with moral justification, intentionally administer a lethal drug dose for the express purpose of terminating life, nor can the patient ever make such a request with moral justification.

Although passive euthanasia is less controversial than active euthanasia, it nevertheless generates a number of perplexing and fascinating issues. Indeed, it is reflection on the moral status of *passive* euthanasia that forces us to consider anew the moral possibility of *active* euthanasia, and it provides, I believe, the greatest insight into the real nature of the euthanasia debate. But not only does passive euthanasia generate fascinating theoretical issues; at the practical level it also provides occasion for difficult and even heartrending decisions to forego or stop treatment. And it is the progress of modern medical technology, which otherwise can be accepted with gratitude, that has created much of our problem. Such technology has enabled the physician to prolong the dying process, on occasion actually increasing the suffering that the patient has to undergo; it has also enabled the physician to keep the patient biologically alive even when he or she is not capable of rational existence and is functioning only at a vegetative level.

A Matter of Definition

No agreement exists on precisely how "passive euthanasia" is to be defined, and there is even a lack of agreement over whether the term should be used at all. It is not uncommon for those who advocate "passive euthanasia" and oppose "active euthanasia" to strongly object to the term "euthanasia" (even when the qualifier "passive" is appended) to describe their own position. In this they are prompted by more than a desire to be faithful to historical usage (after all, "euthanasia" is linked to "mercy killing," not "mercy dying"): tactical considerations also play an important part in their thinking. For "euthanasia" is to many an ugly and frightening term, conjuring up pictures of the euthanasia programs of Nazi Germany; thus many advocates of "passive euthanasia" believe that such a label can only hurt their position. Furthermore, it is easier to get people to accept passive euthanasia than active euthanasia; therefore, once someone persuades people of the moral acceptability of the former (letting die) and also gets them to adopt the term "euthanasia" to describe it, the way has been paved for the acceptance of what "really" is euthanasia. "After all," advocates of mercy killing might argue, "you have already accepted euthanasia in its passive mode. Why not take the next step and accept it in its active mode?"

How, then, should we use the term "passive euthanasia"? There are a number of possibilities, and I shall mention only a few.

First, it could be suggested that passive euthanasia is the rejection of what is called "ordinary means" of preserving and extending life. This would be an understanding of the term characteristic of Roman Catholic thought. This definition trades on a somewhat controversial distinction between ordinary (or obligatory) and extraordinary (or optional) means of preserving life (a distinction that we shall subsequently examine). The idea here is that when extraordinary (i.e., optional) means of preserving life are omitted, then one is *not* carrying out an act of passive euthanasia, even if that omission serves to shorten one's life; if, on the other hand, the means omitted are ordinary (i.e., obligatory), then one *is* engaged in passive euthanasia. Clearly, by virtue of such a definition passive euthanasia is a morally unacceptable practice, since it involves omitting what we are morally obliged not to omit. Indeed, according to such an understanding, to characterize an act or practice as "passive euthanasia" is to pass a negative moral judgment: it is to assert that one has prematurely ended one's life by intentionally omitting treatment that should have been employed.

A second, more broadly construed notion of passive euthanasia includes within its scope the omission of *any* means whatsoever of preserving and extending life. Here no distinction is drawn between ordinary and extraordinary means. It makes no difference whether the patient refuses to undergo a complicated, painful, experimental operation or refuses an ordinary blood transfusion—refusing either the operation or the transfusion, if they are life-extending procedures, is an instance of passive euthanasia. Thus *all* omissions of life-extending treatment involve one in passive euthanasia.

I am inclined to favor (but do not insist upon) a third view, one that equates voluntary passive euthanasia with a form of passive suicide—specifically, passive suicide committed for the purpose of relieving oneself of suffering caused by an illness or injury. Voluntary passive euthanasia is, then, a form of surcease suicide. After all, voluntary *active* euthanasia is suicide (carried out, as we have seen, through the agency of another); thus, if there is another mode of euthanasia denominated "passive," it is reasonable to suppose that it too is a form of suicide, but in this case suicide carried out not by an act but by an omission. However, according to the notion of suicide that I have earlier proposed, not all refusals of life-extending medical procedures are suicide, and therefore not all refusals of life-extending medical procedures would be passive euthanasia. In this regard my position differs from the previous one, for according to it, *all* refusals of life-extending procedures constitute passive euthanasia, whereas, according to my understanding, a refusal of life-extending procedures constitutes passive euthanasia only if the refusal in question constitutes suicide. However, I have previously suggested that persons who are confronted by imminent and inevitable death do not commit suicide when they refuse treatment that serves only to prolong their dying, and it would follow that these are not cases of passive euthanasia, either. Because I am reluctant to characterize any treatment refusal by an *irreversibly dying* patient as suicide, I am also reluctant to characterize it as passive euthanasia.

So what I am suggesting is that passive euthanasia is (a) intentionally ending one's life (b) by a medical omission (c) when death is not imminent and (d) when it is done to relieve oneself of suffering. However, neither this definition nor the others that have been examined are crucial to what follows in this chapter. For we are discussing the withdrawal of life-extending treatment, and that discussion can proceed quite profitably without using the term "passive euthanasia." Indeed, it may even be preferable not to use the term at all, since its use might be seen as giving a polemical advantage to one side or the other in the larger euthanasia debate.

Reflections on a Horror Story

The following account is based on a letter that was published in the *British Medical Journal* on 17 February 1968; it provides an appropriate starting point for our own reflections about refusing life-prolonging treatment:

> The letter told of a doctor of 68 who was admitted to the hospital with advanced cancer of the stomach. An operation revealed that the liver was also affected. Another operation followed for removal of the stomach, and there was evidence of further complications. The patient was told of his condition and, being a doctor, he fully understood. Despite increasing doses of drugs, he suffered constant pain. Ten days after the operation he collapsed with a clot in a lung artery. This was removed by another operation. When he sufficiently recovered he expressed his appreciation of the good intentions and skill of the doctor who had performed the operation. But he asked that, if he had a further collapse, no steps should be taken to prolong his life, for the pain of his cancer was more now than he should needlessly continue to endure. He wrote a note to this effect in his case records, and the staff of the hospital knew of his feelings. Two weeks later he collapsed with a heart attack, and despite his expressed wish, he was resuscitated. The same night his heart stopped again on four more occasions and each time it was restarted artificially. He lingered on for three more weeks, with violent vomiting and convulsions. A whole series of medical techniques was then employed to keep him alive. Preparations were made for using an artificial respirator but the heart stopped before this could be done.[1]

This story underscores the harm that can be caused by an overly zealous use of modern medical technology, and the

1. Reported in *The Humanist* 4 (July 1974): 10.

potential for such harm is even greater today, some twenty years later, because a still more impressive range of life-prolonging medical procedures is available to the physician. Fortunately, physicians are now more sensitive to the possible abuses of these technologies and are more responsive to patients' wishes in such matters. (In this regard, both the medical profession and the larger community have grown together in appreciating patient autonomy and in understanding the ways in which life-extending technologies can be abused.) Therefore, a patient with a terminal illness who today places himself or herself in the hands of a physician should *not* expect to be victimized in this way. Nevertheless, the preceding account does succeed in indicating the kind of harm that *can* be inflicted on a patient should medical technology *not* be used in a wise and humane fashion. And I believe that, as we reflect on this story, two convictions firmly emerge: (1) the patient has the moral right to refuse treatment, even treatment with life-extending potential, and (2) this particular patient would have been justified in exercising that right.

Also, this patient was *not*, according to my understanding, requesting passive *suicide*, even though he was requesting that his physician stop making life-extending efforts. Nor, therefore, was he (again, according to my understanding) requesting passive *euthanasia*. Had his request been honored, as I suggest it should have been, he would not have committed suicide. The reason? He was irreversibly dying and his death was imminent, and to refuse treatment in such circumstances is not suicide.

Withholding Treatment and Stopping Treatment

Allowing a patient to die can take two forms: (1) *withholding* treatment (or a life-support system) before it has begun to be used, and (2) *withdrawing* treatment (or a life-support system) that has already begun to be used. Physicians have tended to be more reluctant to terminate treatment once begun than to withhold treatment from the outset. This reluctance may be attributable to the fact that there is judged to be added legal risk when the physician stops treatment in contrast to withholding treatment from the outset. For the law has not always spoken clearly to the point of whether a physician's discontinuing medical assistance to a terminal patient is an act or an omission. As George Fletcher points out, "If turning off the respirator is an 'act' under the law, then it is unequivocally forbidden: it is on par with injecting air into the patient's veins. If, on the other hand, it is classified as an 'omission,' the analysis proceeds more flexibly. Whether it would be forbidden as an omission would depend on the demands imposed by the relationship between doctor and patient."[2] In the past this legal ambiguity has made the physician more vulnerable to a charge of killing a patient when the physician has turned off a life-support system but less vulnerable when he or she has simply not placed the patient on the system to begin with. But perhaps the physician's greater reluctance to withdraw treatment is the product of the physician's *own* belief that in the case of stopping treatment once it is begun, he or she is "doing something" to cause the patient's death (e.g., unplugging a life-support system), whereas in the case of withholding treatment, he or she is simply "refraining from doing something." This belief may be accompanied by the more or less conscious conviction that "doing something" to shorten the life of a patient (i.e., removing a plug or turning a valve) is always morally more serious than "refraining from doing something" to shorten that life. I believe this constitutes a confusion, however.

Here we need to notice that both withholding and withdrawing treatment are instances of allowing something to happen—in this case, allowing the patient to die a natural death. And, in general, something can be *allowed to happen* in two ways: (1) by doing something (e.g., I unlock the door so you can get in the car) and (2) by refraining from doing something (e.g., I do

2. Fletcher, "Prolonging Life: Some Legal Considerations," *in Euthanasia and the Right to Death,* ed. A. B. Downing (Los Angeles: Nash Publishing, 1969), p. 76.

not lock the door so you can get in the car).[3] Both are cases of letting something happen, in the one instance by removing an impediment (i.e., unlocking the door, unplugging the life-support system), and in the other by not creating an impediment to begin with (i.e., not locking the door, not plugging in the life-support system). Perhaps what is significant here is that when we unplug the life-support system, we are removing an impediment that we ourselves have placed in the way of a natural death; we are restoring matters to the state they were in before we interfered. So if our putting the impediment in place was a mistake to begin with or turns out to be a mistake, then we are only correcting our mistake by removing the life-support system or stopping treatment. And there appears to be no moral difference between not starting treatment (allowing something to happen by refraining from doing something) and stopping treatment (allowing something to happen by doing something), since both are instances of allowing a natural death to proceed. Certainly the patient's right to decide extends equally to both, for the patient's right to control what happens in and to his or her body is both a right not to have bodily invasions begun, should that be his or her wish, as well as a right to have bodily invasions stopped, should that be his or her wish.

Moreover, as Joanne Lynn and James Childress have pointed out, health-care practitioners are often in a better position to determine whether a particular treatment will be of value to the patient *after* it has been tried, but if it is believed that withdrawing treatment is morally more serious than withholding treatment, this could have unfortunate consequences: "Caretakers may become reluctant to begin some treatments precisely because they fear that they will be locked into continuing treatments that are no longer of value to the patient."[4] Or the patient may be reluctant to have a course of treatment begun because

---

3. Cf. Douglas N. Walton, *Ethics of Withdrawal of Life-Support Systems* (Westport, Conn.: Greenwood Press, 1983), pp. 234-35.
4. Lynn and Childress, "Must Patients Always Be Given Food and Water?" *The Hastings Center Report* (Oct. 1983), p. 20.

he may view it as a near-irreversible decision, being reluctant to start what he believes he cannot stop.

In summary, then, if in a given instance it was a mistake to place an impediment in the way of a natural death by starting treatment, then one only compounds the mistake by refusing to remove that impediment. The decision to unplug a life-support system is a decision no more serious than—though every bit as serious as—the decision not to plug it in to begin with. So, although technically a distinction can be drawn between these two variants of allowing to die, and although some physicians may be less comfortable with stopping treatment than with not starting it in the first place, the distinction does not seem to carry with it any moral weight: withholding and withdrawing treatment are morally equivalent.

The Right to Refuse Treatment

The right to refuse life-extending treatment is a right that is well established by law. Robert Veatch, author of *Death, Dying, and the Biological Revolution,* surveys the legal data and concludes, "There seems to be a clear consensus that the competent adult has the right to refuse treatments on apparently foolish or misguided grounds, even when the treatments may be as common and clearly life-saving as a blood transfusion."[5] Veatch does indicate that there are exceptions to the general rule that competent adults may refuse treatment: those willing to be coerced, competent adults with dependents (admittedly, this could be a very large category), and prisoners. Nevertheless, the general rule stands. This legal recognition of the right to reject medical treatment is grounded in a respect for the bodily integrity of the individual, for the right of each person to determine when bodily invasions will take place. As Judge Benjamin Cardoza put it, "Every human being of adult years and sound mind has

5. Veatch, *Death, Dying, and the Biological Revolution* (New Haven, Conn.: Yale University Press, 1976), p. 121.

a right to determine what shall be done with his own body; and a surgeon who performs an operation without his patient's consent commits an assault, for which he is liable in damages."[6]

Thus the right to refuse treatment is grounded in the more fundamental right to determine what happens in and to one's own body—that is, the right to exercise sovereignty over such matters as whether something shall be removed from one's body (e.g., a limb amputated or an organ or a growth removed), whether something shall be placed in one's body (e.g., an organ transplant or a pacemaker implant), whether something shall be connected to one's body (e.g., a dialysis machine or IV tubes), and whether features of one's body shall be altered (e.g., through a face-lift, ear piercing, gaining or losing weight). This kind of bodily self-determination represents a basic freedom that warrants respect, and to deny the competent adult that freedom would be an egregious violation of human dignity; indeed, it would violate the person in much the same way that rape does. For the body is not a possession of the person like a car or a television set; the body *is* the person (even if not all there is to the person), and to take liberties with a person's body is to take liberties with that person.

These considerations support the conclusion reached by Pope Pius XII; he declared, "The doctor, in fact, has no separate or independent right where the patient is concerned. In general he can take action only if the patient explicitly or implicitly, directly or indirectly, gives him permission."[7] This acknowledgment of the patient's right to determine whether or not he or she will be treated serves to remind us that when we discuss the moral question of employing life-extending treatment, we should focus on the question "How should the *patient* exercise this right to accept or reject life-extending treatment?" Indeed, the basic question is not "What should the *physician do*?" but "What should the *patient allow to be done*?" To give primary at-

6. *Schloendorff v. Society of New York Hospital*, 211 N.Y. 125, 105 N.E. 92 (1914) at 93.
7. Pope Pius XII, *Acta Apostolicae Sedis*, 49: 1031-32.

tention to the physician's role is to assume that the physician has a sovereignty over the patient's body that the physician does not in fact have. Since it is the patient who is entitled to decide whether or not to accept treatment, we should ponder how the patient should exercise that right. Moreover, since the patient has the right to decide whether or not to accept treatment, responsibility for the consequences that flow from the physician's honoring that right rests firmly on the patient's own shoulders. If the decision that is made is foolish or wrong, then the patient has acted foolishly or wrongly, not the physician, who only does what he or she is obliged to do—that is, honor the patient's right to decide. The patient may intend his or her own death by rejecting life-extending treatment, but by complying with the patient's request the physician does not thereby intend the patient's death; the physician intends only to honor the patient's right to decide. Full responsibility for what happens lies with the right-holder, who in this instance is the patient. This serves only to raise another significant question: How should the patient responsibly exercise his or her right to accept or reject life-extending treatment?

Dying Morally

From a Christian perspective, dying morally involves fulfilling at least two conditions: (1) honoring the value of one's life by avoiding a premature submission to death and (2) honoring the divine sovereignty over death by not dictating the details of death's occurrence. This is not all there is to a spiritually and morally satisfactory death, but fulfilling these conditions is a part of it. None of this, of course, entails that dying Christians are to glorify pain and suffering. On the contrary, Christians will do for themselves what they also do for others who are dying—seek to control pain and eliminate suffering—but they will do this within the parameters established by their moral beliefs and their spiritual vision of existence. That is, pain and suffering will be controlled in a manner consistent with the beliefs that life is a divine trust and that God is Lord of death. It is these twin beliefs that render suicide morally problematic as a means of dealing with pain and suffering, suicide being in conflict with both of these beliefs, since it may well bring life to a premature close and dictates the precise time and place of death's occurrence.

These two beliefs may seem to pull us in different directions. For doesn't the belief that life is a divine trust to be preserved and protected prompt us to a flurry of human activity to stave off death, while belief in God's lordship over death prompts us to submit to what God himself ordains? Indeed, the first belief activates and the second pacifies; the first prompts us to control events and the second to acquiesce to events. Nonetheless, because these two beliefs are mutually interpretive, they do not, I suggest, have contrary implications. That is, the belief that life is a divine trust to be cared for informs and qualifies our understanding of God's lordship over death, and belief in God's lordship over death informs and qualifies our understanding that life is a divine trust. Accordingly, to postpone death and keep oneself alive by availing oneself of life-extending medical procedures is not a denial of the divine lordship over death, as if one were taking from God the right to determine when life is to end, because through this act one affirms the value of one's life, and by doing so one aligns one's will with the divine will, thereby making oneself an instrument of that lordship, not a violator of it. Therefore, preserving and protecting one's life by holding death at bay or by temporarily defeating it (e.g., by curing an otherwise fatal illness) is not to compromise the divine sovereignty over death but is in fact to express it—God's will is thereby being done. Thus respect for divine sovereignty is to be qualified by our understanding of life as a divine trust—in other words, we actually respect that sovereignty by faithfully honoring our lives as a divine trust.

Similarly, what it means to preserve and protect our lives as a divine trust is qualified by our recognition of the divine sovereignty over death. In the case of the irreversibly dying person, therefore, we have an individual who is moving inexorably toward an imminent death, and nothing is going to change that fact; thus we may see in these circumstances an indication of the divine will—God's will is being declared through events. Accordingly, to cease battling (especially when pain is great), to cease staving off death is not a failure to adequately respect the value of one's life but a submission to what is discerned as God's providential will working itself out in the natural order. So by acquiescing to death, one is acquiescing to what God has ordained, and therefore one is not failing to honor the value of one's life, not failing in the exercise of a divine trust. In this way, belief in God's lordship over death shapes our understanding of what it means to faithfully preserve our lives. To take seriously the belief that life is a divine trust and to act conscientiously on that belief does not require that one do everything humanly possible to prolong one's life, because in the face of inevitable and imminent death one may well judge that to stop battling and to submit to death is to submit to the sovereignty of a good and gracious God who is bringing one's life to a close.

Of these two beliefs, the more problematic of the two is the second (recognition of God's lordship over death), involving as it does the claim that there is a dimension to human dying that is off-limits to human control and is not an appropriate arena in which to exercise our human judgment about what is best. Joseph Fletcher, of situation ethics fame, challenges this very belief:

> People often feel that death should be "natural"—that is humanly uncontrolled and uncontrived. Sometimes they say that God works through nature and therefore any "interference" with nature by controlling what happens to people in the way of illness and death—interferes with God's activity. This argument has a specious aura of religious force. For example, one doctor with an eighty-three year old patient, paralyzed by a stroke and a half dozen other ailments, tells that compassionate family that he will do nothing, "leave it to God." But God does not cooperate; their mother goes on gasping. Maybe the doctor needs a better and more creative theology. . . . The right of spiritual beings to use intelligent control over physical nature, rather than submit beastlike to its blind workings, is the heart of many crucial ques-

tions. Birth control, artificial insemination, sterilization, and abortion are all medically discovered ways of fulfilling and protecting human values and hopes in spite of nature's failures or foolishness.[8]

Why indeed, we may ask, should we submit, beast-like, to nature's capricious ways, being obliged to allow an agonizing dying to proceed at its own slow rate? Why not place dying fully under human control and judgment? This, the argument goes, would not mean ending life on a whim or doing so without moral scruples, but it would mean being open to the moral possibility of taking active steps to end life. To be sure, certain stringent conditions would have to be met, and tough questions would have to be asked. For example, is my situation hopeless and known to be such? Have I been faithful in discharging my responsibilities to preserve my life, including the bearing of appropriately heavy burdens? However, has the burden of my suffering now become intolerable, with nothing but an agonizing, sputtering death (dying) lying ahead for me? Should the answer to all these questions be "yes," could I not throw myself on the mercy of God and end my life? Why not show that we respect the divine lordship over death not by letting nature have its way in these matters but by seeking to make dying captive to values expressive of *God's* nature—love, mercy, compassion, the best interests of all concerned, and so on?

In contrast to this, to say that God is Lord of death (in the traditional sense and in the sense that I believe needs defending) is to say that there is indeed a dimension to our dying that should *not* be subject to human control, subject to what we think is best. So even though it is within our power to bring life to a quick and merciful close, and even though *we* should judge that recognized values would be served by doing so, we are not authorized to assert such a control over our dying, not even when that dying is long and hard. But why this hesitancy to

8. Fletcher, *Moral Responsibility* (Philadelphia: Westminster Press, 1967), p. 151.

assert human control in the name of human well-being when in so many other areas we are quite willing to assert a mastery over nature in order to better the human condition?

There is something spiritually dangerous, I would suggest, in seeking to engineer one's own death. For controlling nature in this area is not like controlling nature in other areas; it is not like seeding clouds, damming rivers, draining swamps, or seeking cures for disease. In controlling nature we are usually affecting people (for better or for worse) as they continue their lives' sojourn, but here we are talking about *ending* that sojourn, about terminating earthly existence. As we have already had occasion to note, Christian faith affirms that we have been placed in this fallen world to live out our lives, to shape an eternal destiny, to act out the drama of the soul. And the world in which all of this is to transpire is characterized by unavoidable pain and suffering; it is a world of apparent capriciousness, unfairness, and—at times—severity. This is the divinely chosen context in which we are to affirm and live out our ultimate loyalties. Dying is part of that life we are called to live, and dying is not always short and "easy." Pain and suffering that cannot be fully controlled by human agency are a significant aspect of the world in which we have been placed by divine design; it is in this world that we are to live, choose, respond, struggle, and—importantly—learn what it means to trust God and to engage in soul-making. For this reason Christians will be extremely cautious in contemplating active means to end life and to cut short the dying process. Nevertheless, we will struggle to determine when and under what circumstances life-extending treatment can be rejected with moral legitimacy. In all this we will recognize that life is a divine trust and will seek to preserve that life even under difficult circumstances; we will also recognize that God's will can be carried out not only through our faithfulness but through natural events, the point coming where the struggle to ward off death can cease and death, with its proximity and inevitability, be accepted as God's will.

Release from the Obligation to Prolong Our Lives

One critical factor in comprehending the case for rejecting life-extending treatment is understanding the full relevance of the suffering that the dying patient may have to endure. For, generally speaking, suffering involved in carrying out our obligations or in achieving good ends may become sufficiently grave that it releases us from our obligation or it relieves us of the necessity to pursue the good. For it is not true that all obligations have to be carried out no matter what the personal cost, or that the good always has to be pursued no matter what the suffering endured by the pursuer of the good. Quite the contrary. It may actually be wrong to impose great sacrifices on ourselves in order to benefit others in small ways or in order to keep relatively inconsequential commitments (e.g., I sacrifice thousands of dollars to keep a promised appointment with a student). Even where the sacrifice made or the suffering endured is for more substantial ends, it may no longer be wrong or foolish but actually meritorious, worthy of praise if pursued—but *not* worthy of condemnation if foregone (e.g., I sacrifice my life in order to save a stranger from a burning building). Certainly there are circumstances in which it *is* mandatory that one be willing to undergo considerable suffering and even to sacrifice one's life in the name of duty. Should a person in such circumstances fail to make the required sacrifice, that failure may rightly be condemned. Soldiers, for example, may find themselves in such circumstances, but even here there are limits to what we expect. But the point is this: we do recognize a class of cases where the suffering an individual might have to undergo is sufficiently great to absolve him or her from obligations that otherwise would hold.

We do, of course, have a duty to preserve our lives, and this does involve seeking and receiving medical treatment when necessary. To reject life-preserving medical assistance would normally be foolish, irresponsible, and ultimately a failure to care for what is a divine trust. But the obligation to preserve and extend one's life need not be construed as an obligation that holds no matter what the cost, no matter how much pain and agony it brings, no matter how imminent and inevitable one's death, no matter how great one's incapacity to function fully as a person. For surely these considerations are relevant in determining whether or not a person is morally obliged to accept life-extending medical treatment. And it is reasonable to believe that there can come a point where the suffering is so intense, where relief consistent with rational existence is unavailable, where one's ability to carry out responsibilities to family and friends is virtually nil, where one's capacity to participate in the higher goods that invest life with much of its value and meaning can be sufficiently jeopardized—in short, where so many negative factors converge that one can say "no" to life-prolonging treatment and do so in good conscience before the Lord and Giver of Life. There are no biblical proof texts that will suffice either to establish this point or to successfully contradict it, but it is a conclusion that seems consistent with the portrait of a compassionate God who does not demand of his creatures more than they are able to endure or more than there seems any reasonable point to endure. We are not obliged to grasp for life no matter what. As John McEllhenney has commented,

> Such grasping for straws is not necessary for the Christian. He believes that his dying has been caught up in the death and resurrection of Jesus Christ. As birth is a gift of God, so is death. Therefore, the Christian is not bound to strive officiously to prolong that living which is truly dying. Christ harrowed hell. . . . Hence, it is not obligatory to fetch hell into the hospital by prolonging the agony of dying. The doctor may permit death to enter as a conquered enemy who is now to be greeted as a friend.[9]

A word of caution is appropriate at this point. What I have just said—even if true—needs to be accompanied by the warning that it is possible for a person to be guilty of a hasty and premature submission to death. For one can yield to despair in the

---

9. McEllhenney, *Cutting the Monkey-Rope: Is the Taking of Life Ever Justified?* (Valley Forge, Pa.: Judson Press, 1973), p. 110.

face of suffering when a courageous Christian response that has point and meaning is still possible and reasonable to expect. Indeed, to recognize that some suffering is *un*bearable is also to recognize that other suffering is bearable; to recognize that life can be robbed of much of its value and significance in the face of an imminent death is also to recognize that this is by no means always so; to recognize that the possibility of personal relationships can be seriously jeopardized during the final stages of a terminal illness is also to recognize that such relationships can also (more often than not) be intensified and deepened. What is called for is discernment adequate to the task of determining the nature of the case. Formulas cannot be provided, but this is *typical* of the moral life, which for the most part is not a matter of strict rule-following but rather a matter of growing, maturing, sensitive discernment. This is not to suggest that there are never any moral principles to strictly adhere to, for there are, but it is to observe that much moral decision-making does not lend itself to such easy resolution. In fact, we find ourselves confronted with a spectrum of cases, ranging from those cases where the rejection of life-extending treatment is clearly morally permissible, to those cases where it is clearly wrong. In between, things may be less certain and more ambiguous, and the right moral decision not easy to come by.

Ordinary vs. Extraordinary Treatment

To assist people in determining when they can appropriately reject life-extending treatment and when they are obligated to accept it, a distinction has been introduced between what is called "ordinary" and "extraordinary" treatment. This distinction has its roots in the Roman Catholic moral tradition, but it has also been widely employed by physicians and ethicists who are not a part of that tradition; certainly the terminology, despite its ambiguities, is extensively used. It represents an attempt to provide moral guidance by helping us distinguish treatment we are required to accept from treatment we are not required to accept. It is also a distinction that has come under much criticism; nevertheless, one cannot discuss the morality of rejecting life-extending treatment without coming to terms with this distinction, either by way of acceptance, rejection, or qualification. In general, ordinary treatment is treatment that one is morally obliged to accept, whereas extraordinary treatment can be rejected even though such rejection involves shortening one's life.

The distinction was fashioned by Roman Catholic moralists in the sixteenth century and thus before the introduction of anesthesia (which would render tolerable the pain associated with most operations), before antisepsis (which would greatly reduce the chance of lethal infections), and before blood transfusions (which would enable one to lose blood and yet survive).[10] During the sixteenth century virtually any operation was a horrible ordeal characterized by excruciating pain; it often left the patient either grossly disfigured or dead (often from shock or loss of blood). Being members of the Christian community, these moralists recognized that one has an obligation to preserve one's life, but a crucial question understandably arose: How much does that obligation demand of us? Must we accept all surgical operations that hold out some hope of extending our life—no matter how much pain, agony, and horror are associated with them? The answer given was "no," for it was contended that the pain may be too great or the prospects for success too remote or one's condition after the operation too horrible (disfigured with limbs missing). Life-extending treatment in such circumstances is not morally required, and one can reject it without failing in one's obligation to preserve and protect one's life.

It was the Roman Catholic theologian Domingo Bañez

10. The remarks found in this and the succeeding paragraph draw heavily upon a helpful article by James J. McCartney called "The Development of the Doctrine of Ordinary and Extraordinary Means of Preserving Life in Catholic Moral Theology Before the Karen Quinlan Case," *Linacre Quarterly* 47 (Aug. 1980): 215-24.

who, in 1595, introduced the terms "ordinary" and "extraordinary" to distinguish the two kinds of treatment. He argued that one is required to accept life-extending treatment that brings with it only *ordinary* pain and suffering, but that one is not required to accept treatment that brings with it *extraordinary* pain and suffering. Notice that what makes a treatment ordinary or extraordinary is the effect it has on the patient: it is the ordinary or extraordinary nature of the pain and suffering to be borne by the patient that in turn renders the treatment ordinary or extraordinary.

From the outset, however, the drawing of this distinction was ambiguous, and this ambiguity has plagued discussions about ordinary and extraordinary treatment ever since. Indeed, this ambiguity can be found in the argument of Bañez himself, who also contended that in order to preserve our lives we are obliged to accept nourishment and clothing "common to all" and medical treatment "common to all." Here a second standard for determining obligatory treatment has been introduced—namely, its *common use,* not its impact on the patient. So what is it, then, that makes treatment ordinary? Is it that the treatment causes only ordinary (i.e., tolerable) suffering, or is it that the treatment is the kind ordinarily used (i.e., is common to all)? An additional complication is that these two criteria may have differing implications. A treatment that is widely used and therefore "common to all" may in particular circumstances cause terrible suffering. By the standard of commonness it is mandatory, but by the standard of suffering it is optional. And what of the treatment that is not common to the physicians' trade but nevertheless may, with little pain, serve to preserve one's life? Again, the two standards—commonness and suffering—might dictate different moral conclusions. So a particular treatment may or may not be obligatory depending on which criterion one uses.

Ethicists and physicians have tended to differ over their interpretations of the distinction between ordinary and extraordinary treatment, a divergence that was present already in the sixteenth century. Ethicists work with and have developed the criterion of suffering, whereas the medical profession has frequently adopted the criterion of commonness. Ethicists ask, "Will this treatment benefit the patient without causing undue suffering?" Physicians (more often) ask, "Is this a standard method of treatment?" Thus for ethicists, unlike physicians, the classification of treatment into categories of ordinary and extraordinary is *not* rooted in distinguishing between standard, orthodox treatment and experimental, unorthodox treatment. Rather, they have other factors in mind. A particular treatment is an ordinary means of preserving life when it offers "a reasonable hope of benefit for the patient and . . . can be obtained and used without excessive expense, pain, or other inconvenience."[11] Conversely, a particular treatment is extraordinary when it "cannot be obtained or used without excessive expense, pain, or other inconvenience, or . . . if used would not offer a reasonable hope of benefit."[12] This is what ethicists stress.

It would seem that the ethicists' criterion is preferable to the physicians', for in certain circumstances standard medical procedures may not benefit the patient at all but only prolong an agonizing dying. To insist that such treatment is obligatory because it is a standard part of the physician's arsenal to fight death and disease is unconvincing. Or to insist that a beneficial and painless course of treatment is not mandatory solely because it is not yet part of that standard arsenal would be equally arbitrary and unconvincing. To underscore the point, one can simply look back on the horror story of the dying physician who was kept alive by a series of procedures, most of which are standard medical procedures, procedures that surely were *not* obligatory in those circumstances but would be obligatory if the criterion for ordinary treatment were commonness or standard

11. Gerald Kelly, *Medico-Moral Problems* (St. Louis: The Catholic Hospital Association of the United States and Canada, 1958), p. 129. Father Kelly's book has for many years been a standard Roman Catholic text in the area of medical ethics.

12. Kelly, *Medico-Moral Problems*, p. 129.

medical techniques. So ethicists have argued that treatment need not be accepted by the irreversibly dying patient when any one of the following conditions is fulfilled:

(1) Treatment would involve excessive financial expense to oneself, one's family, or others. Thus, in waiving treatment, the patient might be able to avoid encumbering others with financial liabilities that would work a genuine hardship on them.

(2) Treatment would cause excessive pain or other gross inconvenience, necessitating a heroic response from the patient in order to face it.

(3) Treatment could not reasonably be expected to benefit the patient; that is, the treatment would in all likelihood prove to be practically useless, little more than a futile gesture or a shot in the dark.

Such treatment is optional, which is to say that it is extraordinary. And we determine whether a proposed course of treatment is ordinary or extraordinary by determining in turn whether or not any of the preceding conditions have been fulfilled, this being a matter of prudent judgment. Admittedly, many of the phrases used are vague—for example, "genuine hardship," "excessive pain," "gross inconvenience," "heroic response." What precisely do these phrases mean? There is, of course, no way to define them precisely, but this kind of vagueness is—we need to again remind ourselves—characteristic of the moral life, where we often must struggle with just such broad and imprecise notions. Although the key notions may be imprecise and such that they do not lend themselves to a calculus whereby we can crank out answers from a properly programmed computer, there are nevertheless many cases in which we judge with confidence that one or more of the preceding conditions has been fulfilled. Of course, there will be other cases in which we are torn and fluctuate in our judgment. But that, again, is the nature of the moral life: often there are simply no easy solutions, be they biblical, theological, or rational. The significance of the preceding conditions is not that they provide easy answers to difficult cases but that they point out relevant considerations that are to be taken into account when seeking moral answers.

Strict vs. Liberal Interpretations of Extraordinary Treatment

The distinction between ordinary (required) and extraordinary (optional) treatment and the discussion surrounding this distinction is rendered more complex when we note that treatment may be pain-producing in two different ways: treatment may be painful in its very application, or treatment may be painful solely because it simply prolongs an already painful dying. The point can be illustrated by comparing major surgery with a blood transfusion. Either procedure, if undertaken in the appropriate circumstances, might serve to prolong the life of a dying patient and thereby cause the patient considerable suffering by lengthening an already painful dying; conversely, rejection of either one of the procedures could serve to cut short the dying process and thereby reduce the patient's suffering by reducing the length of his or her dying. In this regard the two procedures are similiar, because they both have life-extending potential; the difference between them, however, is that blood transfusions by themselves cause no suffering (i.e., the transfer of plasma from a container to a human body is a painless procedure), whereas major surgery itself inflicts additional suffering (i.e., all the pain involved in the surgery and its postoperative effects).

So we rightly wish to have a critical question answered: Must extraordinary treatment be treatment that is painful in application, or can it also be treatment that is painless in application but serves only to extend an already painful dying? The liberal interpretation would conclude that what is important is simply the pain caused the patient, and since pain can be caused both by treatment that is painful in application as well as by painless treatment that extends an already painful dying, then *both* should be considered extraordinary treatment. The strict interpretation, on the other hand, requires that optional life-extending treatment be that which causes pain directly, as a result of its application. And to a considerable extent the latter understanding was the focus of the Roman Catholic moralists of the sixteenth century: they confronted surgical procedures that were sheer torture to endure, involving the direct imposition of enormous suffering on the patient. By all accounts, both strict and liberal, the patient was not morally required to undergo such treatments, which demanded an extraordinary or heroic response from the patient. Today, similarly, a particular surgical procedure may inflict terrible suffering on an irreversibly dying patient, directly causing considerable pain and making the patient's remaining days even more agonizing than they otherwise would have been. And according to all interpretations, such surgery is not required.

But how do we apply these concepts to specific forms of treatment that are not necessarily painful—blood transfusions, resuscitations, the use of oxygen tents and respirators, antibiotics, intravenous feeding, and so on? Consider a case in which a person is dying from gastrointestinal cancer and begins to hemorrhage. If she refuses transfusions, she may die of the hemorrhaging, but this may be preferable to the more painful and prolonged dying that she would otherwise endure. Is it morally permissible to *reject* a blood transfusion in such circumstances? According to the strict interpretation, the answer is "no" because this treatment involves little or no pain in application. Certainly one need not shrink back in horror because one is to be given a blood transfusion or be fed intravenously, because these treatments cause virtually no pain or inconvenience. They are therefore ordinary treatments, and it would be wrong, according to this interpretation, to forego them should they have life-extending value. But, of course, although such procedures cause no direct pain and suffering, they can *indirectly* cause a great deal of pain and suffering simply by keeping the patient alive, prolonging what is a painful existence. Still, according to the strict interpretation, this consideration is not relevant, and these modes of treatment are therefore not optional.

In contrast, according to the liberal interpretation, should these procedures (blood transfusions, resuscitations, etc.) cause excessive suffering in any way, they would be judged to be extraordinary treatment and hence not required; it matters not whether pain and suffering are caused directly in application or indirectly by prolonging an agonizing dying. The important consideration is the ultimate effect on the patient. In either case, it would be argued, the patient is being made to suffer, and that is what is morally significant. Indeed, a life prolonged by blood transfusions may be as painful as another life prolonged by means of major surgery, and surely what is pertinent is the burden of pain and suffering that the patient has to bear, not how that burden was imposed. What difference does it make, it would be asked, whether one rejects painful life-extending treatment because it is painful or one rejects *painless* life-extending treatment because it prolongs a dying that is painful? In either case one is rejecting the prospect of great pain in one's life, and in each case one shortens one's life by doing so. Indeed, in each case what defeats one's resolve to prolong one's life is the anticipated pain. Of course, major surgery would normally impose a greater burden of suffering on the terminally ill patient than would blood transfusions, even after both direct and indirect consequences are taken into account, so typically it would be easier to justify the refusal of major surgery than the refusal of blood transfusions. However, this is true not because major surgery causes suffering directly rather than indirectly but because overall it causes more suffering. Certainly these are persuasive considerations.

Despite such arguments, we may still be less comfortable with the notion of rejecting life-extending treatment that is painless in application, for to reject blood transfusions or intravenous feeding does give some of us pause, even if the patient is irreversibly and painfully dying. In part that may be because when in the rejection of such life-extending treatment, we more clearly see that one is *intentionally* shortening life, that one is choosing between two deaths, one sooner and one (a bit) later, and that one is doing so by rejecting a painless, easily applied, and inexpensive form of treatment. Obviously in such circumstances one is rejecting treatment not because the treatment is burdensome but because *life* is burdensome. In contrast, when one rejects life-extending treatment that is burdensome in its very application, one can do so not because it is life-extending but because it is burdensome, making one's remaining days even less tolerable. Consider again the sixteenth-century Christian for whom surgery without anesthesia would be the physical equivalent of submitting to torture. The Christian could reject surgery under such circumstances, not because she doesn't want her life extended but because she fears the horrendous ordeal that would be involved in the surgery that would extend it. By rejecting such treatment, she doesn't reject the life extension that it promises, and she doesn't *intend* her death; rather, she rejects the pain that the surgery brings with it.

Accordingly, we need to introduce at least a cautionary note whenever we consider rejecting *painless* life-extending treatment. For if we wish to say that painless, convenient, and inexpensive treatment that serves only to extend an agonizing dying is optional (and I do), then we are legitimating one's role as shaper of one's own dying, saying that in difficult circumstances one can proceed to choose (by omission) a death that comes sooner rather than one that comes later. To be sure, one has not thereby instigated one's own dying, since that already is an irreversible fact of one's situation; still, one is shaping that dying process, intentionally abbreviating it by omitting medical treatment.[13] However, there are several considerations that

---

13. Admittedly, even to *accept* life-extending treatment and thereby *postpone* death is to shape our own dying, so whether we accept treatment or reject it (and we must do one or the other), *we* decide whether death takes place sooner or later. However, when we accept life-extending treatment, we may have greater confidence that we are acting consonant with God's will, for we are assuming our rightful role as trustees of lives that are divine gifts to be rigorously preserved and protected. Conversely, when we, by omission, choose a sooner death, our justification is less obvious and our decision more problematic. Decisions to intentionally shorten life by omission thus run a greater risk of encroaching on divine sovereignty.

might satisfy the conscience of a Christian who contemplates omitting such painless treatment: suffering is great, death is imminent, God is merciful, and one's dying at least is not a condition of one's own creation, for that remains a product of God's providential working. Therefore, one can in good conscience stop the struggle to ward off death and accept a sooner death as God's will. In saying this we should be clear that we are admitting the legitimacy of our shaping our own dying (deciding to die sooner rather than later) and affirming that this is consistent with the important affirmation that God and not the individual is Lord of death.

Rejecting Artificial Feeding

The suggestion in the previous section that artificial feeding and hydration may in some circumstances be construed as extraordinary treatment and therefore not required needs a special note, for many people think that artificial nourishment and hydration are *not* like other modes of treatment; they are feeding and providing drink, ministrations which we have a special obligation to accept and which others have a special obligation to provide. According to this view, for care-givers not to provide nourishment and fluids is to abandon the patient, and for the patient to reject nourishment and fluids is to prematurely sever his or her ties with the caring community. As Joanne Lynn and James Childress point out, "One of the most common arguments for always providing nutrition and hydration is that it symbolizes, expresses, or conveys the essence of care and compassion. Some actions not only aim at goals, they also express values. Such expressive actions should not simply be viewed as means to ends; they should also be viewed in light of what they communicate. From this perspective food and water are not only goods that preserve life and provide comfort; they are also symbols of care and compassion."[14]

14. Lynn and Childress, "Must Patients Always Be Given Food and Water?" p. 20.

Certainly providing food and water for a dying patient is a significant expression of care and compassion; it is a way of being with the patient ("companying" the patient, as Paul Ramsey puts it) as his or her life draws to a close. It is not merely a means of physical nourishment but a means of emotional support. Failure to provide this support is a failure in caring. Moreover, just as there is an obligation on our part to care for the dying, so there is some responsibility on the part of the dying to accept the care and compassion that is extended. Certainly this is so at the most basic level of sustenance (food and water), pain control, and comfort. To reject this would be to sever oneself from the caring community—a community constituted by a partnership of those who provide care and those who need and accept it. Stanley Hauerwas puts it this way: "We take on a responsibility as sick people. That responsibility is simply to keep on living, as it is our way of gesturing to those who care for us that we can be trusted and trust them even in our illness."[15]

Are the sick, then, always obliged to accept artificial feeding and hydration? I think not. For the symbolic significance of nasogastric tube feeding (often uncomfortable for the patient) or a gastrostomy (a surgical procedure that involves implanting a tube directly into the stomach) seems far removed from the sip of water and the spoonful of broth. Since these forms of feeding—including intravenous feeding—are artificial, mechanical, and automatic in nature, lacking the human touch, they are not the conveyors of meaning that orally taken nourishment and fluids are. So for the patient to reject artificial feeding and fluids is not for him or her to fly in the face of the important symbolism associated with food and drink. Lynn and Childress appropriately comment, "Medical procedures to provide nutrition and hydration are more similar to other medical procedures than to typical human ways of providing nutrition and hydration, for example, a cup of water. It should be possible to evaluate their possible benefits and burdens, as we evaluate any other medical procedure."[16]

Some Intriguing Complications: Another Look at Mercy Killing

If the dying patient can in certain circumstances reject life-extending treatment that in other circumstances might be mandatory, why can't he or she in certain circumstances also take active, "life-ending" steps that in other circumstances would be forbidden? If it is acceptable to say "no" to life-extending treatment when dying, why wouldn't it also be morally acceptable to say "yes" to a lethal dose of a drug? After all, one is dying and death is imminent, no matter what one does. Furthermore, it is argued, when an irreversibly dying patient rejects life-extending treatment, he or she is not choosing death over life but choosing a slightly sooner death over a slightly later death. And this is exactly what an irreversibly dying patient does when he or she takes a lethal overdose: chooses a sooner rather than a later death.

It might be said in response to this argument that when one who is dying takes a lethal dose of a drug for the express purpose of ending one's life, one creates one's own dying—even though one is already dying—by superimposing a drug-induced dying on an already present dying condition. That is, one replaces one dying condition (say, dying of terminal cancer) with another dying condition (say, dying of a drug overdose). One dies, then, of the second condition, which is to say that one dies by one's own hand. This, Christians may feel, is to pre-empt the divine sovereignty over death and therefore is morally problematic in a way that treatment refusal is not. For when one rejects life-extending treatment, one does not create one's own dying; one simply allows an inescapable but already present

16. Lynn and Childress, "Must Patients Always Be Given Food and Water?" p. 20.

dying condition to run its course. That one is dying is not one's own doing; it is exclusively the product of circumstances over which one has no control. That one is dying is not something one willed or chose or intended. So the Christian, out of respect for divine sovereignty, may balk at *creating* his or her own dying (mercy killing) but feel greater freedom to *shape* his or her own dying by allowing it to run its inevitable course (mercy dying), especially when pain is excessive and the quality of life severely compromised. From this perspective it follows that endorsing non-treatment to enable an unalterable dying condition to run its course more quickly does not commit Christians to endorsing mercy killing because there is a theologically significant difference between *shaping* one's dying and *creating* one's dying.

Unfortunately, although this suggestion is in many ways attractive, it poses difficulties. For if rejecting treatment when one is irreversibly dying is a moral possibility because one does *not* thereby create a dying condition but only allows an already present dying condition to proceed unimpeded, then what do we say about those treatment refusals that actually *do* create a dying condition? And there are some treatment refusals, we should note, that do exactly that: they do what the administration of a lethal drug overdose does—create a secondary preemptive dying condition. Consider the diabetic dying of incurable cancer who decides to stop taking insulin and as a consequence dies of his diabetic condition. He makes this decision because he prefers to die a bit sooner (from diabetes) rather than a bit later and more painfully (from cancer). By stopping his insulin intake, the patient brings about, by his own act of will, his death by diabetes, permitting to become lethal a condition that he could have warded off indefinitely, had he so chosen, via insulin injections. To be sure, the diabetic did not create his diabetic condition. Nevertheless, he is not dying of that condition until he makes the decision to stop taking insulin and acts on it, by so doing he creates or willfully causes his own dying. So the rejection of insulin and the administration of a lethal drug overdose appear to share a crucial property, a property which may make them both morally suspect: a dying condition is created by a human act of will. Such treatment refusals have the following features: (a) there is a withholding of treatment for a *curable/treatable* illness or medical condition, (b) the withholding of this treatment results in the patient dying from *that* illness or medical condition, and (c) the withholding is done to avoid a more prolonged death by *another* illness (the primary illness) for which there is no cure.

Think back on our earlier discussion of suicide. There we judged that the otherwise healthy diabetic commits suicide when, in a state of depression, he goes home, locks his doors, stops his insulin injections, falls into a diabetic coma, and dies. Morally speaking, his deed seems indistinguishable from that of the woman who in the same state of depression goes home, locks her doors, takes a lethal overdose of sleeping pills, and dies. Both, it was concluded, are suicides (the one a *passive* suicide and the other an *active* suicide), and both incidents appear to share the same moral status—if the one is wrong, so is the other. In both instances an act of human will brings into being one's dying condition.

Nevertheless, many moralists—both Protestant and Roman Catholic, both liberal and conservative—have judged that it is morally permissible for the diabetic dying from cancer to stop taking insulin.[17] Possibly part of our unease over this case (and over similar cases where a terminally ill patient rejects treatment for a secondary condition that is treatable but potentially lethal) is that we clearly see possibilities for irresponsible behavior here—for example, the diabetic who, upon being diagnosed with terminal cancer, immediately stops taking insulin, thus sacrificing several years of meaningful life. But, of course, one could do much the same thing by rejecting treatment that was aimed at the cancer itself—for example, by rejecting chemotherapy that could extend one's life for an equal or an even greater amount of time. So why should a diabetic who is

17. Cf. Gerald Kelly, "The Duty to Preserve Life," *Theological Studies* 12 (1951): 215-16; also Paul Ramsey, *The Patient as Person* (New Haven, Conn.: Yale University Press, 1970), pp. 115-16.

dying from a painful and difficult-to-palliate case of bone cancer be morally required to keep himself alive by insulin injections in order to insure that he die a little later from bone cancer rather than a little earlier from diabetes? Why indeed? Or why should the dying cancer patient who gets pneumonia be required to use antibiotics in order to cure the pneumonia so that he may be kept alive only to die a little later from cancer? Certainly one can feel the force of the contention that the insulin and the antibiotics are optional forms of treatment. But if one can create one's dying condition by refusing insulin, why can't one create one's dying condition by a lethal drug overdose? If the one is acceptable, isn't the other? Or if the one is morally wrong, isn't the other also? The two seem to share the same moral status.

There are three different positions that can be taken on this issue, none of which may strike us as fully satisfactory, but one of them must be taken nevertheless. The three alternatives are as follows:

A dying diabetic with terminal cancer rejects insulin and dies.	**Moral status:**		
	1	2	3
	wrong	permissible	permissible

A dying diabetic with terminal cancer takes a lethal drug overdose and dies.	**Moral status:**		
	1	2	3
	wrong	permissible	wrong

In other words, there are three possibilities here: (1) both the actions are wrong, (2) both the actions are permissible, or (3) the one action is permissible and the other is wrong.

First, one can argue that for the dying diabetic, both rejecting insulin and taking a drug overdose are wrong. The fact that one is dying does not change the moral status of either action: rejecting insulin and taking a drug overdose are wrong when a person is healthy, and they continue to be wrong when a person is dying. The dying diabetic, then, is morally obliged to take his insulin, and for him to fail to do so is as wrong as taking a lethal drug overdose. This position has the advantage of consistency. After all, both the rejection of insulin and the taking of an overdose create a dying condition, and they do so whether one is already dying or not. If to intentionally create the dying condition that ends one's life is the crucial property that makes either an omission or an action morally objectionable, and if that property attaches both to the rejection of insulin and to a drug overdose, and if it attaches whether the person is already dying or not, then it follows that the dying diabetic should no more reject insulin than he should take a drug overdose. The problem with this position is that rejecting insulin does not seem as morally problematic as taking a drug overdose. At least it doesn't "feel" that way. This theory and our intuitions, then, appear to be at odds with each other. This theory says that the rejection of insulin by the dying diabetic is as wrong as his taking his life by a drug overdose, but intuitively it does not seem as wrong—possibly it doesn't seem wrong at all.

Second, one can argue that when a diabetic is dying, rejecting insulin and taking a drug overdose are *both permissible*, but not when the diabetic is otherwise healthy. This would be the reverse of the previous position. Here we are asked to trust our intuition that the rejection of insulin by the *dying* diabetic patient is *not* wrong and then encouraged to draw the further conclusion that his taking a lethal drug overdose would not be wrong, either. That one is dying *changes* the moral status of both rejecting insulin and taking a drug overdose: what was wrong in a non-dying context becomes permissible in a dying context. That is, both the (otherwise) *healthy* diabetic who intentionally stops his insulin intake and the *healthy* diabetic who intentionally takes a lethal drug overdose, thereby ending life, act equally wrongly, but when these two individuals are irreversibly dying and *then* reject insulin or take a lethal drug overdose, they act in a permissible fashion, both deeds continuing to share the same status. It would be argued that if the dying diabetic's rejection of insulin is not wrong, then neither is his taking a drug overdose, since there is no relevant property that distinguishes the one from the other. Again, if it is permissible for the dying diabetic to create a pre-emptive dying condition by rejecting insulin, then it is permissible for the dying diabetic to create a pre-emptive dying condition by a drug overdose. Dying changes the moral status of both insulin rejection and drug overdose from forbidden or wrong to permitted, because in both cases one is no longer choosing between life and death (as one would be doing if one were otherwise healthy) but choosing between a slightly sooner and a slightly later death. For many of us, however, the problem with this position is its full acceptance of the dying committing suicide. Certainly if we have reservations about killing dying patients at their request, then we will have reservations about this view of matters.

Third, one can argue that when a diabetic is dying, his rejecting insulin becomes permissible but his taking a drug overdose remains forbidden. Thus dying changes the moral status of rejecting insulin (from forbidden when one is healthy to permissible when one is irreversibly dying), but the moral status of taking a drug overdose does not change: it continues to be forbidden. This position is more in keeping with the intuitions of many of us (including mine, though I know there are those who would intuit matters differently). The challenge, however, is to explain why the change of context (from healthy to dying) changes the moral status of insulin rejection but not that of overdosing.

When one is healthy, the rejection of insulin and the taking of a drug overdose seem more alike, whereas when one is irreversibly dying, they seem less alike. Why is this? Only two factors can be relevant, both of which are introduced when one is dying: the imminence of death and the presence of a primary terminal condition. When one is healthy, those two features are absent, but when one is dying, both features are present. We might note that a drug overdose produces death in a manner that is certain and immediate whether or not one is dying, and that in taking an overdose one is asserting total control over one's dying, whereas when one rejects insulin *in the context of dying*, the control is less certain and more ambiguous. Indeed, when the dying diabetic rejects insulin it may not be clear whether he will die from the diabetes or from the primary terminal condition. For death is, in any case, imminent, and his rejection of insulin will not bring immediate death but may take a week or so to culminate in death. Consequently, it is not clear which condition is going to cause death, and when death does occur, it may not be clear which of the two conditions in fact caused it. But a drug overdose is less ambiguous in this regard, since it is more certainly the cause of death. Moreover, when one takes a drug overdose, one indicates that one is willing to take whatever steps are necessary to insure one's death, to exclude *every* possibility of one's life continuing. In contrast, when one rejects insulin, one indicates that one is prepared to exclude only *some* possibilities of one's life continuing (only those possibilities that depend upon continued treatment). If it turns out that the rejection of insulin does not bring death earlier than the primary illness, then "so be it"—one simply accepts that fact. In other words, in this situation one shows a greater willingness to resign oneself to circumstances; one leaves open the possibility of confessing "Death will come in God's own good time." This, for the Christian, may be a significant consideration.

Insulin Rejection and Active Euthanasia

Tom Beauchamp has argued that there is a significant difference between active euthanasia on the one hand and treatment refusal on the other. Active euthanasia rules out the possibility of the patient profiting from a mistaken diagnosis. In contrast, Beauchamp claims that to withdraw or withhold treatment is to "allow for the possibility of wrong diagnoses or incorrect prediction and hence to absolve oneself of moral responsibility for the taking of life under false assumptions."[18] This is so because

18. Beauchamp, "A Reply to Rachels on Active and Passive Euthanasia," in *Social Ethics*, ed. Thomas A. Mappes and Jane S. Zembaty (New York: McGraw-Hill, 1977), p. 71.

when treatment directed at the diagnosed terminal illness is simply withdrawn, the illness is still allowed to run its natural course, and if it turns out that the illness is not terminal, then that will become manifest in time as the patient—counter to the diagnosis—continues to live. For Beauchamp the important distinction is that treatment refusal at least preserves the possibility of mistaken diagnosis, whereas active euthanasia, because it causes the immediate death of the patient, eliminates that possibility altogether. Therefore, to engage in active euthanasia is to assume a graver moral responsibility than that involved in treatment refusal.

However, it should be noted, contrary to Beauchamp's suggestion, that not all forms of treatment refusal allow the diagnosed terminal illness to run its natural course. This is not the case when a terminally ill patient rejects treatment for a secondary condition that is treatable but potentially lethal. Here it is helpful to return to our earlier example of the diabetic who, confronted by a diagnosis of terminal cancer, rejects insulin and dies of his diabetes rather than of his cancer. He does exactly what a person does who chooses active euthanasia: he ends his life *before* the diagnosed terminal illness can run its full course and thereby demonstrate beyond all doubt that it was terminal. So in this regard active euthanasia and treatment rejection that creates a secondary, pre-emptive dying condition share a crucial property: both prevent the primary terminal illness from running its course. In contrast, standard cases of treatment refusal do, as Beauchamp points out, allow the primary illness or medical condition to play itself out and demonstrate its terminal character beyond question. But how significant is this feature?

Here it is important to stress that there is such a thing as medical knowledge, and at some point short of the illness actually killing the patient, we can be justified in claiming to know that the illness is terminal and that the patient will die. And to the extent that we are in possession of this kind of knowledge, the difference between active euthanasia or insulin rejection by the diabetic with cancer (and similar treatment refusals) and standard cases of treatment refusal (i.e., treatment directed at the primary terminal illness) is not significant, the possibility of taking life under false assumptions having been ruled out in *all* of these cases. Since we don't have to let an illness run its course before we can know that it is terminal, we need not always fear that insulin refusal by the cancer patient and similar treatment refusals involve ending a life under the *false* assumption that the primary illness is terminal. Medical knowledge can, at some point, eliminate that fear. Nevertheless, Beauchamp's observation is still relevant, for it may imply that insulin rejection and similar treatment refusals are more appropriate at the latter stages of terminal illness, when diagnoses can be made with the highest degree of certainty, and at which point health-care professionals can, with a high degree of confidence, assert that death will result from the primary terminal condition.

It also needs to be pointed out that the possibility of mistaken diagnoses is also a problem for some *standard* forms of treatment refusal, though in a slightly different way. For when a patient terminates treatment directed at the primary illness that is diagnosed as terminal, he or she may decide to do so because competent medical authorities have judged that the treatment will not succeed in curing the illness but will only prolong a painful dying. Crucial to the patient's decision is the diagnosis provided by the physician: continued treatment will not cure the illness but will only prove futile. But if this diagnosis is mistaken and continued treatment would have cured the illness, then the decision to forego treatment would be a fatal one, and treatment would be terminated under false assumptions. Therefore, to continue treatment is also to preserve whatever chance for life there is should there be diagnostic error; to discontinue treatment is to abandon that chance. Accordingly, if it is the case that insulin rejection and similar treatment refusals cause problems by not allowing the *illness* to run its full course and demonstrably prove itself terminal, then standard cases of treatment refusal can cause problems by not allowing the *treatment* to run its full course and demonstrably prove itself futile and ineffective. But, again, what most of us assume is that we can reach the point where the possibility of diagnostic error has been excluded, and we have a rational basis for fully informed decision-making.

The Options: A Review

At this juncture we need to gather together the various observations we have made about life-extending treatment and to systematize the available alternatives. This will help clarify a number of issues already presented as well as provide a context in which to review our conclusions. Accordingly, the following options represent differing attitudes toward the acceptance or rejection of life-prolonging treatment *by the dying patient:*

1. Life-extending treatment is always to be accepted.
2. Life-extending treatment can be rejected only when the treatment itself is especially burdensome.
3. Life-extending treatment can be rejected not only (a) when the treatment itself is especially burdensome but also (b) when the treatment (though not itself burdensome) extends an agonizing or burdensome dying (but not when the treatment is directed at a secondary medical condition that is treatable).
4. Life-extending treatment can be rejected (a) when the treatment itself is especially burdensome, (b) when the treatment (though not itself burdensome) extends an agonizing dying, and (c) even when the treatment is directed at a secondary medical condition that is treatable.

Let us examine each of these in turn.
Option #1: Life-extending treatment is always to be accepted. The rationale for this option is that the obligation to preserve life always overrides the obligation to relieve suffering. The argument is that there is never a point at which the disvalue of pain and suffering negates the commanding value of personal life. Not to attempt to prolong one's life (and one's dying) because of pain and suffering is to wrongly conclude that such a negation has taken place. All life-prolonging procedures are impera-

tive as long as one is conscious. Therefore, one is always morally obliged to accept life-prolonging treatment no matter how much pain and suffering are involved.

This is an extreme position that has few—if any—advocates, even among conservative moralists. It is in essence a formula for torture. In this regard, think back on the "horror story" presented earlier in this chapter. There we looked at the case of a sixty-eight-year-old physician who was admitted to a hospital suffering from advanced cancer of the stomach. It was known that his death was imminent. In the course of his stay in the hospital, physicians operated to remove his stomach, operated to remove a clot in one of his lung arteries, resuscitated him after he suffered a heart attack (his heart being restarted artificially on five occasions), and subjected him to a series of medical techniques that served to keep him alive for three more weeks, during which time he suffered from violent vomiting, convulsions, and intense pain. It so happened that his request that life-prolonging treatment be stopped was ignored. But surely his request was a morally legitimate one; not only was he within his rights in making the request, but he was making a request that was beyond, I suggest, moral fault. Surely most of the treatment that this physician-patient wished to reject was morally optional. Yet, on the basis of the position we are now considering, all of that treatment—and more, if it could serve to prolong life—was morally required. This position simply places no limits on the pain and suffering that one should endure in order to prolong one's life.

To argue for such a conclusion flies in the face of common moral sense. In the final analysis there may not be any formal argument that can be given to refute this position; perhaps all we can do is present cases like our "horror story" and ask ourselves whether we can embrace the implications of a position that requires an acceptance of life-prolonging treatment no matter how much pain and suffering are involved, and no matter how close death is. Indeed, the merciful and compassionate God we envision would seem more gracious than this. Further, in saying that life-extending treatment can be rejected, we need not argue that a dying patient's life, plagued as it may be with extreme pain and suffering, has no value or that its value has been negated by that pain and suffering; we need only contend that this pain and suffering relieves the individual of the necessity to preserve that value.

Option #2: Life-extending treatment can be rejected only when the treatment itself is especially burdensome. Although such treatment may have life-extending potential, it is not to be rejected for that reason; rather, it is to be rejected because it brings with it more burdens than one would otherwise have to bear, more burdens than one can reasonably be expected to bear. The crucial point here is that in refusing such treatment one does not intend one's death, one does not undertake shortening one's life, one does not seek to cause one's death sooner rather than later; one intends only to die free from the burdens that such treatment would impose. Indeed, if the treatment could be rendered burden-free, one would accept it even though it would extend an already burdensome dying.

The fundamental moral conviction here is that we are never to intentionally shorten our lives, either by act or by omission, which is exactly what we do when we reject life-prolonging treatment solely because it extends an agonizing dying—that is, because it extends life. By so doing we would be wrongly rejecting life, albeit life in a dying mode. And it is argued that if we do not draw the line right here and declare that such treatment refusal is morally unacceptable, we will be hard-pressed *not* to go on to endorse active euthanasia. For intentionally ending one's life by omission is morally no different from intentionally ending one's life by commission, and if we endorse the former, we appear committed to endorsing the latter as well. Indeed, this is one of the strengths of this option: it clearly enables us to refuse some life-extending treatment (though there is other life-extending treatment that we must accept) without committing us to an acceptance of active euthanasia, and it has a clear rationale for drawing the line where it does: one must not intentionally shorten one's life by action or omission.

When one rejects life-extending treatment because it is burdensome in its own right (the only kind of life-extending treatment that can be rejected, according to this position), one does *not* intend one's death; one intends only to escape the burdens that the treatment brings with it. To be sure, one *foresees* that this omission is life-shortening, but such a result is a "foreseen though unintended consequence" of one's omission. For just as with actions, so with omissions—both can have foreseen but unintended consequences. And there are some things that one is not to intend, and ending one's life is one of them. There are no circumstances (short, perhaps, of the catastrophic) in which such an intention is morally allowable. Therefore, ending one's life, whether actively or passively, is not to be made a project of the will.

Thus there are some circumstances in which one might, with moral justification, either do or omit doing something that will have the foreseen consequence of shortening one's life. Just as a dying patient might have painkillers administered for the purpose of controlling intense pain even though those painkillers may accelerate his or her dying, so also the dying patient can omit certain burdensome treatments even though this omission may be life-shortening. The patient does not intend to shorten life (though that result is foreseen), and if there are adequate justifying reasons for such an action or omission, it may be permitted. Thus *intending* to shorten one's life is absolutely banned, whereas foreseeing-though-not-intending the shortening of one's life may in some (though not all) circumstances be morally allowable.[19]

More specifically, according to this option, major surgery might be rejected because it will bring considerable suffering and gross inconvenience to an already dying patient who wants

19. It is important to stress that this position does not sanction every rejection of life-extending treatment where the life-shortening consequences are merely foreseen but not intended. It only says that such life-shortening consequences, because unintended, *might* be morally permissible. To determine whether or not they are, one must look to the amount of suffering and gross inconvenience that they cause the patient, along with death's proximity.

instead to die free of that burden, able in his or her last days to rest comfortably and to focus attention not on fighting pain and recovering from an operation but on relating to family and friends, and having the mental clarity to engage in the task of attending to spiritual concerns. What is important is that in this instance one does not reject surgery because it extends one's life or one's dying—that is not one's purpose at all. Rather, one is concerned with the quality of one's dying, not the duration of it, and one rejects the surgery because it worsens the quality of one's remaining days, not because it increases their quantity.

So also one might reject highly intrusive medical technology that physically overwhelms one, makes communication difficult, is psychologically repugnant, and hinders humane and warm interaction with others. Again, the treatment is rejected not because of its life-prolonging potential but because it seriously disturbs the quality of one's dying. Although this notion is admittedly an amorphous one, it is part of what many people are getting at when they speak of "death with dignity," avoiding a dying in which one is enveloped by machinery and tubes that seriously threaten the humane nature of one's dying. One physician put it this way: "I submit that the death bed scenes I witness are not particularly dignified. The family is shoved out into the corridor by the physical presence of intravenous stands, suction machines, oxygen tanks and tubes emanating from every natural and several surgically induced orifices. The last words, if the patient has not been comatose for the past forty-eight hours, are lost behind an oxygen mask."[20] In saying "no" to such treatment, one is seeking only to protect the quality of one's dying, not intending to shorten one's life.

Crucially, this option does require that the dying patient accept all life-prolonging treatment that is painless, convenient, and inexpensive, even though that treatment serves only to prolong an agonizing dying. For a person can have only one reason

20. Quoted by Kieran Nolan, "The Problem of Care for the Dying," in *Absolutes in Moral Theology,* ed. Charles E. Curran (Washington: Corpus Books, 1968), p. 250.

for rejecting such treatment—to die sooner rather than later—and that, it is claimed, is a morally unsatisfactory reason for refusing life-extending treatment. For some, this implication alone is sufficient to render this position untenable, for why should a horrible and painful dying have to be prolonged simply because the means of prolonging it are painless, convenient, and inexpensive? Consider one specific problem area: the use of cardiopulmonary resuscitation techniques. In certain restricted circumstances physicians write a so-called no-code order, an order not to resuscitate the patient should he or she suffer cardiac arrest. Resuscitation techniques are not painful, since the patient is unconscious; in addition, they are neither inconvenient nor expensive. This means that to reject cardiopulmonary resuscitation (by prior request) can be based on one reason only—to die sooner rather than later—and thus it is an omission that intends death. Therefore, resuscitation techniques must *always* be applied as long as there is some prospect of continued personal existence, no matter how brief that existence due to death's proximity or how agonizing one's continued dying. Arguably this imperative is too restrictive, and if it is judged to be so, then one has opened the door to omissions that intend death.

Option #3: Life-extending treatment can be rejected by the dying patient not only (a) when the treatment itself is especially burdensome but also (b) when the treatment (though not itself burdensome) extends an agonizing or burdensome dying. This means that life-extending treatment can be rejected even though it entails intentionally shortening one's dying—that is, one *can* reject treatment for the express purpose of ending one's life. This option, unlike the previous one, allows the patient to reject painless, convenient, and inexpensive treatment that only prolongs an agonizing dying, and thus it avoids what some may see as the difficult implications associated with the previous position. Admittedly, this does mean that one can undertake shortening one's life when one is dying, although only when the dying is of a distressing character. This option attempts, however, to respect God's providential ordering of events and to avoid the slide into acceptance of active euthanasia by placing what is judged to be a significant restriction on the rejection of life-extending treatment: *one must not create one's own dying*—one can shape it, yes, but not create it. Creating one's own dying, of course, is just what one does when one commits suicide via active euthanasia—one superimposes a death by lethal injection or some other means on an already present dying condition. But a morally acceptable rejection of life-extending treatment (even though death is intended) does not create a dying condition; it is merely the refusal to impede the progress of an already present but irreversible dying condition. Therefore, to reject treatment in such circumstances does not commit one to active euthanasia, which involves the intentional creation of a dying condition. So some treatment refusals that intend death are actually *acceptable* (those that do not create a dying condition), and some treatment refusals that intend death are *unacceptable* (those that intentionally create a dying condition).

Here there is a serious attempt to recognize the divine sovereignty over death by placing certain matters outside human control: one is not to create one's own dying (by omission or commission), and one is not to do so even when human judgment would say it is for the best. This is a judgment not to be executed by human beings; it is to be left in God's hands. And, of course, in order to leave matters in God's hands, one must recognize a sphere that is off-limits to human control, which is exactly what this option does, while at the same time providing greater latitude than the previous option in the rejection of life-extending treatment, since it includes the rejection of treatment that serves only to extend an agonizing dying but is itself painless. Thus it does grant the human agent the authority to reject treatment for the sole purpose of dying sooner rather than later, but in so doing it does not endorse suicide (active or passive) because suicide, it would (or might) be argued, involves *creating one's own dying* by act or omission (not simply intending one's death), and a morally acceptable treatment refusal does not do this.[21]

21. This introduces a different definition of suicide than that which would be used by the previous option. Option #2 would define suicide as the intentional bringing about of one's own *death*. Option #3 would define suicide as the

But with this option, too, there are difficulties, at least if one believes that it is sometimes legitimate for the dying person to reject treatment and thereby create his or her own dying, the very sort of thing that this option precludes. A case in point is the diabetic who rejects insulin so that death might come sooner from diabetes rather than later from bone cancer. The rejection of antibiotics to cure pneumonia in comparable circumstances serves to further illustrate the point. If one is receptive to these and other such refusals as legitimate moral possibilities, then one must continue one's search for an acceptable option.

Option #4: Life-extending treatment can be rejected (a) when its application imposes an excessive burden on the patient, (b) when it— although painless, convenient, and inexpensive—extends an agonizing dying, and (c) even when it creates a dying condition that in turn pre-empts a primary dying condition of burdensome proportions. This theory says, very simply, that there is no type of life-extending treatment which the dying patient could not in good conscience refuse in the appropriate circumstances. Here the sole focus is on the patient and the suffering that he or she has to endure, and if that suffering constitutes a grave burden and can be reduced by rejecting life-extending treatment, then such rejection is morally permissible, and it matters not what kind of treatment is rejected.

The theoretical difficulty with this option is how to avoid sliding into an acceptance of active euthanasia, a difficulty created by the fact that by accepting this position we have thereby accepted *omissions* that intend death by creating a dying condition—and, that being the case, why not also accept *commissions* that intend death by creating a dying condition? Of course, if we do not find active euthanasia objectionable, then there is no theoretical difficulty to be resolved. But suppose we do find it objectionable. How can we endorse this flexible attitude toward the rejection of life-extending treatment while with

---

intentional creation of one's own *dying*. Definition #3, then, *excludes* from the category of suicide those treatment refusals that shape one's dying by allowing an irreversible dying to proceed unimpeded.

good reason drawing back from the endorsement of active euthanasia? It seems to me that the answer to this question is somewhat problematic, though I have struggled to provide just such an answer.

It can still be said of a dying individual who rejects the full range of life-extending treatment previously mentioned, including those treatments that create a dying condition, that he dies a *natural* death and does so, we are supposing, in a context where prolonging life is burdensome and futile. He judges that he has no obligation to continue waging a battle that is already lost and therefore no obligation to accept any kind of life-extending treatment. Nevertheless, there is still in this approach a respect for the natural unfolding of events. For example, although the diabetic who is dying of cancer foregoes insulin, he is merely taking advantage of a contingency that was not of his own making (i.e., his diabetes), and he does exercise restraint by not forcing events by active means. He thereby refuses to assert a blanket control over his dying, which would be getting what he wants immediately and painlessly by a lethal overdose. To be sure, he is surrendering to the inevitable, but he is not going beyond that, and therefore he does not completely make his dying a project of the will. This dying patient plays the hand that he has been dealt, and part of that hand is diabetes, which in this instance brings with it certain possible advantages: he can, when dying a painful death, shorten his death by rejecting insulin. Others, of course, may be dealt a different hand, and therefore they may not be in a position to bring about a pre-emptive dying condition by means of treatment refusal—they don't have diabetes or pneumonia or whatever—but they too must play the hand that they have been dealt. Part of the challenge for faith is to accept the circumstances of one's dying (that is, one's hand) as coming from God. This becomes an occasion for trust—"Yes, there is a God of providence who controls the events and the circumstances of my dying, and therefore I accept them as his will." We are still able to take seriously the belief that God has placed us in this world and that a natural death is part of the journey that he has ordained for each of us.

The argument comes down to a single crucial point. The diabetic dying of cancer who rejects insulin at least leaves intact a natural death and in appropriate circumstances does not violate the trust given by God to faithfully preserve and protect his life. In contrast, the *non*-dying diabetic who has considerable time ahead of him and who ends his life by rejecting insulin also dies a natural death, but he does not exercise appropriate fidelity in caring for his life. His rejection of insulin is a failure of massive proportions, and such a rejection is morally indistinguishable from intentional overdosing. So the refusals of insulin by the dying diabetic and the non-dying diabetic are morally distinguishable on the basis of the latter not adequately caring for his life. Further, a natural death distinguishes the diabetic dying from cancer who rejects insulin from the patient dying from cancer who chooses active euthanasia. In drawing back from endorsing active euthanasia, this position shows respect for God's providential ordering of events, and recognizes a sphere that is to remain outside human control and judgment. Thus it is consistent for proponents of the present option to disapprove of the non-dying diabetic who rejects insulin (a failure to adequately care for one's life) and to disapprove of the dying patient who elects active euthanasia (a rejection of a God-ordained natural death). In so arguing, however, we have made appeal to distinctly theological considerations.

Summary

The rejection of life-extending treatment by a *dying* patient is not passive euthanasia, I argued, because it is not suicide, and I have suggested that passive euthanasia is to be understood as a form of passive suicide. So if treatment refusal by the dying patient is not passive suicide, then neither is it passive euthanasia.

I maintained that it is reasonable to believe that the point can come, certainly in the case of the dying patient, when one can reject life-extending treatment and do so in good conscience before the Lord and Giver of Life—when suffering is sufficiently intense, when relief consonant with rational existence is not available, when one's ability to carry out responsibilities to family and friends is radically diminished, and when one's ability to participate in the higher goods that invest life with much of its value is sufficiently jeopardized.

In addition, I argued that withholding treatment and stopping treatment are morally equivalent. Therefore, we should be no more reluctant to stop treatment once it is begun than not to start it to begin with. To think otherwise, as we saw, may create serious problems: patient and physician may become reluctant to start what they cannot as readily justify stopping, and this may serve only to deny the patient a form of treatment that should at least be tried. Further, the right both to refuse and to stop treatment is grounded in our right to bodily self-determination and need not be viewed as an implication of any supposed right to die. This right to reject and/or stop treatment is a strong right that ought to be recognized and fully honored by the law (which, to a considerable extent, it already is), but the recognition of this right does not imply any recognition of a right to die.

From a Christian point of view, dying morally involves (a) honoring the value of one's life by avoiding a premature submission to death and (b) honoring the divine sovereignty over death by not dictating the details of death's occurrence. These twin beliefs, I suggested, are mutually interpretative. In other words, preserving and protecting one's life is to honor the divine sovereignty over life and death, because in so doing one affirms the value of one's life and thereby aligns one's will with the divine will; and recognizing the divine sovereignty over death means that at some point one is to stop resisting the inevitable and allow death to come at God's behest, one's obligation to stave off death having come to an end.

I presented the distinction between ordinary (required or obligatory) treatment and extraordinary (optional) treatment, and I concluded that this distinction, while not providing formulas for answering tough questions about treatment termination, nevertheless points to considerations that are relevant to deciding whether or not certain life-extending treatments are obligatory. Thus certain treatments are extraordinary or optional for the dying patient when they involve excessive financial expense, cause excessive pain or other gross inconvenience, and/or cannot be reasonably expected to benefit the patient (i.e., are futile shots in the dark). I concluded that treatment is to be considered extraordinary and therefore not obligatory when the treatment itself directly causes pain and suffering as well as when the treatment itself—although inexpensive, painless, and convenient—causes pain and suffering indirectly by merely prolonging an agonizing dying. Further, I contended that artificial feeding and hydration can be construed, in certain circumstances, as extraordinary and therefore optional treatment.

I argued that there are circumstances in which the dying patient may reject the full panoply of life-extending treatment: (a) when treatment itself is especially burdensome, (b) when treatment, though not itself burdensome, extends an agonizing dying, and (c) even when treatment is directed at a secondary medical condition that is treatable. In regard to the latter type of treatment, I argued that a diabetic who is dying from a painful and difficult-to-palliate case of bone cancer is not required to keep himself alive by insulin injections in order to insure that he die a little later from bone cancer rather than a little earlier from diabetes. The patient, if his dying is especially burdensome, can reject the insulin even though he intends his death and brings about a pre-emptive dying condition of his own making. I also argued that although this is morally permissible, one is not thereby committed to endorsing active euthanasia, because when the diabetic rejects the insulin, he still dies a natural death, does not assert a blanket control over his dying, does not make his dying a project of the will, and leaves room for God's providential ordering of events—none of which pertains with active euthanasia. This is theologically significant and, for the Christian, morally significant.

CHAPTER SIX

The Permanently Unconscious Patient

Introduction

Up until this point in our reflections we have focused on the conscious patient who confronts choices about treatment termination or active assistance in dying. But what do we say about the patient who is permanently unconscious due to accident or illness? Here a number of distinct questions emerge, especially if the patient has given no indication about what he or she might want in such circumstances. Is a permanently unconscious individual dead? Indeed, should we consider dead an individual who has sustained an irreversible cessation of consciousness and whose heart and lungs continue to function only with the aid of an artificial life-support system? And should we consider dead the individual who has sustained an irreversible cessation of consciousness but whose heart and lungs continue to function even *without* the aid of a respirator?

If the answer is "yes" and these individuals are to be pronounced dead, then—granting our cultural and moral understanding of death—a number of things seem to follow. We could, in good conscience, terminate life-sustaining medical efforts; we could stop nourishment and hydration; with appropriate authorization, vital organs could be removed and made available to others; spouses could consider themselves widows or widowers and the mourning process could begin, along with

157

the appropriate rituals that culminate in burial or cremation. Obviously, being pronounced dead constitutes a radical change in one's status and dramatically alters the manner in which one is to be treated. Accordingly, much depends on the decision to pronounce an individual dead and much, therefore, depends on our concept of death.

A Christian Understanding of Death

Our concept of death is not something to be settled by the expertise of the medical profession. For should we first conclude, according to a particular concept of death, that permanently unconscious individuals are dead, then we can turn to the medical profession to diagnose the presence and permanence of such an unconscious state, but the initial decision about what constitutes death and whether or not the permanently unconscious are dead is not a medical decision—rather, it is a conceptual one, possibly a theological and moral one as well. So not only is this decision fraught with momentous implications, but also it is not one that we can turn over to the medical profession to settle for us. Although the medical profession may provide us with diagnostic criteria to determine when a patient is dead, it is society that determines the fundamental character of death and thereby determines which criteria are relevant.

Robert Veatch has argued that in arriving at an adequate concept of death, we must first determine what is significant about human beings, for only then will we be in a position to characterize death. For him death would be the total and irreversible loss of that special significance.[1] Given such an understanding of matters, it follows that before we can delineate a concept of death in more detail, we must first determine what is centrally significant about human beings, and this clearly takes us outside the realm of the medical profession's expertise. Here,

1. Veatch, "The Whole-Brain-Oriented Concept of Death: An Outmoded Philosophical Formulation," *Journal of Thanatology* 3 (1975): 15.

it would seem, we are involved in a momentous act of moral valuation. Is it biological life that provides human beings with their special value? Is it animal consciousness? Is it personal consciousness? Or is it something else? The answers to these questions will determine our concept of death—they will do so, that is, if we adopt the crucial premise that death is the total and irreversible loss of what is centrally significant about human beings.

If we grant the legitimacy of such a general strategy (and it is not without its problems), then those operating within a Christian belief-system may be attracted to the conclusion that death is the total and irreversible loss of the capacity to participate in God's creative and redemptive purposes for human life. For it is reasonable for Christians to believe that it is precisely this capacity which endows human life with its special significance. More specifically, this is the capacity to shape an eternal destiny by means of decision-making and soul-making, requiring as it does both spiritual agency and spiritual receptivity—all of which presuppose conscious existence (that is, psychic life) and not mere organic functioning (that is, somatic life). Indeed, it is reasonable to suppose that human organic life has no value in its own right but receives its significance from the fact that it can make possible and sustain personal consciousness and thereby make possible the capacity to participate in God's creative and redemptive purposes. However, when the human biological organism can no longer fulfill that function, its significance has been lost.

The same point can be made by putting matters in a slightly different way. When an individual becomes permanently unconscious, the *person* has passed out of existence, even if biological life continues. There cannot be a person where there is neither the capacity for having mental states nor even the potentiality for developing that capacity (e.g., as with infants). For persons are beings who have the capacity (potentially or actually) to think, will, affirm moral and spiritual ideals, love and hate, desire, hope, plan, and so forth. The concept of a person may not be a concept over which there is perfect agreement.

159

Indeed, in the case of an individual in whom the capacities just listed are attenuated but not totally absent, we may not be altogether certain whether or not we have a person (in cases of such uncertainty, of course, we should act on the assumption that we *are* dealing with a person). But where *no* such capacities exist *at all* due to permanent loss of consciousness, there we no longer have an individual who commands the special respect due a person because we no longer have a person. And when the person passes out of existence, so do a range of obligations that formerly held. This is not to suggest that we have no remaining obligations to the person who has died, for we may still have an obligation to dispose of the person's body and possessions in accord with the person's wishes and to treat that person's bodily remains with appropriate respect. But if the person is dead, then the obligation to persist in life-sustaining efforts no longer holds.

However, when we press matters, problems emerge with the suggestion that psychic life is what is essentially significant about human beings. For what kind of psychic life is it that endows one with this special significance? It cannot be mere consciousness, because animals are conscious, yet they lack that special significance we wish to attribute to human beings. It must, therefore, be *personal* consciousness that is crucially significant about human life. But what then do we say about the individual suffering from advanced stages of senile dementia whose mental capacities have deteriorated to the point where she can no longer remember, judge, reason, engage in purposeful action, and so on, but who nevertheless is conscious and has a certain primitive awareness of her environment? If this individual can function only at the level of an animal, then it would seem that what is special and significant about human beings has been lost. What appears to follow is that—even though the woman is conscious—the *person* is dead. It would be outrageous, however, to treat this individual as if she *were* dead. In part that may be because we would actually be uncertain that the person is dead. For how do we know that there is not, deep in the recesses of that personality, a personal awareness that still flickers from time to time and has not been completely extinguished? And in such cases of uncertainty, surely we must operate on the assumption that there is still personal life present that warrants respect. To pronounce such an individual dead would be to arrogantly assume an authority beyond our capacities as diagnosticians.

It has been argued that much of the debate over how death is to be defined is really a covert debate about what should be done with the patient (e.g., should he or she be kept on the life-support system or disconnected from it?) and not a debate about whether the patient is really dead or not.[2] Accordingly, Veatch's proposal that death is the irreversible loss of what is essentially significant about human life would be understood as actually being a proposal about how we should handle certain patients. And perhaps it doesn't matter whether we construe Veatch as proposing that (1) a patient who has totally and irreversibly lost what is essentially significant about human life *is dead*, or that (2) a patient who has totally and irreversibly lost what is essentially significant about human life *can be allowed to die*. In either case we must decide matters based on an act of valuation. For the fact is that psychic death can occur without somatic death, and this fact forces us to judge whether mere organic functioning without any psychological life provides us with a value sufficient to justify life-preserving effort. If we say "no" —if we say, in other words, that human biological functioning without any conscious life (actual or potential) is of no special value— then we are saying that it is the presence or absence of psychic life and not the presence or absence of somatic life that should control our decision either to declare the individual to be dead or—if we prefer—to declare that the individual can be allowed to die. If we say "yes," then we recognize the presence or absence of somatic life as the determining factor. In either case we are making our decision based on what we believe gives human

2. Cf. Hans Jonas, "Against the Stream: Comments on the Definition and Redefinition of Death," in *Ethical Issues in Death and Dying,* ed. Tom L. Beauchamp and Seymour Perlin (Englewood Cliffs, N.J.: Prentice-Hall, 1978), pp. 51ff.

life its special significance. The brain-death statutes that many states have adopted favor the former way of putting matters (that is, the individual who has totally and irreversibly lost what is essentially significant about human life is dead). For these statutes do not declare that the brain-dead individual can be taken off the respirator and allowed to die; rather, they declare that the individual can be taken off the respirator because he or she is *already* dead. The declaration of death is made, then, *before* the patient is removed from the life-support system.

Unfortunately, tangled discussions of the concept of death often intrude themselves in a way that doesn't help us determine whether or not we should pull the plug. John Harris makes the point this way: "What matters is whether or not the organism is still a person, not whether or not it is dead. . . . What we need, then, is not a definition of death but an account of when it is right to say that personhood is lost."[3] I believe that to be correct.

Brain Death vs. Persistent Vegetative State

At a certain level of application most of us would not find the preceding suggestions problematic. For example, a person suffering from total brain death who is on a life-support system that makes breathing and heartbeat possible would be considered dead (or considered to be in such a state that he or she could be allowed to die), since there will never again be a center of consciousness connected with that body (short of the Christian hope of the Resurrection). Therefore, most of us would feel free to disconnect the life-support system and allow the biological organism to die—the *person* having already died. We might have some emotional difficulties in doing this but not, I suggest, any serious moral reservations. For to keep the physical organism alive (apart from the need to do so for purposes of organ transplants) would serve no useful purpose, since what is significant

3. Harris, *The Value of Life* (London: Routledge & Kegan Paul, 1985), pp. 241-42.

about human life has been irretrievably lost—death in its important sense has already occurred. The life-support system is keeping not the *person* but only the *body* alive and therefore may be removed.

Many states now have brain-death statutes that enable the physician to pronounce dead the individual who has suffered irreversible loss of total brain function and to remove the life-support system that makes breathing and heartbeat possible. According to such an understanding of death, the life-support system is not removed in order to allow the patient to die; rather, the patient is already dead, and for *that* reason treatment can be stopped. So, in addition to the traditional criteria for death (i.e., permanent cessation of heartbeat and respiration), the states have been adopting a brain-death criterion which, when applied with due care, permits a legal declaration of death. These brain-death statutes, however, concern *total* brain death. This means not only that the individual will not regain consciousness but that he or she will never again breathe independently because the respiratory centers in the brain stem have been destroyed. It is also the case that the totally brain-dead individual typically expires in a matter of weeks even with ventilator support, so what is achieved by removing such an individual from a ventilator will usually occur in a week or so in any event. However, what justifies the removal of such an individual from a ventilator is not, I suggest, that he or she will expire shortly anyway but that he or she will never again be conscious. So even if it were possible to maintain artificial breathing *in perpetuity,* that would not alter the central consideration which justifies removal from the life-support system: the existence of an irreversible unconscious condition.

But consider a troublesome variant of this case. Suppose that removing the permanently unconscious individual from the life-support system does not result in the death of the body, that breathing and heartbeat continue without the aid of a ventilator. This can occur when the individual has suffered *partial but not total* brain destruction. In such cases there may be a flat EEG, indicating that the cerebral cortex is no longer able to function, although the lower-brain portion that regulates breathing and heartbeat continues to perform *its* function. Such individuals are in what is called a "persistent vegetative state," which is to be contrasted with total "brain death." The persistent vegetative state has been described as follows: "Personality, memory, purposive action, social interaction, sentience, thought, and even emotional states are gone. Only vegetative functions and reflexes persist. If food is supplied, the digestive system functions and controlled evacuation occurs; the kidneys produce urine; the heart, lungs, and blood vessels continue to move air and blood; and nutrients are distributed in the body."[4]

This is what occurred in the well-known case of Karen Ann Quinlan, whose heart and lungs continued to function after she was weaned from the respirator;[5] she continued in this state for about 10 years (the record in such cases is an amazing 37 years and 111 days[6]). However, the body of Karen Ann Quinlan would not have continued to live had it not been fed artificially by means of nasogastric tubes. But why, we may wonder, continue artificial feeding (whether by nasogastric tubes, gastrostomy tubes, or IV tubes) when the person as a center of continuing consciousness can no longer be the object of our life-sustaining concern because the body has ceased to serve its significant role as sustainer of a conscious being. Why should artificial feeding be any more mandatory than artificial respiration? Indeed, it is difficult to see why the one (artificial feeding) should be re-

4. President's Commission for the Study of Ethical Problems in Medicine and Biomedical and Behavioral Research, *Deciding to Forego Life-Sustaining Treatment: A Report on the Ethical, Medical, and Legal Issues in Treatment Decisions* (Washington: GPO, 1983), pp. 174-75.

5. In many cases in which a person's breathing has been assisted by a ventilator, especially for an extended period, the individual has become physically dependent on the ventilator, and it must be removed gradually, not abruptly. Thus the individual is taken off the ventilator for increasingly extended periods of time, enabling the lungs to adjust to the physical demands of functioning on their own.

6. This is the case of Elaine Esposito, a five-year-old girl who never regained consciousness following surgery on 6 August 1941. See President's Commission, *Deciding to Forego Life-Sustaining Treatment*, p. 177n.16.

quired and the other (artificial breathing) not required if neither can bring any benefit to the *person*. Of course, if there is some possibility that the unconscious condition might turn out *not* to be permanent, then there is reason to keep in place not only a ventilator that makes breathing possible but also an apparatus that makes the assimilation of nutrients possible. However, our present assumption is that there is no such possibility, and on that assumption both forms of life support seem to be equally dispensable. They appear to be morally equivalent: circumstances that render the one dispensable render the other dispensable as well.

Yet many of us are more hesitant about withdrawing artificial feeding (from an individual in a persistent vegetative state) than about withdrawing a ventilator (from an individual suffering from total brain death), even should we judge chances of recovery to be equally non-existent. But why is this? Perhaps we feel that removing artificial feeding is tantamount to starving an individual to death, and that this is unacceptable in much the same way that intentionally administering a lethal dose of a drug is unacceptable. Of course, we could—to take matters one unpleasant step further—bury the still breathing but irreversibly comatose individual. This would strike us as ghoulish and shock the sensibilities of most people. But why do we have these feelings? If the individual is truly dead—dead in the most significant sense of that term—why would we have scruples about any of these practices? Can't we stop feeding the dead? Can't we bury them? Yet clearly we do have such scruples. Can we justify them, or are they merely irrational reactions to what looks alive but has in fact lost all value?

Appropriate Care for the Permanently Unconscious

Even though the permanently unconscious individual is, as I have suggested, no longer a person, it is not true that we can treat that individual in just *any* manner we choose. The grotesque suggestion that the permanently vegetative individual be buried, heart still beating, serves to make that point for most of us. Such conduct is out of bounds. But why? In attempting to answer this question, let me make two suggestions.

First, respect for persons does involve respect for a person's body, even though the person is dead. For example, to disinter a body from a grave, place the decomposing corpse on display, and scrawl graffiti on the headstone would be an act of desecration more serious than a mere breach of etiquette. Whereas what constitutes disrespect toward a human corpse may be culturally variable, a breach of those culturally conditioned forms of respect is nevertheless a failure at a fundamental level to honor that which was a divine creation and through which personality once manifested itself. We may surmise, therefore, that an even *greater* sensitivity and respect is required in handling a human body in which the heart and lungs still function despite the brain damage that renders conscious existence impossible (where we have, in other words, psychic death but not somatic death). This is one reason why the irreversibly comatose patient is to be kept clean and presentable: it is a form of respect for the person whose body this was and for the body itself as a divine creation. So also to bury the still-breathing but irreversibly comatose patient would manifest, among other things, an undue haste, a precipitous pushing of the individual into the grave, and therefore a failure to show a decent respect. It is not that we would be murdering anyone by so doing (only *persons* can be murdered), but that we would be failing to pay a form of respect appropriately due a person's bodily remains. The administration of a lethal dose of a drug to a still-breathing but permanently unconscious individual would *not* be murder, but might be (though less obviously) a failure of respect.

A second relevant consideration is the *symbolic* significance of the care that we extend to the irreversibly unconscious. Such care, though it may be minimal, symbolizes our commitment to the value of human life and the commitment on the part of the medical profession to faithfully provide for those entrusted to its care. In all such symbolism we need to maintain sensitivity so that we do not become lax in the care that is offered and thereby communicate to many minds an indifference to and a premature discharge of our responsibilities. Indeed, we want to avoid treating the permanently unconscious "in ways that deaden the sensitivities or shock the conscience of the public, of professionals, or of the family involved, that violate the secure expectations that people reasonably have about the way they will be treated if they are ever unconscious or that degrade the trust and confidence required for health professionals."[7] Burying the individual who is in a persistent vegetative state, heart still beating, would certainly shock the conscience of the public. On the other hand, we do not want to be blindly fanatical about death, incapable of "letting go" of a patient, acting as if death is not merely the last enemy but the only enemy.

Accordingly, sensitivity involves drawing a line somewhere along a continuum that stretches from a willingness to keep a permanently unconscious individual on a ventilator *in perpetuity* (were that possible), to burying the still-breathing but permanently unconscious individual. Most of us would concur that both ends of the continuum represent unacceptable extremes. There is less agreement, however, when it comes to drawing lines along the continuum: some will hesitate over removing an artificial feeding apparatus, arguing that respect involves feeding; others will sanction stopping artificial feeding but will hesitate at the point of using positive means (e.g., a lethal drug); still others will approve the lethal injection of a drug but draw back from the suggestion that the drug need not even be administered and the permanently unconscious simply be buried. The point is that we all draw lines somewhere. The question is, Where should we draw those lines?

In seeking to determine the correct level of treatment for the permanently unconscious, we should, I suggest, walk a middle course. I am inclined to conclude that in such cases it would be appropriate, with family concurrence, to remove a ventilator and to stop both artificial feeding and the intake of

7. President's Commission, *Deciding to Forego Life-Sustaining Treatment,* p. 188.

liquids. When sustenance is withdrawn, the death of the body will follow shortly and will, of course, be painless, since the individual is unconscious. I would, however, be more reluctant to endorse the use of positive means to end biological human life. And why the drawing of the line at this particular point? Because, I suggest, apart from the possibility that consciousness will be regained—a possibility that has been excluded for purposes of the present discussion—there is no benefit that artificial feeding can secure for the patient. The cost of long-term care for the individual, therefore, represents an expenditure for which there are no compensating benefits. Although precise figures are hard to come by (since there is currently no clearinghouse to which such data is reported), one estimate is that the total number of permanently comatose individuals receiving long-term care in the United States is almost 5,000.[8] And the cost of such care is not inconsequential. For example, two years of care for one individual in a persistent vegetative state reportedly cost $280,000.[9] Costs for such care in a skilled nursing home would be less than in a hospital, but even here costs would be in excess of $25,000 a year.

We may wonder whether this would be a responsible use of a community's financial resources when such efforts secure only a prolonged vegetative existence. Moral consideration may dictate that such resources be directed to those for whom there is a genuine possibility of benefit. Further, the burden on the family may be considerable. As the President's Commission for the Study of Ethical Problems in Medicine and Biomedical and Behavioral Research put it, "The disruption of family life, together with the emotional drain on families which elect to care for their patient at home, can be very significant."[10] On the other hand, to administer a lethal dose of a drug in order to hurry mat-

8. President's Commission, *Deciding to Forego Life-Sustaining Treatment*, p. 176n.15.

9. President's Commission, *Deciding to Forego Life-Sustaining Treatment*, p. 185n.35.

10. President's Commission, *Deciding to Forego Life-Sustaining Treatment*, p. 85n.36.

ters along would be a cost-cutting measure of little financial consequence but would, I believe, be repugnant to public sensibilities and therefore is to be rejected. Further, if as a society we decide against the legalization of active euthanasia, then the symbolism associated with actively terminating the life of the permanently comatose individual (though this would not be the killing of a person and therefore *not* an instance of active euthanasia) may not be at all what we want, since that would communicate a willingness to take the life of a patient where that would serve financial ends.

Is It "Wrong" to Keep the Permanently Unconscious Organically Alive?

It has been argued that there are reasons other than the pointless expense involved for rejecting life-support efforts on behalf of the permanently unconscious. People sometimes speak of the horror of being kept alive in a permanently comatose state and emphasize that they don't want that to happen to them. But this horror may not be rational—no more rational than the horror experienced by some people at the prospect of being cremated or buried at sea. After all, this happens not to the person but only to the person's bodily remains. Nevertheless, some people may anticipate such a prospect for themselves with repugnance and consequently may have provided written directives for the disposal of their bodily remains. The philosopher Richard Brandt has relevantly commented, "If it is morally obligatory to some degree to carry out a person's wishes for disposal of his body and possessions after his death, it would seem to be equally morally obligatory to respect his wishes in case he becomes a 'vegetable.'"[11] And what seems important here is honoring the person's wishes, not saving someone from what is a horrible fate.

However, might there not be indignity involved in being

11. Brandt, "A Moral Principle About Killing," in *Beneficent Euthanasia*, ed. Marvin Kohl (Buffalo, N.Y.: Prometheus, 1975), p. 110.

kept alive in a permanently unconscious state even if it is not indignity that the unconscious person experiences? At least many have thought so as they have looked upon what they see as a "human vegetable"—unconscious, unmoving, kept alive by a respirator, connected to tubes that pump nourishment into the body, pierced by a catheter, needing to be moved frequently to avoid bedsores, fouled by uncontrolled bowel movements, having to be cleaned and washed by others. In every such situation we realize that we are now confronted with flesh that once expressed spirit, manifested personality, lived, loved, reasoned, willed, cared for self, cared for others, and so forth. Looking upon such a spectacle, we may be prompted to view such prolonged biological existence as an indignity.

Robert Veatch has suggested that to treat a dead person as if he or she were alive is an evil.[12] This too may be correct. For one senses that just as it is an evil (clearly) to treat the living as if they were dead, so (to reverse matters) it may be an evil to treat the dead as if they were living—although, to be sure, the latter would not be as objectionable as the former. We may reason that if individuals ought to be treated in a certain fashion because they are persons and only because they are persons, then it would be morally inappropriate to extend that same treatment to what is no longer a person. Thus to keep such an individual alive on a life-support system in the belief that the life being preserved is worthy of such an effort may constitute a moral mismatch, the value of biological human life devoid of any possibility of personal human life not being a value sufficient to warrant heroic life-sustaining efforts. Such efforts may be wrong, I would suggest, in the same way that it would be wrong to make such aggressive and heroic efforts on behalf of a non-human animal—a dog or a cat, for example. This would be not merely eccentric but wrong—wrong because such extraordinary efforts represent an act of valuation disproportionate to the inherent worth of the life being preserved. As Veatch puts it, "To

12. Veatch, "The Whole-Brain-Oriented Concept of Death: An Outmoded Philosophical Formulation," p. 17.

fail to recognize that the essential qualities of humanness have left an individual is a serious assault on the dignity of man. To treat an individual who has lost that which is essential to human life as if he still had it is to say about that individual and about humanity in general that we fail to perceive the essential dignity of human life."[13]

What Veatch has said can be given a theological translation. Indeed, if we understand that a divine image-bearer is an individual capable (actually or potentially) of imaging God by engaging in acts of intellect, emotion, and will, and if we grant that it is this imaging which warrants a special respect, then when that imaging capacity is permanently lost, we should recognize that our manner of treating the individual should be adjusted accordingly. For if it is killing image bearers that is wrong (Gen. 9:6) and it is sustaining and supporting the life of image bearers that is required, then when there is no image bearer present (i.e., when the person is dead), to act as if there were one present is morally inappropriate. It is not that it is merely unnecessary but that it is wrong: to treat what is not an image bearer as if it were an image bearer is a failure to do what is required.

But Do We Know That They Are Permanently Unconscious?

Up to this point we have referred to two differences between a brain-dead individual and an individual in a persistent vegetative state: (1) the brain-dead individual cannot breathe on his or her own but requires ventilator support, whereas the individual in a persistent vegetative state can survive without the ventilator, and (2) the brain-dead individual will expire shortly (typically within a week or so), despite our best efforts, whereas the individual in a persistent vegetative state can, by virtue of artificial feeding, be kept alive for years. I discounted the significance of these differences in the face of the overriding impor-

13. Veatch, "The Whole-Brain-Oriented Concept of Death: An Outmoded Philosophical Formulation," p. 17.

tance of the central feature that unites these two cases: both are conditions in which the individual is irreversibly unconscious. It is this latter feature, I suggested, that justifies the cessation of all life-support and medical efforts. Therefore, just as it is defensible to remove the brain-dead individual from the ventilator, so it is defensible, I would argue, to treat the individual in a persistent vegetative state in a similar fashion: (a) the patient can be removed from the ventilator, (b) the patient need not be *weaned* from the ventilator should weaning be required to make the transition from automated breathing to autonomous breathing, (c) artificial feeding need not be continued, and (d) life-threatening illnesses (e.g., pneumonia) need not be combatted. However, these conclusions are based on an assumption that can be called into question—namely, that the unconscious condition is *known* to be irreversible.

In the case of those who have been diagnosed as suffering total brain death, we know that their condition is permanent; in the case of those diagnosed to be in a persistent vegetative state, we do not have the same certainty. For in the case of those judged to have undergone total brain death, where that condition was properly diagnosed using the accepted diagnostic criteria, there have been *no* instances of recovery of consciousness, and this is an impressive consideration. However, in the case of those diagnosed to be in a persistent vegetative state, there have been a few individuals who subsequently regained consciousness. But we must be cautioned at this point; in the words of the President's Commission for the Study of Ethical Problems in Medicine and Biomedical and Behavioral Research, "The few patients who have recovered consciousness after a prolonged period of unconsciousness were severely disabled. The degree of permanent damage varied but commonly included inability to speak or see, permanent distortion of the limbs, and paralysis.... Thus even the extremely small likelihood of 'recovery' cannot be equated with returning to a normal or relatively well functioning state."[14]

14. President's Commission, *Deciding to Forego Life-Sustaining Treatment*, pp. 182-83.

The moral question that emerges is this: Does the small likelihood (approximately 2 to 3 chances out of 100) of such partial recovery render obligatory the use of artificial feeding and the application of medical techniques to ward off various illnesses? Here opinion is divided; indeed, one may even find one's own convictions wavering between opposite opinions. That a person (anticipating the prospect) would choose *not* to be kept alive in a persistent vegetative state is understandable. Charitable considerations may well prompt such a choice: one could avoid imposing on one's family the severe financial and psychological burdens that often accompany long-term care; one could make available vital organs for life-saving transplant purposes. And what is it that one is "sacrificing" by making such a choice? A slim prospect of a future conscious existence that is likely to be characterized by some combination of paralysis, blindness, and locked-in syndrome (the sufferer is able to communicate only by eye-blinking). On the other hand, as we continue to reflect on this issue, we may have growing reservations about the message that will be communicated to the larger community if we allow individuals in a persistent vegetative state to die. For such individuals do breathe, yawn, grimace, undergo sleep-wake cycles, and simply do not look dead (though it is also the case that brain-dead individuals who are on a ventilator do not look dead, either). To withdraw artificial feeding from someone who looks to be resting or asleep when there is some chance—albeit very slim—of partial recovery may be offensive to the larger community and may be viewed as premature abandonment of a helpless patient. Indeed, I find myself tempted to view it in this way in cases in which it isn't known what the patient would want for himself or herself.

However, if we place the emphasis where I believe it properly belongs—on the patient, not on the care-giver—then the fundamental question is this: What should the *patient* have done in such circumstances? How should we as Christians, who value God's gift of life, have ourselves dealt with in such a situation? For suppose that our society does what Robert Veatch has suggested that it should do: permit, within limits, a range of concepts of death that members of society can choose for themselves or can have chosen for them by their appropriately designated agents.[15] Death may be variously defined as (a) heart-lung death, (b) total brain death, or (c) neo-cortical death. As we survey these options, which should we choose? It is the last—neo-cortical death—that includes the individual who is in a persistent vegetative state, and unquestionably it is the problematic option. But what choice should Christians make?

In trying to answer this difficult question, we should note that we have already introduced two important considerations: the probability that one will regain consciousness (low), and the quality of that conscious existence (likely to be poor). However, we may well ponder the place that quality-of-life considerations should have in our deliberations. Specifically, can a Christian value system accommodate such considerations? That is, should we be open to a line of reasoning which suggests that the chance of regaining consciousness is not worth the effort, not because the chance is remote but because the quality of life is likely to be substandard? Of course, if quality-of-life considerations are relevant indicators of one's capacity to participate in God's creative and redemptive purposes, then they could—consistent with Christian values—be taken into account. And, indeed, there may be a certain correlation between the two such that drastic reduction in the quality of life reduces our capacity to participate in God's creative and redemptive purposes. However, in the kind of case before us, where the individual emerges from what was diagnosed as neo-cortical death, the person is conscious and despite severe limitation is not, I believe, totally beyond participating in those purposes. Moral and spiritual response by the individual to what would admittedly be a difficult set of circumstances is still possible, as are various restricted forms of interaction with other human beings. Unquestionably, the situation is a limited and even grim one, but it is not one totally devoid of all significance and value. Nevertheless, we

15. Veatch, "The Whole-Brain-Oriented Concept of Death: An Outmoded Philosophical Formulation," p. 29.

may wonder whether it would be *sufficiently* limited and the burden of living such a twilight existence *sufficiently* great so that an individual would not be obliged to have organic life maintained on the outside chance that psychic life might be restored in what most likely would be a drastically attenuated form.

It is arguable that an individual is not so obliged and that a properly executed directive to that effect—which would request the removal of all life-support devices, including artificial feeding apparatus—ought to be honored. For certainly there are charitable considerations that might prompt one to sign such a directive: the saving of money and health-care resources that can be more beneficially used for others who have a realistic hope of recovery and cure; the termination of the protracted burden that will fall upon the family, who must look upon their loved one suspended between life and death and be forced to make the heartrending decisions (as months and years pass) about what it means to be faithful and loyal in such circumstances; the making available of vital organs for transplant and life-saving purposes. These are good and honorable reasons to give such a directive, and the fear of the slim chance that one will actually recover and be blind, deaf, and paralyzed is not itself ignoble. I believe that to so act, prompted by such considerations, is to act responsibly and with due regard for life as a gift of God. The Christian can, therefore, select the third option, neo-cortical death, as a valid concept of death. And to grant the individual the authority to make such a choice seems reasonable, since there appear to be no overriding societal interests sufficient to warrant a denial of individual autonomy in these circumstances.

Summary

This chapter has dealt with the peculiar problems attaching to decisions about the appropriate level of treatment for the permanently unconscious. Here there are two categories of patient: (1) the brain-dead patient who has suffered total brain death, cannot breathe without ventilator support, will expire shortly even with the assistance of a ventilator, and whose condition, when properly diagnosed, permits no possibility of recovery; (2) and the patient in a persistent vegetative state who has suffered partial brain death (neo-cortical death), who *can* breathe without the aid of a ventilator, who can in many cases be kept biologically alive for years, and for whom there is a 2 to 3 percent chance of some very limited recovery.

I argued that what is of special value about human life is personal consciousness, which makes it possible for the individual to participate in God's creative and redemptive purposes for human beings; biological human life is valuable because it sustains and makes possible personal consciousness, but where there is only biological or somatic human life, that special value no longer attaches to the individual, and biological or somatic death may be allowed to proceed unimpeded. Indeed, I suggested that it may even be wrong to sustain biological human life where there is no possibility of personal human life because that which is of special value and warrants life-sustaining efforts has in fact been lost; in fact, it is morally inappropriate to treat what no longer images God (in acts of intellect, emotion, and will) as if it did.

In searching for a Christian concept of death, I expressed sympathy for Robert Veatch's suggestion that death is the total and irreversible loss of what is supremely significant about human life, which, from a Christian perspective, is the capacity (potential or actual) to participate in God's creative and redemptive purposes for human life. Such participation presupposes future personal consciousness, but when personal consciousness is known to be permanently lost, the *person* is dead, and therefore the following are justifiable: (a) the patient can be removed from the ventilator, (b) the patient need not be weaned from the ventilator, (c) artificial feeding need not be continued, and (d) life-threatening illnesses need not be combatted. Should there be any doubt, however, about the level of consciousness of the patient—is it personal or sub-personal?—we must proceed on the assumption that what is there is personal consciousness, and our appropriate response will be to continue life-sustaining efforts.

The use of lethal drugs to accelerate the biological death of a patient who is permanently unconscious was rejected not because it would be murder (it would not be murder, since the *person* is already dead) but because it is repugnant to public sensibilities and because it may be interpreted as a step toward the endorsement of legalized active euthanasia.

The most difficult issue confronted in this chapter is that posed by the case of the patient who is in a persistent vegetative state and who has only a slight chance (about a 2 to 3 percent chance) of recovery (though typically this recovery is only partial and includes such disabilities as paralysis and the inability to speak or see). I offered a range of reasons suggesting that a properly executed directive from the patient requesting the removal of all life-support devices, including artificial feeding, ought to be honored, and that such a directive (in anticipation of these circumstances) can be a legitimate expression of Christian values.

CHAPTER SEVEN

Legalizing Voluntary
Active Euthanasia

Introduction

Should a terminally ill patient, under carefully controlled circumstances, be legally permitted to request that he or she be given a lethal drug by a cooperating physician? This, of course, would be a classic case of voluntary active euthanasia, which is not legal anywhere in the Western world, although in the Netherlands the law is not enforced, and euthanasia is practiced openly. Euthanasia does, however, have articulate advocates who through a network of right-to-die organizations—the Hemlock Society being the best known in the United States— are seeking to change both public opinion and the law. What is being seriously proposed is that active euthanasia be legally available to those who voluntarily choose it and who are terminally ill or are no longer capable of rational existence. Here, then, we are addressing the legal and not the moral issue of mercy killing. Whatever we may have concluded about the morality of voluntary active euthanasia, the issue of its legality is a separate matter.

The basic argument offered in support of such a proposal is a simple one: it would mercifully permit some terminally ill individuals to escape what is judged to be undesirable suffering and indignity. In terminating the lives of such persons, it is pointed out, we are not harming but are extending mercy, a claim supported by the fact that a *natural* death which cuts short an agonizing dying is something we often view as a benefit or a blessing. But death would be no less a benefit should it be brought about by direct human intervention.

This appeal to mercy is coupled with a powerful appeal to individual autonomy. Indeed, in response to the question "Whose life is it, anyway?" comes the reply "It is the patient's, not society's." The patient, therefore, should be given control over the dying process, should decide whether to accelerate it or retard it. Certainly the patient has a right to life, but that right, so the argument goes, can be waived, which is exactly what the patient who requests active euthanasia does. Therefore, those who cooperate with the terminal patient in bringing life to a close violate no one's rights; on the contrary, they perform a positive act of charity.

Further, it is argued, we live in a pluralistic country and therefore ought not to impose our beliefs on others by means of laws whose only justification is religious in character. Accordingly, if the objection to voluntary active euthanasia is exclusively religious, then, although that may provide a good reason for members of the religious community to abstain from acts of active euthanasia, it does not provide a good reason for passing laws that prevent others who don't share those religious convictions from engaging in such acts.

This, in brief, is the case for legalizing voluntary active euthanasia. It is a case that cannot be easily dismissed; indeed, it deserves careful reflection and consideration even on the part of those who ultimately judge that they must draw back and decline to endorse it.

A Right to Be Killed?

It is characteristic of proponents of euthanasia to speak of a right to die, arguing that since everyone possesses such a right, there ought to be no legal prohibitions preventing either passive or active euthanasia, such prohibitions being in direct violation of one's right to die. Therefore, what justifies legalizing euthanasia is a fundamental human right that each one of us possesses—a right that is in fact violated by current law.

The phrase "a right to die" is, however, ambiguous. It can mean (1) "a right to be allowed to die," which would be a right of non-interference and would be exercised when one simply asked to be left alone and permitted to die a natural death. It also can mean (2) "a right to kill oneself," which would be a right to take one's own life free from interference by others (i.e., a right to *unassisted* suicide). Finally, it can mean (3) "a right to be killed by another at one's own request" (i.e., a right to *assisted* suicide). So we have at least three separate (putative) rights that should not be confused:

(1) a right to be allowed to die
(2) a right to kill oneself (unassisted suicide)
(3) a right to kill oneself through the agency of another (assisted suicide)

And it is the third of these rights that needs to be invoked to make a case for legalizing voluntary active euthanasia, because *opponents* of legalized voluntary active euthanasia can grant that people have a right to be allowed to die and even that they have a right to kill themselves but deny that they have a right to be assisted in their endeavor by others, especially by physicians. So at issue in the debate over legalizing voluntary active euthanasia is the existence of a right to kill oneself through the willing agency of another.

Insisting as a Matter of Right That Others Kill Us

It seems that we do *not* have a right to be killed *if* by that we mean that we can insist, as a matter of right, that others kill us— willing or not. For surely others would be within *their* rights in rejecting our request to be killed, which would not be the case if such a request were in fact backed up by a legitimate moral right. As Peter Williams puts it, "One cannot give a priest a hand gun and demand that the priest use it. One might ask, or beg, or plead to get shot with a gun or hypodermic but not as an assertion of right."[1] Thus as a matter of religious or moral principle I might refuse to accede to a patient's request to be killed, and I would be acting well within my moral rights; indeed, to coerce me into acceding to that request would appear to be a violation of *my* rights.

However, matters are quite different when a person simply requests to be permitted to die. Suppose, for example, that a terminally ill individual requests that he not be operated upon but be allowed to die. Suppose, further, that this request is ignored, and the individual is forced to undergo a life-saving operation: despite his protests, he is strapped to a stretcher, removed to the hospital, taken to an operating room, and subjected to surgery. This is objectionable even if the operation is a low-risk, life-saving procedure. Thus, whereas refusing on religious or moral grounds to cooperate with a patient who wants to be killed does not violate that patient's rights, forcing an operation on that patient does violate his rights. Indeed, to use force to prevent the surgeon from operating would protect the patient's rights but would not violate the surgeon's rights, since she has no right to force an operation on another despite her religious convictions that the patient ought to have such an operation. To operate against the will of the patient, then, would be a clear violation of the moral rights of the patient.[2] We might disagree about the identity of the right that is violated, but most would agree that a right *is* violated.[3] Therefore, whereas one can-

1. Williams, "Rights and the Alleged Right of Innocent to Be Killed," in *Bioethics and Human Rights,* ed. Elsie L. Bandman and Bertram Bandman (Boston: Little, Brown, 1978), p. 142.

2. For another point of view, see Donald Van De Veer, *Paternalistic Intervention: The Moral Bounds on Benevolence* (Princeton: Princeton University Press, 1986), pp. 248-60.

3. Is the operative right here the right to be allowed to die? Or is it, as I

not give a physician a hypodermic and demand to be killed, one can demand, as a matter of right, that the physician forego operating or stop medical treatment.

A Right to the Free Cooperation of Others?

What has just been said, however, does not settle matters. Indeed, simply because I cannot demand, as a matter of right, that others kill me (others are within *their* rights in refusing) does not mean that I don't have a right to the cooperation of others in ending my life when such cooperation is freely offered. Consider this parallel: I cannot demand as a matter of right that others talk with me (others are within their rights in refusing), but my rights would be clearly violated should the law prohibit others from engaging in conversation with me. Clearly, then, I can have a right to receive something that is freely offered to me even though it is not something I can demand from others as a matter of right. So it is at least possible that both of the following propositions could be true: (a) I cannot insist as a matter of right that others kill me, and (b) I have a right to the cooperation of others in ending my life when that cooperation is freely offered. And it is the second proposition—the right to *willing* cooperation—and not the first—the right to cooperation, willing or not—that is relevant to the debate over legalizing voluntary active euthanasia. This is the case because there are physicians who are quite willing to assist the terminally ill in actively ending their lives; further, advocates of voluntary active euthanasia are not proposing that unwilling physicians be coerced into participating in the practice of active euthanasia. So all that is necessary for patients to have access to active euthanasia is that the law not stand in the way of those physicians willing to offer their assistance; it is not necessary that the

---

am inclined to believe, the right to bodily self-determination, which includes the right to reject bodily intrusions initiated by others?

law require unwilling physicians to offer assistance. But do we actually have such a right to freely offered assistance?

To speak of such a right is ultimately to appeal to two fundamental and powerful moral considerations: (1) the right to define ourselves as moral beings (moral autonomy) and (2) the right to make those decisions that vitally affect our own interests (prudential autonomy). It is this twofold appeal that renders plausible the claim that we have a right to freely offered euthanasia. A comment on each of these considerations is therefore in order.

First, to shape one's own death by intentionally accelerating it or retarding it, as one judges best, is surely—if one is mature and mentally competent—to express one's values and thereby to exercise one's *moral autonomy* in a crucial sphere; it is to give one's own personal answers to a range of morally significant questions and to live out these answers in one's own life. Thus, do I or do I not see myself under an obligation to preserve and protect my life, and if I do, what kind of obligation is it, and under what circumstances—if any—am I relieved of that obligation? What does death with dignity look like, and how do I preserve my dignity while dying—by waiting patiently for death or by seizing the initiative and determining its time and place? How shall I confront death so that I give a final expression to those values for which I have lived my life and provide for my family and friends an example of dying well? In answering these questions and in shaping my dying in accord with *my* answers, not someone else's, I exercise my moral autonomy and contribute to my self-definition as a moral and spiritual being; I also express my particular vision of life, be it secular, religious, humanist, or whatever. But for society or for anyone else to dictate to me how I am to die based on answers that *they* have given to these questions is, it would be asserted, to abridge my moral autonomy at a fundamental level. But, it would be added, this is exactly what happens when I desire active euthanasia for myself and the law prohibits it from being freely offered to me.

Second, in the shaping of my death my *prudential autonomy* is at stake, for if I am confronted by a distressing and painful dying that I can escape only by means of active euthanasia, then it is my interests that are crucially at stake, and I am the one, it would seem, who should be allowed to make the decision whether or not to avail myself of active assistance. To criminalize voluntary active euthanasia, as society now does, is to restrict my options in pursuing my own interests, a limitation thereby being placed on my prudential autonomy. Of course, an individual electing active euthanasia may be making both the wrong moral choice and the wrong prudential choice (that is, the individual may be both sinful and foolish), but if liberty means anything, it must include at least some latitude to make *wrong* choices. To say that we are free to choose so long as we make the right choice is not to possess genuine liberty at all. For to respect individual autonomy is to acknowledge the right of people to make wrong choices—choices that we may preach and counsel against but that we may not legally preclude.

A Partial Response

How can an opponent of legalized voluntary active euthanasia respond to these remarks?

First, it can be pointed out that the legal prohibition of voluntary active euthanasia does not take from us all freedom to shape our dying. In addition to fighting to preserve and extend our life, the following options are legally open to us: (a) we can reject life-prolonging treatment, (b) we can be given drugs that control our pain but that incidentally accelerate our dying, and (c) we can even commit *unassisted* suicide. None of these is a criminal action. The only option that *is* denied us by law is assisted suicide, being killed by someone else at our own request. This does mean, of course, that when we are sufficiently incapacitated, suicide is effectively precluded, because we would require active assistance, and active assistance is legally forbidden. To that extent the law does indeed place limits on our freedom to shape our own dying; nevertheless, considerable legal latitude does remain.

184

Second, moral and prudential autonomy, though undeniably powerful considerations that must be respected, do not function in an absolute fashion, overriding all considerations that are in conflict with them. The law justifiably places limitations on both our moral and our prudential autonomy, and it does so when it thereby protects fundamental interests of other members of society or prevents us from seriously harming ourselves.[4] For these very reasons we have laws that forbid various forms of consensual homicide (killing an individual who consents to being killed). Accordingly, we do not legally permit dueling, nor do we permit human sacrifice where *consenting* adults are used as sacrificial offerings, nor do we permit a living individual to offer all his transplantable organs (heart, kidneys, etc.) to save the lives of those in desperate need of them, including members of his own family. It follows, as the philosopher Philip Devine has pointed out,[5] that the law—correctly—does not permit killing even when all of the following conditions are fulfilled: (a) the individual to be killed both wants and requests to be killed, (b) the person doing the killing does so willingly, and (c) no third-party rights are violated. Each of these forms of consensual homicide—dueling to the death, voluntary human sacrifice, and so on—fulfills all of these conditions, but since such homicide ought not (we judge) to be legalized, then it follows that these conditions by themselves are not sufficient to warrant the legalizing of consensual homicide, including euthanasia.

4. The law frequently interferes with our prudential autonomy, pre-empting our decision-making power when our interests are at stake. Numerous examples are available: (a) Social Security laws that compel contribution to a government-controlled fund to care for our retirement, even though we might wish to use that money differently; (b) laws forbidding swimming at public beaches when lifeguards are absent; (c) laws requiring people to obtain licenses to engage in various professional activities, thereby limiting options available to the consumer; (d) laws limiting the availability of potentially harmful drugs that might hold out some possible (even if slim) benefit to the user. All laws of this nature place restrictions on the exercise of our prudential autonomy, and, unless one is a thoroughgoing libertarian, some such laws are judged to be warranted.

5. Devine, *The Ethics of Homicide* (Ithaca, N.Y.: Cornell University Press, 1978), pp. 180-84.

In reply, an advocate of legalized voluntary active euthanasia would observe that there is a difference between these cases of consensual homicide that we find objectionable and voluntary active euthanasia—namely, that *euthanasia doesn't harm anyone,* whereas these acts of consensual homicide do. In fact, euthanasia actually benefits the person who is killed, whereas these objectionable practices *harm* the person who is killed, even though he or she willingly consents to that harm. The person killed in a duel is not benefited but harmed, as is the person who offers up his or her life in an act of religious sacrifice or gives all of his or her (healthy) transplantable organs to save others. These practices, though willingly engaged in by all parties, do *not* benefit everyone involved but seriously harm certain parties. In this regard they are in sharp contrast to voluntary active euthanasia, which benefits everyone. Indeed, as James Rachels contends, "If an action promotes the best interests of *everyone* concerned, and violates no one's rights, then that action is morally acceptable."[6] And not only is it morally acceptable, but also it ought to be permitted by law. Crucially, then, it is claimed that the legalization of voluntary active euthanasia for the terminally ill, unlike these objectionable practices of consensual homicide, will promote "the best interests of everyone concerned," *in addition to* fulfilling the three conditions just cited.

This, of course, is exactly what *opponents* of legalized euthanasia deny. While they do not deny that euthanasia might, in a given instance, benefit an individual, they do argue that the overall consequences coming in the wake of its legalization are likely to be negative. So to such arguments we now turn, asking ourselves, "Is euthanasia in the best interests of everyone concerned, and if it is not, whose interests would be jeopardized by its legalization?"

6. Rachels, "More Impertinent Distinctions and a Defense of Active Euthanasia," in *Social Ethics: Morality and Social Policy,* 3rd ed., ed. Thomas A. Mappes and Jane S. Zembaty (New York: McGraw-Hill, 1987), p. 79.

Two Types of Arguments

Reservations over the wisdom of legalizing voluntary active euthanasia characteristically center on the possibility of negative social consequences following in the wake of such legalization. Whatever immediate good may be secured by legalizing voluntary active euthanasia, it will be outweighed, so the argument goes, by a wide range of bad consequences. Such arguments are of two basic kinds: (1) *negative-fallout arguments*, in which it is contended that even if euthanasia is effectively restricted to the terminally ill, there will be serious repercussions of an undesirable kind that make the legalization of voluntary active euthanasia a hazardous undertaking; (2) *slippery-slope arguments*, in which it is contended that euthanasia first extended to the terminally ill will later be unacceptably extended to other categories of individuals—euthanasia once extended to the dying will next be extended to incurable but non-terminal patients, to handicapped infants, to the senile, to the insane, and so on.

Negative-Fallout Arguments

What I dub "negative-fallout arguments" all attempt to point to undesirable consequences that allegedly will ensue even if the legalization of voluntary active euthanasia is never extended to groups other than the terminally ill. It is claimed that such legalization will have various bad consequences, sufficiently impacting vital societal interests so as to justify retention of the current legal prohibition or at least to contribute to the making of such a case. These bad consequences will occur, it is claimed, whether or not legalizing voluntary active euthanasia for the terminally ill puts us on a slippery slope that leads to euthanasia for various socially unwanted groups.

Argument #1: It is feared that voluntary euthanasia, once legalized, will increasingly lose its voluntary character. That is, the terminally ill will be manipulated—consciously or unconsciously—into viewing themselves as unnecessary burdens and thereby pressured into opting for euthanasia. A social atmosphere (or at least pockets of such an atmosphere) may be created such that people are expected to "move on" and not become a drain on society's limited resources, euthanasia becoming "the only decent thing to do." A patient's *own* suffering may be merely the legally required excuse for his requesting euthanasia; his real motivation may be a concern for family and friends and the suffering that *they* will be caused by his protracted dying. That patient may choose death not because he feels his life is too burdensome but because he views himself as a burden to others, not because he is tired of life but because he judges that others are tired of him.

Thus one merit that attaches to the current law is that it provides a buffer against certain pressures that might prompt one to end one's life for the sake of others. In part it protects one from one's own altruistic promptings as well as from external pressure that might take advantage of those promptings, be that pressure from family, friends, or society. In large measure the rationale for laws that prohibit dueling, human sacrifice, and the sacrificial offering of one's vital organs is to provide a similar buffer against pressures (honor, religious zeal, altruism) that would prompt one to seriously harm oneself. Granted, voluntary active euthanasia is designed to benefit the persons killed; nevertheless, though it may benefit some (as intended), it may also expose others to pressures (unintended) from which they would be better off shielded. As Yale Kamisar put it, "Will we not sweep up, in the process, some who are not really tired of life, but think others are tired of them; some who do not really want to die, but who feel they should not live on, because to do so when there looms the legal alternative of euthanasia is to do a selfish or cowardly act?"[7]

7. Kamisar, "Some Non-Religious Views against Proposed 'Mercy Killing Legislation,'" in *Death, Dying, and Euthanasia,* ed. Dennis J. Horan and David Mall (Frederick, Md.: University Publications of America, Inc., 1980), p. 427. This article, a rich source of information and argument, is one of the most significant critiques of proposals to legalize voluntary active euthanasia; it was originally published in the *Minnesota Law Review* 42 (May 1958): 969-1042. For a well-known rejoinder to Kamisar, see Glanville Williams, "'Mercy Killing' Legislation—A Rejoinder," in *Death, Dying, and Euthanasia,* pp. 480-91.

Especially vulnerable in this regard would be the old and the institutionalized. To be sure, they may have earlier signed a euthanasia directive, but that will not by itself guarantee that their *eventual* request for euthanasia will be an authentic expression of what they *then* want for themselves. Indeed, what people antici- pate they will want and what they do actually want when con- fronted by death are often two quite different things. This may happen because, as an unnamed former officer of no less an or- ganization than the Euthanasia Society of America is reported to have admitted, "Very few incurables have or express the wish to die. However great their physical suffering may be, the will to live, the desire for life, is such an overwhelming force that pain and suffering become bearable."[8] Thus many who sign a euthanasia directive will not be inclined to exercise the euthanasia option when actually confronting death but will become candidates for a range of pressures that might prompt them to act in a way that runs counter to what they really want for themselves.

Argument #2: In assessing the consequences of legalized active euthanasia, we also need to take into account those can- didates for euthanasia whose lives would be impacted nega- tively even though they themselves do not choose euthanasia. As Richard Trammell has commented, "It would seem that the vast majority of people who go through an agonizing process of deciding whether or not to be euthanatized, and choose not to, would have been happier if this agonizing choice had not been put before them."[9] These may be people who are resisting family pressures (of a subtle or not-so-subtle variety) to opt for eutha- nasia, and who are emotionally torn between guilt over not having chosen euthanasia and resentment toward those they view as trying to pressure them into electing euthanasia. They feel guilty because they see the benefits that euthanasia will bring their family (perhaps an increased inheritance, along with a shortening of time that the family has to care for and ago-

---

8. Cited by Neil Elliot in *The Gods of Life* (New York: Macmillan, 1974), p. 132.
9. Trammell, "Euthanasia and the Law," *Journal of Social Philosophy* 9 (Jan. 1978): 17.

nize over them), and perhaps they also feel resentful because they suspect (rightly or wrongly) that the pressure for euthanasia arises from mixed motives. Ultimately they resist this pressure and reject euthanasia, but by no means has the legal possibility of euthanasia eased their dying and contributed to their peace of mind—quite the contrary.

Argument #3: Euthanasia might come to be viewed as the answer to tough medical cases. Rather than focusing on the need for improved health-care systems, improved treatment for pain, improved nursing, and so on, instead we might feel that we already have, in the form of voluntary active euthanasia, the answer to these cases. The result could be that the terminally ill who do not choose euthanasia will be increasingly neglected. Of course, some might surmise that, on the contrary, legalization will have just the *opposite* effect—at least initially, as long as there is widespread anti-euthanasia sentiment—prompting society in general and health-care professionals in particular to show an *increased* concern for the dying and focus more attention and energy on improving the lot of the terminally ill, these reactions being prompted by a desire to make the option of natural death more attractive than the newly legalized euthanasia option.

In time, however, when the public at large and the health-care community in particular have made their peace with euthanasia, we should not be surprised to see increasing reliance upon it as the accepted mode of handling "difficult" cases, along with an increasingly liberal understanding of what constitutes a "difficult case." Consider the dramatic change in attitudes toward abortion that resulted from its legalization and the consequent acceptance of abortion as virtually the standard mode of dealing with unwanted pregnancies. To be sure, today there are still groups that seek to keep alive the alternative of bringing such pregnancies to term, and to some little extent these groups have had their successes, but the reality is that ours has become a society in which the abortion clinic, not the home for unwed mothers, is the solution to unwanted pregnancies. In a similar manner, euthanasia may become society's accepted solution to difficult cases of dying. This may reduce our concern and sympathy for those who choose a lingering, painful, and expensive death rather than electing euthanasia; after all, we might observe, they have willfully chosen their lot. With this reduction in sympathy may come a reduction in funds directed at helping those who face such difficult deaths.

Argument #4: The legalization of voluntary active euthanasia may engender additional and unnecessary fears and anxiety among the terminally ill. The message they might receive is "Dying can be *so* bad that you'd better choose euthanasia now rather than face the horrors that await you later." This will not, of course, be a spoken message, but it may nevertheless be what some will "hear" when euthanasia is legalized. On the other hand, it must be acknowledged that it may comfort the terminally ill individual to know that, should his dying be more than he thinks he can bear, the euthanasia option is available. Like the lethal pills at the bedside of the terminally ill patient that are never used but that bring comfort by their mere presence, so euthanasia can fill that same role even if it is never actually chosen as an alternative. Nevertheless, this does not eliminate the negative message that legalizing voluntary active euthanasia might send to some terminally ill patients.

Argument #5: Legalizing euthanasia may mean that some doctors will be considerably less hesitant to inject fatal doses whenever they deem it appropriate to do so. Such "euthanasia free-lancing" (i.e., euthanasia without legal authorization) will be encouraged, and this will be more a fact of medical life than it now is. "After all," the physician might reason, "society does accept active euthanasia. If a piece of paper hasn't been signed, so what? Surely what is important is compassion and mercy, not legal niceties." The physician would thus view himself as acting in the spirit of the law even if technically outside its parameters. However, it might be argued in reply that the availability of legal euthanasia will actually reduce the necessity for such euthanasia free-lancing.

Here two responses are in order. First, we may at least question whether the legalization of euthanasia will significantly reduce the number of tough cases "crying out" for a "merciful release." For who will actually opt for euthanasia should it be legalized? Will it be those who are dying especially painful deaths? Or will it be those who for a variety of *other* reasons are prompted to choose euthanasia—that is, those who are especially frightened by pain and death, or those who simply wish to be in control of their own dying, or those who view suicide as an acceptable and preferable alternative to a longer natural dying? One would, for example, suppose that more Hemlock Society members than members of the general population would commit suicide when confronted by a terminal illness, but one would not suppose that Hemlock Society members confront more difficult terminal illnesses than the general population. So it may very well be that it is the dynamics of individual personalities rather than the degree of suffering attaching to terminal illness that determines who decides to end their lives and who decides not to.

Second, even if legalizing euthanasia would reduce the need for free-lancing, it would nevertheless increase the number of free-lancers, and that is what is crucial. For even in a world of legalized voluntary active euthanasia, there will still be many dying patients who have not signed a euthanasia directive, who may not be in a position to clearly communicate their wishes on this matter, and who, in the physician's eyes, would be mercifully served by an act of euthanasia. So even if with the legalization of euthanasia there would be *fewer* such cases, that does not mean that there would be *few* such cases, and granting that the stigma that has hitherto attached to euthanasia would be largely removed (due to its legalization), a greater number of physicians would be less hesitant to take what they would deem appropriate action. The decisive factor in determining whether there will be more free-lancing is the number of free-lancing physicians, not the number of cases calling for free-lancing.

Slippery-Slope Arguments

Slippery-slope arguments are also referred to as "wedge" arguments, and it is sometimes observed that there are two kinds of slippery-slope arguments which posit that accepting X in one way or another leads to accepting Y: logical slippery-slope arguments (accepting X logically commits one to accepting Y), and empirical or prudential slippery-slope arguments (once X is accepted, then Y *will in fact be accepted* and put into practice). It is assumed, of course, that Y is an objectionable practice that many if not all would want to repudiate. It is the empirical type of slippery-slope argument that I am examining, though clearly the logical form could help support the empirical form. Thus, if acceptance of practice X *logically* commits one to the acceptance of practice Y, then, since people often act on the implications of what they believe, that provides reason for believing that people will also come to both accept Y and put it into practice. Of course, things are complicated by the fact that people and societies are often not logical: sometimes they fail to draw the implications that are there just waiting to be drawn; at other times they draw the wrong implications; at still other times they don't act on the implications that they do draw.

Slippery-slope arguments are nevertheless widely used in the law. As Frederick Schauer has commented,

> These arguments appear commonly in discussions about freedom of speech. The warning is frequently heard that permitting one restriction not by itself troubling and perhaps even desirable, will increase the likelihood that other increasingly invidious restrictions will follow. The *Skokie* controversy provides one of the most notorious modern examples of this type of argument in freedom of speech debates. The argument there was not that freedom of speech in theory *ought* to protect the Nazis, but rather that denying free speech protection to Nazis was likely to start us down a slippery slope, at the bottom of which would be the denial of protection even to those who should in theory be protected. More generally, slippery slope arguments have been employed to argue against racial classifications for benign purposes, certain forms of warrantless searches or seizures, arguably inconsequential forms of state support for religion, and all forms of euthanasia.[10]

10. Schauer, "Slippery Slopes," *Harvard Law Review* 99 (Dec. 1985): 363. The editorial summary of the article offers this comment: "He [Schauer] argues

So the form of argument known as "slippery slope" is widely used in the law; whether in any given case the argument is rationally persuasive depends on the particulars of the case and the considerations adduced in support of the contention that the slide downward is likely to occur. We now turn to such a slide in the case of euthanasia. What is being suggested is that euthanasia ultimately will be extended, by law, to classes of persons other than the dying.

Euthanasia for the Non-terminal. Once voluntary active euthanasia for the terminally ill is legalized, one can reasonably expect pressure to mount to secure legalized euthanasia for those individuals whose illness or physical impairment is incurable, of a distressing character but *not* terminal. Mary Rose Barrington, an articulate advocate of euthanasia, puts it this way: "Certainly some of the most tragic cases crying out for euthanasia arise out of accidents, and unlike terminal cases, the agony might stretch over many years."[11] It is true that the incurable but non-terminal have longer to live, but they have more time to suffer as well; therefore, they become fitting candidates for euthanasia. Indeed, the British Voluntary Euthanasia Bill of 1969 included what is called an "accidental-injury provision"—that is, euthanasia for the non-terminal—and it was the inclusion of this provision that in part caused the bill's defeat in the House of Lords. Current euthanasia proposals typically make provisions *only* for the terminally ill, but for many euthanasia advocates this is not a matter of principle but a matter of tactics—"better half a loaf than no loaf at all." In time, after the legalization of active euthanasia for the terminally ill, there will be occasion for more *outspoken* advocacy of euthanasia for the incurable but non-terminal. Of course, such advocacy, if premature, might jeopardize the push to legal-

---

that slippery slope arguments depend for their persuasive power on the currently perceived inability of future decisionmakers to recognize, comprehend, or defend doctrinal lines drawn by their predecessors. . . . Slippery slope arguments may flourish in law because of the unique way in which law, set apart from other disciplines, pays allegiance to the past while guarding the future."

11. Barrington, "Voluntary Euthanasia Act, 198-?" in *Beneficent Euthanasia,* ed. A. B. Downing (Los Angeles: Nash Publishing, 1969), p. 212.

ize euthanasia for the terminally ill and therefore is better post-poned to a more propitious time.

The logic for such advocacy is straightforward, even if pragmatists counsel a temporary restraint on such advocacy. Indeed, if the merciful termination of excruciating suffering is what warrants euthanasia, what reason can be given for restrict-ing the range of mercy to those who are terminally ill? Why, in other words, should the *non-terminal* nature of one's illness and suffering exclude one from qualifying—or at least make it more difficult for one to qualify—as a fitting object of mercy killing? To be sure, those with a non-terminal illness have longer to live, and, should they choose to have their lives ended, they would be eliminating a greater span of temporal existence than persons who end their lives when confronted by a *terminal* illness. But these persons are also, *ex hypothesi*, eliminating a propor-tionately greater quantum of pain and suffering, and if the smaller quantum justifies elimination of the shorter span, then the proportionately greater quantum—one reasonably would suppose—justifies the elimination of the longer span.

Now I judge euthanasia for the non-terminal patient to be more problematic than euthanasia for the terminal patient, and therefore I would view such an extension of euthanasia as a par-tial slide downward. For in the case of a non-terminal but in-curable illness or impairment, one runs a greater chance of error in evaluating the future, since there are more variables that have to be taken into account—for example, the possibility that in time one will learn to cope with the suffering, that what is now experienced as unbearable will not continue to be so, that medi-cal advances will at a later time be able to alleviate or possibly even eliminate the suffering. Furthermore, not only is there this greater risk of error in assessing the future, but also there is a known future that awaits one, a future of considerable duration that one is rejecting, a future that holds open the possibility of something more than merely enduring existence—namely, a life of fulfillment in which one discharges substantial ongoing ob-ligations to one's family, one's society, and one's God, even if under trying and difficult circumstances. It is for this reason that

195

I think that a case of suffering associated with non-terminal illness or injury is to be viewed differently from a case of suffering associated with terminal illness.

However, although I find these considerations persuasive, others may not—indeed, a very high percentage of those now advocating euthanasia for the terminally ill are *not* persuaded and consequently will be advocates of euthanasia for the incurable but non-terminal. What's more, there are emphases in the euthanasia movement that would make such an extension of euthanasia a logical one. Here I have in mind the strong emphasis on autonomy—the right of the individual to make those decisions that vitally impact his or her own welfare. For in the kind of case we are now considering, the individual is suffering sufficiently to raise the question "Would I be better off dead or alive?" And who, we may ask, should be given authority to answer that question and act on that answer? Respect for individual autonomy suggests that the suffering individual should be granted that right. On the grounds of autonomy, then, it is a very short step from euthanasia for the terminally ill to euthanasia for the incurably but non-terminally ill.

Euthanasia for Those Suffering from Degenerative Diseases. If we legalize euthanasia for the incurable but non-terminal, we have in essence introduced euthanasia for those who suffer from senile dementia, Alzheimer's disease, and various other degenerative diseases associated with old age, and who declare in advance, by means of a properly signed and witnessed euthanasia directive, that they want their lives to be mercifully brought to a close rather than suffer the indignity of an existence that is mentally disoriented, out of touch with reality, and possibly bordering on the subpersonal. That an individual who is suffering from senile dementia or Alzheimer's disease cannot at the time rationally request active euthanasia is no more problematic than the fact that an individual who is in an irreversible coma cannot request the termination of all life-support systems. In both cases it will suffice that a properly executed directive was signed in advance that empowers another individual (referred to as an attorney-in-fact) to make those decisions on the sufferer's behalf. Again, the rationale for extending euthanasia in this way is that it honors individual autonomy and the right of each person to construe for herself or himself what constitutes an existence lacking in full human dignity. Further, through the mechanism of a previously signed directive, the act of euthanasia retains its voluntary character, and we have not crossed the boundary that demarcates euthanasia *with* consent from euthanasia *without* consent.

Although such a proposal will be repellent to many, it will not be without sympathetic support both among many euthanasia advocates and among at least some members of the general public. These supporters will view the proposal as expressive of individual autonomy, merciful in character, and in keeping with human dignity. Such a proposal means that at some point in the course of a patient's degenerative disease, the specially appointed attorney-in-fact will judge that the patient's life has become sufficiently lacking in dignity, and the administration of euthanasia will be ordered. Of course, it might also be proposed that the patient be allowed to request and undergo euthanasia at the outset of the particular degenerative disease, precluding altogether his or her falling into the grips of the disease and perhaps facing the compromise of his or her rational faculties.

Euthanasia Invoked by Substituted Judgment. The doctrine of "substituted judgment" is a currently recognized legal mechanism whereby an incompetent person, though unable to make a decision to have life-prolonging treatment discontinued, may nevertheless have his needs and hypothetical desires recognized and acted upon. Thus it is asked, "What decision would this incompetent person make were he in fact competent?" If the answer is—after a range of factors has been considered—that the patient would have wanted to have life-extending treatment discontinued, then it is permissible to discontinue that treatment.

In this regard, consider the important case of Earle N. Spring, a gentleman in his late seventies who was suffering from a kidney disease requiring that he undergo hemodialysis. This necessitated that Mr. Spring, who was also suffering from "chronic organic brain syndrome" (senility) and had been de-

197

clared legally incompetent, be placed on a dialysis machine three days a week for five hours a day. With continued treatment, Mr. Spring might live for years; without it, he would die in a fairly short time. Mr. Spring's wife and son sought court authorization to discontinue treatment. The court-appointed guardian for Mr. Spring opposed cessation of treatment, but the judge nevertheless sided with the family and authorized its discontinuance. The guardian appealed this decision to the Massachusetts Appeals Court, but without success: here the earlier decision to discontinue treatment was upheld, and the doctrine of "substituted judgment" was reaffirmed.

Judge Christopher J. Armstrong, who rendered this decision, pointed to eight factors which, he argued, supported the contention that Mr. Spring, were he competent, would choose to have dialysis treatment terminated. They are worth carefully noting. In the words of Justice Armstrong, his decision was supported by "(1) the fact that [Mr. Spring] had led an active, robust, independent life; (2) the fact that he has fallen into a pitiable state of physical dependence and mental incapacity; (3) the fact that no improvement can be expected in his physical or mental condition, but only further deterioration; (4) the fact that dialysis treatments exact a significant toll in terms of frequency and duration of treatments and uncomfortable side effects; (5) the fact that the ward has no understanding of the nature and purpose of his treatments and cannot cooperate and does not reliably acquiesce in their administration; (6) the fact that his wife and son, with whom the ward had and has a very close relationship, feel that it would be his wish not to continue with dialysis in the present circumstances; (7) the fact that it is their wish that dialysis not be administered; and (8) the fact that the attending physician recommends against a continuation of dialysis treatments in these circumstances."[12]

Now it takes little imagination to anticipate that once active euthanasia is legalized, the doctrine of substituted judg-

12. Armstrong, "Opinion in the Matter of Earle N. Spring," in *Social Ethics: Morality and Social Policy*, p. 83.

ment may find application here as well. Indeed, the very considerations that led Judge Armstrong to conclude that Mr. Spring would want dialysis treatment discontinued could equally well lead—in a world of legalized active euthanasia—to the conclusion that Mr. Spring would want active assistance in terminating his life. So it is easy to imagine that legally incompetent patients could be the subjects of active euthanasia made possible by the doctrine of substituted judgment. And certainly the more we ourselves are inclined to view active euthanasia as a boon, the more easily we can be convinced that incompetent patients would want it for themselves, for it is hard for us to believe that someone would not actually want a benefit, and surely if there is any doubt it is better to resolve matters in favor of their receiving that benefit. Indeed, mercy is mercy whether people ask for it or not.

The doctrine of substituted judgment, although it opens the door for mercy in the difficult case of the incompetent patient, also opens the door to possible mischief. For how easy it is for us to *want* to be convinced that discontinuance of treatment or active assistance in dying is what the patient would want—our own positive attitude toward euthanasia inclining us to judge matters in a particular way. An offhand remark by the patient when he or she was competent now looms large as an important indication of what he or she would want, the testimony of relatives (so easily colored by the burdens they have to bear and their desire to bring matters to a close) is assigned authoritative status, and our own view of what *we* would want for ourselves may incline us to conclude that the patient would want the same for himself or herself. In all of this it is easy for our own needs and our own values to determine the fate of the patient, though all the while we are supposedly attempting to determine what the patient would have wanted.

The point that needs to be emphasized is that the doctrine of substituted judgment coupled with the legalization of voluntary active euthanasia for the terminally ill would extend euthanasia to the incompetent terminally ill patient who has not signed a euthanasia directive, and if active euthanasia for the incurable but non-terminal is legalized and then coupled with the doctrine of substituted judgment, we will extend active euthanasia into the nursing homes to provide relief for those suffering from Alzheimer's disease, senile dementia, and other similar degenerative diseases. These are not, I suggest, unrealistic projections. The serious point of difference may rather be over how we view these projections—positively or negatively.

Infanticide. It is also to be feared that seriously handicapped infants will become more vulnerable, being judged fitting candidates for "mercy" in the form of active euthanasia. In fact, there is already a momentum of logic and sentiment in this direction sufficiently strong that one might suppose that active euthanasia for seriously handicapped infants will be legalized before active euthanasia for terminally ill adults. However, should the latter be legalized first, it might prove to be the push sufficient to secure legalization for euthanasia for seriously handicapped infants as well.

There are a number of considerations that might prompt one to view matters in this way. First, seriously handicapped infants already are objects of passive euthanasia. Second, there is much confusion over whether or not infants have a right to life, and if they do, what property is it that imbues them with that right—is it or is it not a property also possessed by the seriously handicapped? Third, there is the near-universal temptation to construe self-interested actions in altruistic terms—that is, ending the lives of seriously handicapped infants is supposedly done for their sakes when in fact self-interested motivations are prominent, though unacknowledged. Fourth, there is a widespread notion of dignified existence, a kind of existence judged to be absent in the case of the seriously handicapped. Let us look briefly at each of these factors.

Consider infants with Down's syndrome, a condition sometimes referred to as mongolism. As they develop, these infants will fall into one of the three recognized categories of feeblemindedness: idiocy (these individuals have an IQ ranging from 0 to 25 and a maximum mental age of up to 3 years; they require constant, lifelong supervision), imbecility (these individuals have an IQ ranging from 26 to 50 and a mental age ranging from 3 to 7 years; they can be trained to carry out simple tasks), and moronity (these individuals have an IQ ranging from 51 to 70 and a mental age ranging from 8 to 12 years; they can perform manual labor of moderate complexity). Most will fall into the second of these three categories (i.e., imbecility). Now some Down's syndrome infants are born with physical abnormalities which, if not corrected by surgery, will cause death— for example, an intestinal blockage that precludes the proper intake and assimilation of food is fatal if untreated. The courts have given parents the power, in consultation with their physicians, to make the decision not to operate. As a consequence of such decisions, the infants so afflicted will die; these are cases of passive euthanasia. Other parents, however, are not so "fortunate." They have Down's syndrome infants who require no operation in order to continue to live; they need only nourishment and normal care. If these parents wish to deny continued existence to their infants, they have no legal options available to them because they cannot do what is required to end their infants' lives—that is, they cannot deny the infants nourishment or liquids, or order the administration of a lethal drug.

But what, it might forcefully be asked, is the difference between refusing to remove an intestinal blockage and thereby allowing an infant to starve/dehydrate (the infant is sedated and apparently feels no pain) and simply not providing the liquids required for survival (sedation also being provided)? Indeed, to take matters one step further, why not give the parents of both "kinds" of infants the authority to order the administration of a lethal drug and thereby avoid the protracted unpleasantness of watching their infants slowly wither and die? Indeed, why not? Does it not seem more humane and more caring for all concerned to do just that?[13] Further, it is frequently argued (at least

13. Certainly it seems so to James Rachels, who in the course of a forcefully argued and much-anthologized article quotes Anthony Shaw:

When surgery is denied [the doctor] must try to keep the infant from suffering while natural forces sap the baby's life away. As a surgeon

in the professional literature) that there is no moral difference between letting a person die and ending that person's life at his or her request—in both cases the intention is to end life, and in both cases the end is effectively accomplished, so what is the moral difference between the two acts? And if letting Down's syndrome infants die is already deemed morally and legally acceptable, then it would follow that so also is actively terminating their lives. If, additionally, it turns out that we are already ending the lives of the terminally ill by means of legalized voluntary active euthanasia, the question can be pressed—"Since we are doing it in those cases, why not in these cases as well?" It is hard to introduce for the first time a practice that conflicts with long-standing moral, social, and legal prohibitions; it is easier the second time. And if the precedent has been set with legalized voluntary active euthanasia for the terminally ill, it will be that much easier to lobby for just one more exception.

The second factor that renders seriously handicapped infants vulnerable is the growing uncertainty over whether infants, handicapped or not, have a right to life, and if they do, what property endows them with such a right? In the professional literature there have been capable voices denying that

---

whose natural inclination is to use the scalpel to fight off death, standing by and watching a salvageable baby die is the most emotionally exhausting experience I know. It is easy at a conference, in a theoretical discussion, to decide that such infants should be allowed to die. It is altogether different to stand by in the nursery and watch as dehydration and infection wither a tiny being over hours and days. This is a terrible ordeal for me and the hospital staff—much more so than for the parents who never set foot in the nursery.

Rachels proceeds to comment, "I can understand why some people are opposed to all euthanasia, and insist that such infants must be allowed to live. I think I can also understand why other people favor destroying these babies quickly and painlessly. But why should anyone favor letting 'dehydration and infection wither a tiny being over hours and days'? The doctrine that says that a baby may be allowed to dehydrate and wither, but may not be given an injection that would end its life without suffering, seems so patently cruel and to require no further refutation" ("Active and Passive Euthanasia," in *Social Ethics: Morality and Social Policy*, pp. 61-62).

any infant (normal or not) has a right to life.[14] The general public does not (I suppose) share that belief; nevertheless, that same public is confused over just what it is that invests infants with a right to life. The widespread and easy acceptance of abortion has contributed to that confusion, since the very principles that could be invoked to protect infants have been implicitly rejected in the permissive stance on abortion.[15] In any case, the confusion exists, and when people lack a clear focus on what it is that endows infants with a right to life, they can be more easily persuaded that terminating the lives of seriously handicapped infants is not a violation of their right to life.

A third source of concern is the almost universal tendency to seek altruistic accounts for self-interested actions. Thus it is often said that infanticide (like certain abortions) is carried out for the sake of the infant, sparing it an intolerable existence. But few mentally and / or physically "defective" individuals in fact find life so intolerable that they themselves want to die, and in light of that fact it is not fully convincing to suggest that we are benefiting such individuals by terminating their lives and that infanticide is therefore an act of mercy. To construe an act of in-

14. The individual most prominently associated with the denial that infants have a right to life is Michael Tooley. Among Tooley's publications are the following: "A Defense of Abortion and Infanticide," in *The Problem of Abortion,* ed. Joel Feinberg (Belmont, Calif.: Wadsworth, 1973), pp. 51-91; "Is Abortion Murder?" (co-written with Laura Purdy), in *Abortion: Pro and Con,* ed. Robert Perkins (Cambridge, Mass.: Schenkman, 1974), pp. 129-49; and *Abortion and Infanticide* (New York: Oxford University Press, 1983). Other proponents of this position include Mary Ann Warren, "On the Moral and Legal Status of Abortion," in *Today's Moral Problems,* ed. Tom Wasserstrom (New York: Macmillan, 1975), pp. 120-36; Joel Feinberg, "Abortion," in *Matters of Life and Death,* ed. Tom Regan (New York: Random House, 1980), pp. 183-216; and Jonathan Glover, *Causing Death and Saving Lives* (New York: Penguin Books, 1977), pp. 150-69.

15. The principles I have in mind are these: (a) the species principle, which says that members of the human species have a right to life and (b) the potentiality principle, which says that those who will naturally and in due course develop into persons (retarded or not) have a right to life. These principles protect infants, but they also protect fetuses. In adopting a liberal stance on abortion, we implicitly reject these principles, making it less clear what basis remains to protect infants.

fanticide (or abortion) in altruistic terms is attractive because it enables us to avoid confronting the truly self-interested character of such an act and to avoid having to construct a self-interested justification of it. And what is wrong with such an altruistic construal of matters is that it doesn't give the infant a fair chance; since everything is purportedly done for the infant's sake, we don't have to struggle with a justification that must weigh our benefits over against its life. Indeed, if we construed matters in this way (our needs versus the infant's value), the decision might favor sparing the infant's life. However, when the justifications for infanticide are cast entirely in terms of benefits to the infant, there is no call for a struggle of conscience.

The fourth and final source of concern is the notion of death with dignity, a notion that is amorphous and ill-defined but widely used in discussions of euthanasia. A prolonged and painful dying, complete or almost complete dependence on others or on machines for one's functioning, prolonged or permanent rational disorientation—all these are said to be human conditions lacking in dignity. In such circumstances death voids the indignity, thereby providing justification for acts of mercy killing or active euthanasia. Notice that even in situations in which individuals (presumably) do not suffer physically or emotionally, human dignity may still be said to be lacking. So the more-or-less seriously handicapped individual or the more-or-less seriously retarded individual may not be suffering or in pain but may nevertheless exist in a state allegedly lacking in full human dignity. Thus acts of infanticide may be rationalized not because they relieve pain but because they void a condition of indignity.

To believe that infanticide may become a social reality is not, then, a groundless fear. And should active euthanasia for the terminally ill be legalized, those forces that advocate euthanasia for infants will be emboldened to press their case with new rigor and will be able to point to an already accepted logic that leads in that direction.

Euthanasia for Children. Finally, let me point out that many who would want euthanasia for themselves should they be suffering from a distressing terminal illness would likely want to provide euthanasia for their children (under the age of consent) should they be suffering from a distressing terminal illness. Indeed, if euthanasia brings a good and merciful death, why should we deny euthanasia to children, especially when their parents or guardians concur that it is in the children's best interest? Another possible ramification is endorsing euthanasia for children *without* the consent of their parents, in much the same way that our society has endorsed abortion for children (under 18) without parental consent. The rationale in both cases would be straightforward: abortion and euthanasia are beneficial practices, and for parents to allow their scruples to get in the way of something that would significantly benefit their children would be for them to violate the children's rights. Euthanasia for children, then, would be a natural outgrowth of legalized active euthanasia; it is yet another possible outcome the desirability of which we need to ponder.

I do not believe that the preceding concerns are excessive or overstated. It is not unreasonable to expect that the legalization of voluntary active euthanasia for the terminally ill adult would provide a significant beachhead from which euthanasia could be extended to several other groups: (a) the non-terminal but incurable, including those suffering from accidental injuries, degenerative diseases associated with old age, and so on (in these cases euthanasia would be effected both by signed euthanasia directive and by the doctrine of substituted judgment); (b) seriously handicapped infants; and (c) terminally ill children. Many of those who are in the forefront of the euthanasia movement today or are sympathetic with its aims would in fact embrace these extensions; they would not be a slide down any slope for these individuals. Others would not view such moves quite so positively. Further, to have active killing institutionalized so widely in the fabric of our society might create an atmosphere, set certain forces in motion, and involve the acceptance of a logic that would lead to even more objectionable acts of killing—acts that only a few now advocate, but that in time, with a new generation socialized by the presence of institutionalized active killing, might begin to develop a receptive audience and ultimately win general social acceptance.

Further Down the Slope

If active killing became widely institutionalized in our society in the ways just indicated, is there any reason to expect that this in turn might prepare the way for further extensions of legalized active killings, extensions that we would find far more objectionable than those already contemplated? Certainly this is a fear shared by many critics of legalized active euthanasia: that legalized euthanasia would lead to truly grotesque forms of killing. It is also true that there have been capable advocates of these more extreme extensions of active euthanasia; thus the perceived dangers are not solely the product of the frenzied imaginations of irresponsible critics of euthanasia. Although it is extremely difficult to assess the likelihood that these more remote though more objectionable possibilities would occur, this does not mean that they should be ignored or passed over lightly.

Euthanasia for the Mentally Ill. The argument has been advanced that if *physical* pain and suffering can justify mercy killing, then so can *mental* pain and suffering, which for the mentally ill individual can be equally as hopeless and agonizing as its physical counterpart. Eliot Slater—a distinguished psychiatrist, a founding member of the World Federation of Neurology, and a former vice-president of Britain's Voluntary Euthanasia Society—has argued that a right to suicide should be extended to the incurably mentally ill. Speaking of the irretrievably psychotic patient, Slater issues the following challenge: "What is the value of saving the life, say, even of a suicidal recurrent depressive, if it is only to force him to face again, in a few weeks or months, the same predicament? How can we be sure that the impulsive psychopath, who has opted for death, is not really doing his best, both for himself and [for] everyone else?"[16] Glanville Williams, former professor of English law at Cambridge University and one of the most prominent advocates if not the most prominent advocate of legalized voluntary active euthanasia in the twentieth century, shares Slater's sympathies, arguing that the mentally ill individual may be competent to make one and only one decision—the decision to end his or her own life. Williams comments, "The opinion I hold as to the patient's rights [to decide whether he or she wishes to continue to exist or not] applies also to mental hospitals. I reject the argument that mental patients as a class are unable to form competent decisions to commit suicide. This may be the one rational decision that they are able to make."[17] Additionally, Walter Alvarez, former professor of medicine at the University of Minnesota, makes a remarkable—indeed, startling—statement when he forthrightly declares, "Right now I know of a woman who is not insane enough to be put in a hospital. Instead, she will live for some months with a married sister, and as a result her brother-in-law generally must leave the house and go to his club, where he remains until the half-insane woman is transferred to the home of another sister. If this psychotic person were to ask for voluntary suicide, I would be for granting her the right, because she is mildly insane and for no useful reason she is almost ruining the lives of others."[18]

We should note that these are distinguished individuals; they are not ill-informed eccentrics who have given the subject little thought and whose words would command no respect in serious circles. In addition, we should honestly acknowledge that their opinions are not (I believe) representative of the majority in the euthanasia movement at the present time. Nevertheless, although theirs is a minority viewpoint, it is one that would

16. Slater, "Choosing the Time to Die," in *Suicide: The Philosophical Issues,* ed. M. Pabst Battin and David J. Mayo (New York: St. Martin's Press, 1980), p. 202.

17. Williams, "Euthanasia and the Physician," in *Beneficent Euthanasia,* ed. Marvin Kohl (Buffalo, N.Y.: Prometheus Books, 1975), p. 161.

18. Alvarez, "The Right to Die," in *Humanistic Perspectives in Medical Ethics,* ed. Maurice B. Visscher (Buffalo, N.Y.: Prometheus Books, 1972), pp. 67-68.

receive at least a sympathetic hearing. Further, we should note that when these individuals assess the desirability of a mentally ill person's committing suicide, they show a willingness to take into account the benefits for the *family and friends* who would thereby be relieved of the burden imposed by the continuing existence of the mentally ill individual. This is a reminder that mercy killing can be prompted by a desire to bring "mercy" to others besides the person whose life is being ended.

Now those who endorse voluntary active euthanasia but would oppose its application to the mentally ill (as most now would) may wish to resist such an extension for the following reasons: (a) some forms of mental illness are in fact curable, (b) mentally ill persons cannot make a responsible decision to end their lives, and (c) mental suffering is not as difficult to bear as intractable physical pain. But, of course, the advocates of a right to suicide for the mentally ill would be unpersuaded, and in response would offer rebuttals: (a) there are in fact serious identifiable mental illnesses that we cannot cure or whose symptoms we cannot satisfactorily control, (b) mentally ill persons are not always without moments of lucidity and sanity during which they could make a responsible decision in favor of suicide, and (c) many who have experienced both mental and physical suffering judge the former to be as bad as or even worse than the latter; furthermore, mental suffering need not be as difficult to bear as the worst physical suffering in order for death to be a merciful release.

In a world where active killing was widely institutionalized, one might anticipate that proposals which would provide euthanasia for the mentally ill would be taken with increasing seriousness and that the preceding issues would begin to be more widely debated. And who, we may ask, would emerge victorious in this debate? Could forces that endorse euthanasia for the mentally ill actually prevail?

Euthanasia for the Feebleminded. Some have thought it desirable to provide euthanasia for those infants who have no prospect of developing any qualities of personhood whatsoever, who are forever doomed to function at the level of an animal—

indeed, who are destined to function *below* the level of many animals. Some such infants have already been the object of passive euthanasia, as we noted when discussing euthanasia for Down's syndrome infants. But medical diagnoses and prognoses are not always as accurate as we might wish; sometimes, for example, congenital idiocy does not demonstrate itself until a number of years have passed, and in some cases it turns out that what was initially *thought* to be congenital idiocy is not that at all. In view of this fact, it might be thought desirable to provide euthanasia for feebleminded individuals at a later stage in their development when the passage of a few years has made their condition demonstrably clear.

Such a proposal has in fact been made; indeed, it was made several decades ago by Foster Kennedy, a psychiatrist who served as president of the Euthanasia Society of America and as a professor at the School of Medicine of Cornell University. And it is reasonable to interpret his proposal as embracing both idiots (who have IQs ranging from 0 to 25) and imbeciles (who have IQs ranging from 26 to 50):

> I believe when the defective child shall have reached the age of five years—and on the application of his guardians—that the case should be considered under law by a competent medical board; then it should be reviewed twice more at four-month intervals; then if the Board, acting, I repeat, on the application of the guardians of the child, and after three examinations of a defective who has reached the age of five or more, should decide that the defective has no future nor hope of one; then I believe it is a merciful and kindly thing to relieve that defective—often tortured and convulsed, grotesque and absurd, useless and foolish, and entirely undesirable—of the agony of living.[19]

Now what are we to think of the prospects of such a proposal? Certainly we do not want to take a proposal made over forty years ago by a maverick psychiatrist and magnify it all out of proportion, turning it into an approaching tidal wave.

19. Kennedy, "The Problem of Social Control of the Congenital Defective," *American Journal of Psychiatry* 99 (July 1942): 14.

Nevertheless, it was a proposal offered by a thoughtful and respected individual, and it was offered, we should note, at a time when active killing was not in any way institutionalized in the medical world; indeed, it was a time when even abortion was not a legal option—not a propitious time, in other words, for this proposal to be given serious consideration by large numbers of people. To be sure, the proposal was interesting and provocative, good for a brief, heated exchange after its presentation at a luncheon, but it was not a proposal that was going to translate into a flurry of political activity calling for a change in our laws to permit terminating the lives of five-year-old congenital idiots (and possibly imbeciles as well).

But what kind of reception might this proposal receive not in the war years of the 1940s (when it was initially made) and not even today, when the focus is on euthanasia for the terminally ill, but rather in a future world in which voluntary active euthanasia both for the terminally ill and for the incurably but non-terminally ill has led to the creation of euthanasia centers, or euthanasia wards in hospitals, or euthanasiasts who make house calls—a world in which active euthanasia for infants with "dim" prospects is an accepted fact of neonatal life, along with euthanasia (executed via the doctrine of substituted judgment) for the elderly suffering from degenerative diseases. In such a world, in which the once-traditional restrictions on the active killing of other human beings have long since been breached, Foster Kennedy's proposal might be on our agenda for serious discussion, consideration, and possible adoption. In such a context, Kennedy's proposal would not be quite the aberrant suggestion that it was when he proposed it or that it might appear to be now.

Reflections on the Preceding Arguments

Now what should we think of all this? We should perhaps begin our reflections by observing that all of us engage in bad-consequence arguments—that is, all of us project future consequences of a good or bad sort in attempting to determine whether or not a particular practice should be adopted or a proposed law enacted. The making of such projections is, of course, an uncertain business, and we should not claim infallibility for ourselves. We should also recognize that our projections are influenced by a range of factors, and we do well to be aware of them. Indeed, why is it so "obvious" to Pope Paul VI that the use of artificial contraceptive devices will tempt men to view women primarily as objects of pleasure and thus lead to men's abusing them, while it is equally "obvious" to others that this is absurd;[20] why is it so "obvious" to some that censoring pornography is likely to lead to the censorship of literary and political works, while it is "obvious" to others that this is nonsense; why is it "obvious" to some that permissive attitudes toward abortion will lead to permissive attitudes toward infanticide, while it is "obvious" to others that this is nothing more than hysterical overstatement?

In part the answer is that everyone brings to such bad-consequence arguments a range of background beliefs that strongly incline one to accept or reject these arguments. Among these influential factors are the following: (1) one's moral assessment of the original activity (euthanasia, abortion, censorship, etc.) from which the bad consequences are expected to flow—one's tendency being to believe that evil will have undesirable consequences and that good will have desirable consequences; (2) one's moral assessment of the anticipated consequences—the more objectionable one finds them, the more fearful and anxious one will be that they will come to pass, while the less objectionable one finds them, the more sanguine one will be,

20. In his 1968 encyclical condemning artificial birth control, Pope Paul VI argued, "It is also to be feared that the man, growing used to the employment of anti-conceptive practices, may finally lose respect for the woman, no longer caring for her physical and psychological equilibrium, may come to the point of considering her as a mere instrument of selfish enjoyment and no longer his respected and beloved companion" (*Humanae Vitae*, in *Vice and Virtue in Everyday Life*, ed. Christina Hoff Sommers [New York: Harcourt Brace Jovanovich, 1985], pp. 508-16). In the same volume by Sommers there is a rejoinder by Carl Cohen entitled "A Reply to Pope Paul's *Humanae Vitae*," pp. 517-27.

calmly assuring others that the projected consequences are only remote possibilities; (3) one's own anticipated relationship to the practice in question—one is more likely to attribute good consequences or at least the absence of bad consequences to practices that one sees oneself participating in and that one wants available for oneself, whereas if one does not see oneself participating in those practices, one will tend to be insensitive to the fact that one may be denying other people access to practices that they desire for themselves; (4) one's own experience with people, institutions, and practices, and one's ability to judge how they will function under varying and changing circumstances; (5) one's view of human nature and one's own estimation of its dark side, and the extent to which one perceives a need for institutions, practices, policies, and laws to inhibit certain evil tendencies in people. Because each of us differs in all these ways (and others as well), we will often disagree over the reasonableness of bad-consequence arguments, and the perspectives that we bring to an argument may be as important as the quality of the argument itself. Indeed, it will frequently be the case that we will not reach any agreement over the legitimacy of particular bad-consequence arguments until we first reach a measure of agreement on these background beliefs, which may be to say that we will not reach agreement at all.

Furthermore, we should not expect that in time, subsequent to the legalization of voluntary active euthanasia (should that occur), all will become clear and that the predictions of bad consequences will *either* demonstrate themselves to have been accurate and realistic projections into the future, the *opponents* of euthanasia emerging triumphant, *or else* turn out to be groundless fears that never so much as even partially materialized, the *proponents* of euthanasia being vindicated. More likely than not, ambiguity will continue, and the same factors that prompted us either to endorse or to debunk these predictions to begin with (evil breeds evil, good breeds good, etc.) will in turn prompt us to interpret subsequent events as tending either to confirm or to refute those predictions.

At this point an admission needs to be made. To argue

successfully that various bad consequences will follow in the wake of the legalization of voluntary active euthanasia does not show that euthanasia should not be legalized; it must also be successfully argued that the bad consequences of its legalization will outweigh the good consequences. However, as one able advocate of legalized active euthanasia, Margaret Pabst Battin, has noted, "Usually . . . when the conclusion is offered that euthanasia therefore ought not to be permitted, no account is taken of the welfare or rights of those who are to be denied the benefits of the practice. Hence, even if the causal claims advanced in the wedge [slippery-slope] argument are true and we are not able to hold the line or avoid the slide, they still do not establish the conclusion."[21] Of course, if it were argued that the legalization of voluntary active euthanasia might lead to something as horrendous as mass genocide, then there would be no doubt that the bad consequences would outweigh the good; however, such an intemperate conclusion is a difficult one to establish. Indeed, it may be the very desire to make it *obvious* that the bad consequences will outweigh the good that has prompted some critics of legalized voluntary active euthanasia to project such cataclysmic consequences, thereby removing any doubt about where the weight of the consequences lies. It seems to be, however, that the more disastrous the projections (genocide, killing the senile, etc.), the less convincing are the supporting arguments.

I have suggested a more modest (though still ambitious) version of the slippery-slope argument, along with some negative-fallout arguments. Together they suggest bad consequences that might reasonably be taken to outweigh the projected good consequences, but I am not sufficiently confident to suggest that this has been demonstrated or that those who dissent from such a conclusion are being unreasonable; projections of both kinds— good and bad—are simply too tenuous for that kind of confidence. But what these arguments do succeed in setting up is a

21. Battin, "Euthanasia," in *Health Care Ethics: An Introduction*, ed. Donald Van De Veer and Tom Regan (Philadelphia: Temple University Press, 1987), p. 82.

conflict, as Battin observes, forcing us to choose between protecting "those who would be the victims of corrupt euthanasia practices" and extending "mercy and respect for autonomy to those who are the current victims of euthanasia prohibitions."[22] Battin chooses the latter, while others of us are inclined to choose the former.

The Nazi Euthanasia Program

I have given my reasons for questioning the wisdom of legalizing voluntary active euthanasia, reasons which are *not* related to the atrocities that were committed in the Nazi euthanasia program. It is, however, incumbent upon all of us who wish to participate in the euthanasia debate to confront this ugly episode in human history and see what implications—if any—it has for the current debate.

What I am referring to is the Nazi euthanasia program, which was implemented in Germany between December 1939 and August 1941; during that time between 50,000 and 60,000 physically and mentally handicapped adults were gassed or given lethal injections.[23] Neither the consent of the handicapped nor that of their families was ever obtained. This, of course, was not *voluntary* euthanasia or assisted suicide; it was simply murder. Many of the handicapped were gassed in a manner that we associate with the extermination of the Jews: unsuspecting persons were taken to what they thought were showers but which in reality were gas chambers, where they were killed. Further atrocities were committed in a special euthanasia program for German and Austrian children, which was begun even prior to the adult euthanasia program and carried out right up until the end of the war. According to one reliable figure supplied by Lucy Dawidowicz, professor of Holocaust Studies of Yeshiva

22. Battin, "Euthanasia," p. 82.
23. Gerald Reitlinger, *The Final Solution* (New York: A. B. Barnes, 1953), p. 132.

University, about 5,000 children were put to death under this program.[24] But parental consent was not obtained—at least not *legitimate* parental consent, according to Gitta Sereny:

> Parents were informed that Kinderfachabteilungen—Special Section for children—was being established all over the country. They were asked to sign an authorization for their severely disabled children to be transferred to these wards and were told that, as these were in fact intensive-care units where highly advanced experiments would be carried out, this represented a unique chance for their children's possible recovery. *This* was how the Nazis obtained authorizing signatures. . . . Eleven Special Sections were involved; each of them had between twenty and thirty beds. . . . The children were "put to sleep" with injections and, from all accounts, were not aware of their fates.[25]

After these children were exterminated, their parents were sent a letter which read in part (there were variations),

> We are sincerely sorry to tell you that your son/daughter who had to be transferred to this Institution . . . died suddenly and unexpectedly here, of a tumor of the brain . . . the life of the deceased had been a torment to him/her on account of his/her severe mental trouble. You should therefore feel that his/her death was a happy release. As this Institution is threatened by an epidemic at the present time, the police have ordered immediate cremation of the body. We would ask you to let us know to what cemetery we may arrange for the police to send the urn containing the mortal remains of the deceased.[26]

What we had in Nazi Germany, then, was a *camouflaged* "euthanasia" program. It could be characterized as "the most secret operation in the Third Reich."[27] Those who participated

24. Dawidowicz, *The War against the Jews: 1933-1945* (New York: Holt, Rinehart & Winston, 1975), p. 132.

25. Sereny, *Into That Darkness: From Mercy Killing to Mass Murder* (New York: McGraw-Hill, 1974), pp. 54-55.

26. Cited in A. Mitscherlich and F. Mielke, *The Death Doctors* (London: Elek Books, 1962), p. 251.

27. Sereny, *Into That Darkness*, p. 49.

in the program were sworn to secrecy and threatened with death if they failed to keep silent.[28] Further, the program had at best a kind of quasi-legal status; it was the product of a secret decree by Adolph Hitler. No law was ever enacted, no change was ever made in the German penal code to provide a legal justification for what was being done. The larger community of Germans was not consulted.

The Nazi euthanasia program served a preparatory function for the Nazis' subsequent attempt to exterminate the entire Jewish population of Europe. Indeed, the administrative center for the euthanasia program subsequently assumed the task of overseeing the mass murder of the Jews. Procedures and techniques that had been employed during the euthanasia phase— procedures for gassing those assessed as having "lives unworthy of living" and disposing of the bodies—were continued when Jews were substituted for the mentally and physically handicapped. In addition, there was a carryover of personnel. And, significantly, as Gitta Sereny stresses, "The work at the euthanasia institutes ... did 'inure' them to feeling and thus prepare them for the next phase."[29]

But this kind of activity could not be kept secret forever. Word got out, and the activities of the Nazi euthanasia program became common knowledge.[30] Both Catholic and Protestant churchmen mounted a strenuous protest from their pulpits and in official communications to Nazi authorities. Referring to the program, the chairman of the Central Committee of the Home Mission of the German Evangelical Church commented, "It is urgently necessary to put a stop to these proceedings with the least possible delay, for they are seriously endangering the very foun-

28. Mitscherlich and Mielke, *The Death Doctors,* p. 240.

29. Sereny, *Into That Darkness,* p. 83.

30. According to Lucy Dawidowicz, "Notifications of death that the medical-killing stations sent to the families concealed the actual manner of death. Families were informed that their kin had died of pneumonia or during an appendectomy. (The lie was detected in instances when the family knew the patient's appendix had been removed many years earlier.)" See "Biomedical Ethics and the Shadow of Nazism," *Hastings Center Report,* Aug. 1976, p. 4 of special supplement.

dation of German morality. The inviolability of human life is one of the cornerstones of any political system."[31] Sereny reports that during the summer of 1941 Hitler had the unusual experience of being jeered by an outraged crowd when his train was being held up while mental patients were being loaded onto trucks for transportation to one of the euthanasia centers.[32] At the end of the summer (on August 25, to be exact), Hitler ordered a halt to the adult euthanasia program. Most commentators have hitherto agreed that pressure from the church and the public forced Hitler to take this action, but Sereny provides evidence that by the time Hitler halted the program the Nazis had already succeeded in killing all those they wanted to kill anyway.[33] But at least public indignation was aroused, and the church spoke to the issue.[34]

To some degree the Nazi rationale for the euthanasia program was crudely economical. The financial "burden" of providing institutional care for the physically and mentally handicapped may have been a factor prompting its creation. This can be seen in the government's attempts to prepare the German people to accept this very kind of rationale. Consider the following excerpts from a mathematics textbook for German children:

> Question No. 95. If the building of a lunatic asylum costs six million marks and it costs 15,000 marks to build each dwelling on a housing estate, how many of the latter could be built for the price of one asylum?
>
> Question No. 97. Daily maintenance of an insane person costs 4 marks, of a cripple 5.50 and of a criminal 3.50. In how many cases does an official earn daily only about 4 marks, a factory employee barely 3.50 and an unskilled labourer less than 2 as the head of the family?
>
> (a) Illustrate these figures graphically. According to calcu-

31. Cited in Mitscherlich and Mielke, *The Death Doctors*, p. 255.
32. Sereny, *Into That Darkness*, p. 59.
33. Sereny, *Into That Darkness*, p. 76.
34. Regrettably, for whatever reason, the church did not protest the extermination of the Jews when similar word-of-mouth communication must have also rendered the genocidal activities of the Third Reich common knowledge.

lations there are some 300,000 insane persons, epileptics, etc.,
in Germany under treatment in institutions.

(b) Give the total yearly cost of such persons at the rate of
4 marks p.d. [per day]

(c) How many State marriage loans of 1,000 marks, not re-
payable, would be issued annually from the amount now
spent on the insane, etc.[35]

Here the message is clear. The mentally and physically handicapped are a drain on the financial resources of the state, and
the conclusion just waiting to be drawn is that if the state were
not economically bound by those in need of institutional care,
money would be freed for other "more important" uses.

But the primary motivation behind the Nazi euthanasia
program is to be found in the Nazi ideology with its fanatical
emphasis on a *pure* Volk (people) who were to rule the world
through the German state. The Volk was pure to the degree that
it was free of any non-Aryan admixture and free of mentally and
physically defective "elements," Aryan or otherwise. A euthanasia program directed at the mentally and/or physically handicapped who needed prolonged institutional care served two
purposes: (a) it purified the Volk, and (b) it freed resources that
the nation needed to fulfill its historical destiny of world domi-
nation. We should be clear that the Nazi euthanasia program
was not motivated by considerations of mercy. Referring to both
the child and the adult euthanasia programs, Lucy Dawidowicz
has commented, "In neither area and in none of the cases was
death administered because of a sick or dying person's intolerable suffering or because of a patient's own feelings about the
usefulness of his life. In no case did the patient ask for death.
Killing was done without the patient's consent and . . . without
the family's knowledge."[36]

In pondering what the Nazi euthanasia program has to tell
us about the wisdom of legalizing voluntary active euthanasia,

35. Cited in Mitscherlich and Mielke, *The Death Doctors*, p. 234n.1.
36. Dawidowicz, "Biomedical Ethics and the Shadow of Nazism," p. 4 of
special supplement.

it is important to notice that there are several lessons that cannot be drawn from it.

First, the Nazi experience does not teach us that voluntary euthanasia would (or might also) lead to involuntary euthanasia, because the Nazi program never progressed from being voluntary to being involuntary; it was involuntary from the outset.

Second, the Nazi experience does not teach us that the mercy killing of the terminally ill would (or might) lead to "mercy" killing of the mentally and physically handicapped. This is so because the Nazi program was not an outgrowth of concern for the terminally ill at all; it was from the beginning and continued to be directed at the mentally and physically handicapped. There was no euthanasia program for the terminally ill.

Third, the Nazi experience does not teach us that a program of euthanasia prompted by mercy could be perverted so that it would lose its original humane impetus and would later be enlisted in the service of corrupt ends. Again, this is so because the program was never prompted by a merciful concern for others but was a corrupt undertaking from the outset.

Thus, whatever we may ultimately conclude from the Nazi experience, I believe that one thing is clear: we do not find any support here for the slippery-slope argument. The Nazis did no sliding down any slope—they started at the bottom. It is true that the Nazis, upon terminating the adult euthanasia program, turned to the task of eliminating the entire Jewish population of Europe. But this was not so much a slide downward as it was a parallel extension of an already utterly immoral policy, an undertaking perhaps more ambitious in terms of numbers but morally no worse than its predecessor. It, too, was part of an attempt to create a pure Volk and thus was ideologically motivated in the same way that the euthanasia program was. The Nazis corrupted everything they touched: the medical and legal professions, the military, the church, and the universities. What the Nazi experience should teach us to fear is not so much voluntary euthanasia for the terminally ill but rather the Fascist mind-set that justified all manner of atrocities to begin with. It is because the goal of creating a pure Volk provided the primary motivation for the

Nazi euthanasia program and because this ideological factor is absent in the United States that Lucy Dawidowicz concludes that the Nazi euthanasia program is "historically irrelevant to the contemporary [euthanasia] debate."[37]

Crucially, the Nazi experience should teach us to value an open society in which ideas are debated, policies are submitted to careful scrutiny by the citizenry and their elected leaders, information flows freely, and government is conducted in the open—none of which was the case in Nazi Germany. For even in Nazi Germany the Nazi euthanasia program could not pass the test of public scrutiny, despite the Nazi ideology that pervaded the land at the time and the crass appeal to social utility that the Nazis were not beyond making. As we have already seen, once the euthanasia program became public knowledge, there was a considerable cry of protest and outrage. In an open and democratic society one would trust that the program never would have gotten off the ground in the first place.

Summary

I have argued that in order for society to be justified in legalizing any form of voluntary active euthanasia, the following conditions should be fulfilled: (a) the individual to be killed both wants and requests to be killed, (b) the person doing the killing does so voluntarily, (c) no third-party rights are violated, and

37. Dawidowicz, "Biomedical Ethics and the Shadow of Nazism," *Hastings Center Report*, p. 10 of special supplement. Daniel Maguire contends that four differences between our current situation and that of Nazi Germany undercut the force of the contention that we might follow the Nazi example: (1) Respect for individual rights is ingrained in our society in a way it was not in Nazi Germany; (2) Our society is not as homogeneous as German society, making it less likely that uniform support for such policies could ever be obtained; (3) We have the ugly example of Nazi Germany as part of our cultural memory; (4) Current discussion of euthanasia is arising not in the context of the utilitarian disvalue of useless lives but in the context of death as a good for the individual, which points in a different direction than did the discussion in Nazi Germany (*Death by Choice* [New York: Schocken Books, 1975], pp. 133-34).

(d) the killing is in the best interest of all concerned, including both the person being killed and other seriously affected persons. As I pointed out, the first three conditions are not by themselves sufficient to warrant the legalization of euthanasia. For we presume that society has justifiably criminalized various forms of consensual homicide that meet these three conditions: we do not legally permit dueling, human sacrifice, the sacrificial offering of one's vital organs to others, and so on. What is required is the fulfillment of an additional condition—namely, that the act be in the best interest of all seriously affected parties. Thus concern over the wisdom of legalizing voluntary active euthanasia properly centers on this last condition, it being argued that legalized euthanasia threatens substantial societal interests which in turn justifies placing restrictions on individual autonomy by denying to the terminally ill (and others) access to physician-assisted suicide.

Thus opponents of legalized voluntary euthanasia argue that its legalization threatens bad consequences that will outweigh good consequences—in other words, it is argued that voluntary active euthanasia is *not* in the best interest of all concerned. In this connection I looked at two kinds of arguments—negative-fallout arguments and slippery-slope arguments—both of which project negative consequences flowing from euthanasia's legalization. I concluded that together they provide grounds for having serious reservations about the wisdom of legalizing voluntary active euthanasia. I did point to a range of background beliefs that one brings to these arguments which strongly inclines one to reject or to accept them; my personal judgment is that society would be better off not legalizing voluntary active euthanasia.

I also examined the Nazi euthanasia program and argued that it is historically irrelevant—at least in any direct way—to the issue of legalizing voluntary active euthanasia. It certainly was a malignant episode in the history of the human race, and it clearly displays the human capacity for evil and underscores the need for proper safeguards to keep that propensity in check. But all participants in the euthanasia debate, both proponents and opponents, would agree that there is a need for socially imposed restraints that limit the human capacity for inhumanity; what they disagree about is where those restraints should be applied. Proponents of voluntary active euthanasia believe that to criminalize that act is to impose restraints at the wrong place, preventing the considerable good that a quick, painless, physician-assisted death can achieve. Opponents feel that the risks involved in legalized euthanasia are seriously underestimated by its proponents and that, on the contrary, the traditional and long-standing prohibitions against killing the terminally ill, even at their request, should be honored and maintained. I identify with the opponents of legalized voluntary active euthanasia.

CHAPTER EIGHT

Concluding Remarks

In this book we have been dealing with terminal choices—reflecting on how we should die and how we should advise others to die. Certainly this is no modest undertaking, despite our not having dealt with all dimensions of dying nobly and well, but only with dying as it relates to that special context provided by modern medicine with its capacity to cure illness and disease, to control pain, to postpone death, to hasten death, to end life quickly and painlessly (if it so chooses), and to forecast (with increasing accuracy) the time remaining to the dying and the quality of that time. It is dying as it relates to *that* context, with its special problems, which has been the focus of our attention as well as the source of our moral consternation. Indeed, society has recently acquired powers and knowledge formerly reserved for God, and that has not made matters easier for us. Rather, these advances have confronted us with new and perplexing options, so that dying, which was never easy, is now not only a test of our endurance and patience but also a severe test of our ethical acumen, forcing us to plot a course through the moral thicket created by the growth of modern medical science and technology.

So in these pages we have been struggling with how we should act on this new medical knowledge and how we should use these newly acquired medical powers. In the course of our struggle we have dealt with a range of moral issues, some complicated and baffling, others apparently more straightforward and manageable. And we have approached them in a manner that takes seriously our membership in the Christian community, construing our task as a search both for God's will and for a way of living and dying that embodies those values to which we are committed by virtue of our Christian faith. For Christians, of course, this is just as it should be, for in fashioning and shaping death, as in fashioning and shaping life, we always make a serious attempt to express a Christian vision of human existence. In this regard, all approaches to death—Christian and non-Christian alike—are the same: how one views life determines how one views death. Indeed, to answer the question "How shall we then live?" is to answer the question "How shall we then die?"

It appears, then, that all along the crucial question has been "What is the point of human existence?" Here, of course, humanity is divided, and people give radically different answers. Is the point of human existence to exercise autonomy, giving expression to one's own individual will? Is it to maximize one's own welfare? Or possibly to maximize the welfare of the community? Or is the point of human existence to achieve moral excellence (in some sense)? Or is it, as the Christian affirms, to gain friendship with God, the Father of Jesus Christ, and to be transformed into the moral likeness of that God via an earthly pilgrimage, the boundaries of which he has established?

Thus how one views life, its point and its purpose, will shape one's approach to death; what one views as a good life will determine what one takes to be a good death. And how one actually deals with death when it comes will often reveal and clarify what one has all along believed about life. Therefore, if the point of life is to exercise autonomy—"after all, it is my life, to do with as I please"—then a death will be satisfactory to the extent that it is dictated by the dying individual. But if the point of life is the happiness and welfare of the individual, then a death will be satisfactory to the extent that it is in the best interest (under the circumstances) of the dying individual, and this will be so

224

whether the individual chooses his or her own death or whether another chooses it for him or her. Or one may have a broader concept of a good life, one that accords with a utilitarian vision of morality. That is, one may believe that a good life is one that maximizes *community* happiness (which includes but is not exhausted by one's own happiness). For such an individual, a good death will be one that is in the best interest of the community—that is, in the best interest of *all* who are affected by it.

On the other hand, one may find all these options unsatisfactory as guides to living and dying. That is, one may have a moral vision about how one is to die that is not reducible to the exercise of autonomy, to the maximizing of one's own welfare, or even to the maximizing of the community's welfare. There may be many such visions, but one of those is the Christian vision, which declares that the point of human existence is to gain friendship with God, the Father of Jesus Christ, and to be transformed into that God's moral likeness as it has been revealed in Jesus Christ, and that this is to be done in the course of an earthly pilgrimage the boundaries of which have been established by God. This is the answer that the Christian community gives to the question "What is the point of human existence?"

To accept this answer is to commit oneself to shaping a death in accord with a Christian vision of human existence—a vision that includes, at its very heart, accountability *to* one's creator, who is the acknowledged source of one's being as well as the source of ultimate purpose and meaning. Significantly, this includes accountability *for* the death one elects to die and *for* the deaths one elects to cause. Thus the Christian rejects at the outset the autonomy thesis, which declares the killing of one individual by another to be morally unobjectionable so long as the person killed is mature and mentally competent, and wants and requests to be killed. Such a view declares that the life of each person is his or her own to dispose of as he or she sees fit, free from any legitimate moral criticism. According to such a view, the individual who kills himself or herself is morally accountable to no one, and the individual who kills another is accountable only to the one who is killed. Voluntary euthanasia (passive or active) is acceptable simply because it is voluntary, being an expression of an autonomous will. When it comes to life and death, therefore, each individual is moral sovereign over his or her own existence.

Of course, the Christian community would judge unacceptable such an elevation of human autonomy. For surely how one lives and how one dies have moral implications that go beyond the exercise of individual autonomy. For both how one lives and how one dies have consequences for the happiness and welfare of others—including one's family, one's friends, and one's community—and one cannot disregard those consequences without denying that other people are to be the object of moral concern. Such a denial would be unacceptable by most standards, but certainly by Christian standards, for Christians are called to love their neighbor as they love themselves, and this they are called to do whether they are living or dying. Human moral connectedness is not severed simply because one is dying; moral responsibility persists even when one's life is drawing to a close. Accountability to God, then, involves faithful concern for one's neighbor even in the midst of death. This is only part of what constitutes a satisfactory death, but it cannot be set aside as morally irrelevant.

It is for this same reason that the personal happiness principle cannot be our guide to ending our own lives. Merely because it is in *my* best interest to end my life does not make it right to do so, if for no other reason than that this principle, like the autonomy principle, fails to take into account my obligations to others. For I have obligations to family, friends, and community, and these obligations are to inform my dying as well as my living.

But we will not make difficulties vanish by setting aside the autonomy principle and adopting utilitarianism with its reduction of all obligations to the single obligation to maximize the happiness of the greatest number. To be sure, with this principle the effects of a death upon family, friends, and community will *not* be ignored but will actually become, along with the benefit that comes to the deceased, the *only* factors relevant in assessing the rightness or wrongness of taking one's own life. According to such a view, ending life (one's own or that of another) is justified whenever the net effect on human welfare is more positive than that of any other available alternative. This perspective, however, renders vulnerable those individuals whose deaths would further the overall interests of society. True, the welfare of such individuals must be taken into account, but those interests are not the only ones to be considered, and they might well be outweighed by the interests of the community. In criticism of such a view it is rightly argued that individuals possess certain fundamental rights—including a right to life— that cannot be overridden for the sake of increasing the overall amount of happiness in the world. Christians would be sympathetic to such criticism, whether or not they couch matters in terms of a right to life, because respect for human life is grounded not in the temporal interests of society but in the absolute claim of God. For it is God who has called the individual into existence for his purposes, and those purposes cannot simply be set aside in the name of the collective interests of society.

It may be granted that of course it is not morally acceptable to end *another* person's life because of the net gain which that death would produce in human happiness, but isn't it different when one ends one's *own* life, sacrificing *it* for the good of society, thereby furthering the general welfare? Perhaps one's own lingering death is causing pain and sorrow for friends and relatives, who must helplessly watch what is judged to be a sad spectacle. Might not a quick, self-inflicted death cut short their emotional suffering while at the same time ending a drain on limited medical resources? It may indeed, and to end one's life in order to further overall human welfare may seem noble, even Christian—but in fact it is not consistent with the Christian perspective on human existence.

A utilitarian moral vision that determines the rightness or wrongness of an action solely by reference to its consequences in maximizing human happiness is not an ethic that has found acceptance within the Christian community. It is not a moral standard that has been judged adequate for living one's life;

therefore, neither would it be judged adequate as a standard for dying. There are, of course, all the commonplace criticisms of utilitarianism (a theory which, admittedly, has its enthusiastic and able defenders): it flies in the face of common moral sense by its willingness to set aside individual rights, offend canons of justice, and violate the moral law in pursuit of human welfare. Such criticism affirms what the Christian community also affirms: the common good is to be sought only within the boundaries established for us by the moral law. Thus, even as I seek to love my neighbor by the death I die, there continue to be moral constraints placed upon me. Suicide, therefore, would rarely be a legitimate expression of love for one's neighbor (which is not to say that it could *never* be). This is so not only because suicide will often *not* in fact further my neighbor's welfare but also because, even if it did succeed in doing so, it would still fail to be a morally acceptable means to that end. And why is this so? Because, very simply, the value of my life is not exhausted by my capacity to further human welfare; it is to diminish that value too much to say that when life best serves the goal of maximizing human happiness, then I am to choose life, but when death most effectually furthers that goal, then I am to choose death. Rather, my life has a value that transcends its capacity to maximize happiness, and this is part of what is recognized by the Christian ban on suicide. Life is not to end in suicide when my happiness and/or the happiness of others can thereby be furthered. For my life belongs to God, to be lived out in providentially ordained circumstances, in trust that a good and wise God directs my paths even in difficult circumstances for purposes he has decreed.

To exercise faith in God's reality, to believe that I am accountable to him for the whole of my life, to trust in his providential ordering, to understand my life in terms of his purpose of spiritual transformation, and to shape my dying as well as my living in the light of this—this is my calling as a Christian. Indeed, as the apostle Paul writes, "None of us lives to himself, and none of us dies to himself. If we live, we live to the Lord, and if we die, we die to the Lord; so then, whether we live or whether we die, we are the Lord's" (Rom. 14:7-8). In all of this there is a challenge both to faith and to understanding. For how should all of this be translated into particular lives and particular deaths? How do we die "to the Lord" in a modern hospital or nursing home? Struggling with these kinds of questions has been the focus of this book; we have grappled with complexity and ambiguity in an attempt to clarify how the Christian vision of human existence is to be expressed as death confronts us in the problematic world that modern medical technology has created for us. We have given our answers—some assured, some tentative—and as difficult as that task may have been, the more difficult task is to take those answers and embody them in our living and in our dying. For that, much grace is required.

SELECTED BIBLIOGRAPHY

Books

Aries, Philippe. *Western Attitudes toward Death*. Trans. Patricia Ranum. Baltimore: Johns Hopkins University Press, 1974.

Arras, John, and Robert Hunt. *Ethical Issues in Modern Medicine*, 2nd ed. Palo Alto, Calif.: Mayfield Publishing, 1983.

Asch, Sholem. *Tales of My People*. Freeport, N.Y.: Books for Libraries Press, 1948.

Augustine. *The City of God*. New York: Modern Library, 1950.

The Babylonian Talmud, Nezikin, vol. IV. London: Soncino Press, 1935.

Bakan, David. *Disease, Pain and Sacrifice*. Chicago: University of Chicago Press, 1968.

Bandman, Elsie L., and Bertram Bandman. *Bioethics and Human Rights*. Boston: Little, Brown, 1978.

Battin, Margaret Pabst. *Ethical Issues in Suicide*. Englewood Cliffs, N.J.: Prentice-Hall, 1982.

Battin, Margaret Pabst, and David Mayo, eds. *Suicide: Contemporary Philosophical Issues*. New York: St. Martin's Press, 1980.

Beauchamp, Tom. L., and James F. Childress. *Principles of Biomedical Ethics*. New York: Oxford University Press, 1979.

Beauchamp, Tom L., and Seymour Perlin. *Ethical Issues in Death and Dying*. Englewood Cliffs, N.J.: Prentice-Hall, 1978.

Bender, David L., ed. *Death and Dying: Opposing Viewpoints*. St. Paul, Minn.: Greenhaven Press, 1980.

Bonhoeffer, Dietrich. *Ethics*. New York: Macmillan, 1955.

Bonica, John J., et al., eds. *Recent Advances on Pain.* Springfield, Ill.: Charles C. Thomas, 1974.

Boros, Ladislaus. *The Mystery of Death.* New York: Seabury Press, 1973.

Brandon, S. G. F. *The Judgment of the Dead: The Idea of Life after Death in the Major Religions.* New York: Charles Scribner's Sons, 1967.

Campbell, Alistair V. *Moral Dilemmas in Medicine.* Edinburgh: Churchill Livingstone, 1975.

Carrick, Paul. *Medical Ethics in Antiquity.* Dordrecht: D. Reidel Publishing, 1975.

Clow, Archie, ed. *Morals and Medicine.* London: British Broadcasting Company, 1970.

Cohen, A. *Everyman's Talmud.* New York: E. P. Dutton, 1932.

Culver, C. M., and B. Gert. *Philosophy in Medicine: Conceptual and Ethical Issues in Medicine and Psychiatry.* New York: Oxford University Press, 1982.

Curran, Charles, ed. *Absolutes in Moral Theology.* Washington, D.C.: Corpus Books, 1968.

Dawidowicz, Lucy S. *The War against the Jews: 1933-1945.* New York: Holt, Rinehart & Winston, 1975.

Devine, Philip E. *The Ethics of Homicide.* Ithaca, N.Y.: Cornell University Press, 1978.

Devlin, Patrick. *The Enforcement of Morals.* New York: Oxford University Press, 1965.

Donagan, Alan. *The Theory of Morality.* Chicago: University of Chicago Press, 1977.

Downie, R. S., and Elizabeth Telfer. *Caring and Curing.* London: Methuen, 1980.

Downing, A. B., ed. *Euthanasia and the Right to Death.* Los Angeles: Nash Publishing, 1969.

Durkheim, Emile. *Suicide: A Study in Sociology.* New York: Free University Press, 1951.

Elliott, Neil. *The Gods of Life.* New York: Macmillan, 1974.

Fedden, Henry Romilly. *Suicide: A Social and Historical Study.* London: Peter Davies, 1938.

Fletcher, Joseph. *Morals and Medicine.* Boston: Beacon Press, 1960.

Frey, R. G. *Rights, Killing and Suffering*. Oxford: Basil Blackwell, 1983.

Fried, Charles. *Right and Wrong*. Cambridge: Harvard University Press, 1978.

Gerstenberger, Erhard S., and Wolfgang Schrage. *Suffering*. Trans. John E. Steely. Nashville: Abingdon, 1980.

Gibson, David. *Down's Syndrome: The Psychology of Mongolism*. New York: Cambridge University Press, 1978.

Glover, Jonathan. *Causing Death and Saving Lives*. New York: Penguin Books, 1977.

Gorovitz, Samuel, et al. *Moral Problems in Medicine*. Englewood Cliffs, N.J.: Prentice-Hall, 1976.

Grisez, Germain, and Joseph M. Boyle, Jr. *Life and Death with Liberty and Justice*. Notre Dame, Ind.: University of Notre Dame Press, 1979.

Harris, John. *The Value of Life*. London: Routledge & Kegan Paul, 1985.

———. *Violence and Responsibility*. London: Routledge & Kegan Paul, 1980.

Hauerwas, Stanley. *Suffering Presence*. Notre Dame, Ind.: University of Notre Dame Press, 1986.

Heinlein, Robert A. *Time Enough for Love*. New York: G. P. Putnam's Sons, 1973.

Hendin, Herbert. *Suicide in America*. New York: W. W. Norton, 1982.

Hick, John H. *Death and Eternal Life*. New York: Harper & Row, 1976.

Horan, Dennis J., and David Mall, eds. *Death, Dying, and Euthanasia*. Frederick, Md.: University Publications of America, 1980.

Humphry, Derek. *Let Me Die Before I Wake*. Los Angeles: Hemlock Society, 1984.

Inge, W. R. *Christian Ethics and Modern Problems*. New York: G. P. Putnam's Sons, 1930.

Jonsen, Albert R., et al. *Clinical Ethics*. New York: Macmillan, 1982.

Josephus. *The Jewish War*. Trans. G. A. Williamson. Harmonds-worth, Eng.: Penguin Books, 1959.

Kelly, G. *Medico-Moral Problems*. St. Louis: Catholic Hospital Association, 1958.

Kluge, Eike-Henner W. *The Practice of Death*. New Haven: Yale University Press, 1975.

Kohl, Marvin. *The Morality of Killing*. New York: Humanities Books, 1974.

Kohl, Marvin, ed. *Beneficent Euthanasia*. Buffalo, N.Y.: Prometheus Books, 1975.

Labby, D. H., ed. *Life or Death: Ethics and Options*. Seattle: University of Washington Press, 1968.

Ladd, John, ed. *Ethical Issues Relating to Life and Death*. New York: Oxford University Press, 1979.

Lifton, Robert J., and Eric Olson. *Living and Dying*. New York: Praeger Publishers, 1974.

Lorenz, K. Y., and John J. Bonica, eds. *Pain, Discomfort and Humanitarian Care*. New York: Elsevier, 1980.

Lyon, Jeff. *Playing God in the Nursery*. New York: W. W. Norton, 1985.

McCormick, Richard, and Paul Ramsey, eds. *Doing Evil to Achieve Good*. Chicago: Loyola University Press, 1978.

Maguire, Daniel. *Death by Choice*. New York: Schocken Books, 1975.

Mannes, Marya. *Last Rights: A Case for the Good Death*. New York: William Morrow, 1974.

Margolis, Joseph. *Negativities: The Limits of Life*. Columbus, Ohio: Charles E. Merrill, 1975.

Melden, A. I. *Rights and Persons*. Berkeley and Los Angeles: University of California Press, 1977.

Mitscherlich, A., and F. Mielke. *The Death Doctors*. London: Elek Books, 1962.

Munson, Ronald. *Intervention and Reflection*. Belmont, Calif.: Wadsworth, 1979.

Oden, Thomas C. *Should Treatment Be Terminated?* New York: Harper & Row, 1976.

O'Donnell, Thomas J. *Morals in Medicine.* Westminster, Md.: Newman Press, 1957.

Ostheimer, John and Nancy, eds. *Life or Death—Who Controls?* New York: Springer Publishing, 1976.

Phipps, William E. *Death: Confronting the Reality.* Atlanta: John Knox Press, 1987.

President's Commission for the Study of Ethical Problems in Medicine and Biomedical and Behavioral Research. *Deciding to Forego Life-Sustaining Treatment.* Washington: GPO, 1983.

President's Commission for the Study of Ethical Problems in Medicine and Biomedical and Behavioral Research. *Defining Death: Medical, Legal and Ethical Issues in the Determination of Death.* Washington: GPO, 1983.

Ramsey, Paul. *The Patient as Person.* New Haven: Yale University Press, 1970.

Rashdall, Hastings. *The Theory of Good and Evil,* 2nd ed. New York: Oxford University Press, 1924.

Regan, Tom, ed. *Matters of Life and Death.* New York: Random House, 1980.

Reitlinger, Gerald. *The Final Solution.* New York: A. S. Barnes, 1953.

Russell, O. Ruth. *Freedom to Die.* New York: Human Sciences Press, 1975.

St. John-Stevas, N. *Life, Death, and the Law.* Bloomington, Ind.: Indiana University Press, 1961.

Sandbach, F. H. *The Stoics.* New York: W. W. Norton, 1975.

Sarjeant, Richard. *The Spectrum of Pain.* London: Rupert Hart Davis, 1969.

Sereny, Gitta. *Into That Darkness: From Mercy Killing to Mass Murder.* New York: McGraw-Hill, 1974.

Skegg, P. D. G. *Law, Ethics, and Medicine.* Oxford: Clarendon Press, 1984.

Society for the Right to Die. *The Physician and the Hopelessly Ill Patient.* New York: Society for the Right to Die, 1985.

Steinbock, Bonnie, ed. *Killing and Letting Die.* Englewood Cliffs, N.J.: Prentice-Hall, 1980.

Steinfels, Peter, and Robert M. Veatch, eds. *Death Inside Out.* New York: Harper & Row, 1974.

Torrey, E. *Ethical Issues in Medicine.* Boston: Little, Brown, 1968.

Van De Veer, Donald. *Paternalistic Intervention.* Princeton: Princeton University Press, 1986.

Van De Veer, Donald, and Tom Regan, eds. *Health Care Ethics.* Philadelphia: Temple University Press, 1987.

Vaux, Kenneth. *Biomedical Ethics: Morality for the New Medicine.* New York: Harper & Row, 1974.

Veatch, Robert M. *Death, Dying, and the Biological Revolution.* New Haven: Yale University Press, 1976.

————. *A Theory of Medical Ethics.* New York: Basic Books, 1981.

Visscher, Maurice B., ed. *Humanistic Perspectives in Medical Ethics.* Buffalo, N.Y.: Prometheus Books, 1972.

Walton, Douglas N. *Ethics of Withdrawal of Life-Support Systems.* Westport, Conn.: Greenwood Press, 1983.

Weatherhead, Leslie. *The Christian Agnostic.* New York: Abingdon Press, 1965.

Wertenbaker, Lael Tucker. *Death of a Man.* New York: Bantam Books, 1957.

Wilcox, Sandra Galdieri, and Marilyn Sutton. *Understanding Death and Dying.* Port Washington, N.Y.: Alfred Publishing, 1977.

Williams, Glanville. *The Sanctity of Life and the Criminal Law.* New York: Alfred A. Knopf, 1957.

Williams, Robert H. *To Live and to Die.* New York: Springer-Verlag, 1973.

Wilson, Jerry B. *Death by Decision.* Philadelphia: Westminster Press, 1975.

Wogaman, J. Philip. *A Christian Method of Moral Judgment.* Philadelphia: Westminster Press, 1975.

Woods, John H. *Engineered Death: Abortion, Suicide, Euthanasia and Senecide.* Ottawa, Can.: University of Ottawa Press, 1978.

Yezzi, Ronald. *Medical Ethics.* New York: Holt, Rinehart & Winston, 1980.

Articles

Alexander, L. "Medical Science under Dictatorship." *New England Journal of Medicine* 241 (1949): 39-47.

Beauchamp, Tom L., and Arnold I. Davidson. "The Definition of Euthanasia." *The Journal of Medicine and Philosophy* 4 (1979): 294-312.

Bernstein, Arthur. "Consent to Operate, to Live, or to Die." *Hospitals* 46 (1972): 124-28.

Biorck, Lunnar. "How Do You Want to Die?" *Archives of Internal Medicine* 132 (Oct. 1973): 605-6.

Boeyink, David. "Pain and Suffering." *Journal of Religious Ethics* 2 (Spring 1974): 85-98.

Bok, Sissela. "Personal Directions for Care at the End of Life." *New England Journal of Medicine* 295 (1976): 367-69.

Boorman, J. Arthur. "To Live or Not to Live: The Moral and Practical Case against Active Euthanasia." *Canadian Medical Association Journal,* 18 Aug. 1979, pp. 483-85.

Cahill, Lisa Sowle. "A 'Natural Law' Reconsideration of Euthanasia." *Linacre Quarterly* 44 (Feb. 1977): 47-63.

Cannon, William F. "The Right to Die." *Houston Law Review* 7 (1970): 654-70.

Cassem, Ned H. "Controversies Surrounding the Hopelessly Ill Patient." *Linacre Quarterly* 42 (May 1975): 89-98.

Cavanagh, John R. "Bene Mori: The Right of the Patient to Die with Dignity." *Linacre Quarterly* 30 (May 1963): 60-68.

Cranford, Ronald E., and Harmon L. Smith. "Some Critical Distinctions between Brain Death and the Persistent Vegetative State." *Ethics in Science and Medicine* 6 (1979): 199-209.

Culliton, B. J. "The Haemmerli Affair: Is Passive Euthanasia Murder?" *Science* 190 (1975): 1271-75.

Daube, David. "The Linguistics of Suicide." *Philosophy and Public Affairs* 1 (1971-72): 387-437.

Dawidowicz, Lucy. "Biomedical Ethics and the Shadow of Nazism." *Hastings Center Report* 6 (Aug. 1976), special supplement.

Devine, Philip E. "Homicide Revisited." *Philosophy* 55 (1980): 329-47.

Dickens, Bernard M. "The Right to a Natural Death." *McGill Law Journal* 26 (1981): 847-79.

Dorpat, Theodore, and John W. Boswell. "An Evaluation of Suicidal Intent in Suicide Attempts." *Comprehensive Psychiatry* 4 (Apr. 1963): 117-25.

Engelhardt, H. Trestram Jr., and Michele Mallory. "Suicide and Assisting Suicide: A Critique of Legal Sanctions." *Southwestern Law Journal* 36 (1982): 1003-37.

Evans, Andrew L., and Baruch Brody. "The Do-Not-Resuscitate Order in Teaching Hospitals." *Journal of the American Medical Association* 253 (1985): 2236-39.

Ewin, R. E. "What Is Wrong with Killing People?" *Philosophical Quarterly* 22 (1972): 126-39.

Exton-Smith, A. N. "Terminal Illness in the Aged." *Lancet*, 5 Aug. 1961, pp. 305-8.

Feldman, Walter S. "Passive Euthanasia Revisited." *Legal Aspects of Medical Practice* 11 (Mar. 1983): 6-7.

Fletcher, George. "Legal Aspects of the Decision Not to Prolong Life." *Journal of the American Medical Association* 203 (1968): 65-68.

———. "Prolonging Life." *Washington Law Review* 42 (1967): 999-1016.

Fletcher, Joseph. "Voluntary Euthanasia: The New Shape of Death." *Medical Counterpoint*, June 1970, p. 13.

Freeman, John. "Is There a Right to Die—Quickly?" *Journal of Pediatrics* 80 (1972): 905.

Frey, R. G. "Did Socrates Commit Suicide?" *Philosophy* 53 (1978): 106-8.

———. "Some Aspects to the Doctrine of Double Effect." *Canadian Journal of Philosophy* 5 (Oct. 1975): 259-83.

———. "Suicide and Self-Inflicted Death." *Philosophy* 56 (Apr. 1981): 193-202.

Fye, W. Bruce. "Active Euthanasia: An Historical Survey of Its Conceptual Origins and Introduction into Medical Thought." *Bulletin of the History of Medicine* 52 (1979): 492-502.

Geddes, L. "On the Intrinsic Wrongness of Killing Innocent People." *Analysis* 33 (1972): 93-97.

Goodrich, T. "The Morality of Killing." *Philosophy* 44 (1969): 127-39.

Gourevitch, Danielle. "Suicide among the Sick in Classical Antiquity." *Bulletin of the History of Medicine* 43 (1969): 501-18.

Graber, Glenn. "Some Questions about Double Effect." *Ethics in Science and Medicine* 6 (1979): 65-84.

Green, Michael B., and Daniel Wikler. "Brain Death and Personal Identity." *Philosophy and Public Affairs* 9 (1980): 105-33.

Green, O. H. "Killing and Letting Die." *American Philosophical Quarterly* 17 (July 1980): 195-204.

Grunman, Gerald J. "An Historical Introduction to Ideas about Voluntary Euthanasia." *Omega* 4 (1973): 87-138.

Habgood, J. S. "Euthanasia: A Christian View." *Royal Society of Health Journal* 94 (1974): 118-22.

Hare, R. M. "Euthanasia: A Christian View." *Philosophic Exchange* 2 (1975): 43-53.

Haslett, D. W. "Is Allowing Someone to Die the Same as Murder?" *Social Theory and Practice* 10 (Spring 1984): 81-95.

Higashi, K., et al. "Epidemiological Studies on Patients with a Persistent Vegetative State." *Journal of Neurology, Neurosurgery, and Psychiatry* 40 (1977): 876-85.

Higgs, Roger. "Cutting the Thread and Pulling the Wool—A Request for Euthanasia in General Practice." *Journal of Medical Ethics* 9 (1983): 45-49.

High, Dallas M. "Death: Its Conceptual Elusiveness." *Soundings* 55 (1972): 438-58.

Ingvor, David H., et al. "Survival after Severe Cerebral Anoxia with Destruction of the Cerebral Cortex: The Apallic Syndrome." *New York Academy of Science, Annals* 315 (1978): 184-214.

Ivy, A. C. "Nazi War Crimes of a Medical Nature." *The Journal of the American Medical Association* 139 (1949): 131-35.

Jamieson, Dale. "Utilitarianism and the Morality of Killing." *Philosophical Studies* 45 (1984): 209-21.

Jorgenson, David E., and Ron C. Neubecker. "Euthanasia: A

National Survey of Attitudes toward Voluntary Termination of Life." *Omega* 11 (1980-81): 282-91.

Kamisar, Yale. "Some Non-Religious Views against Proposed 'Mercy Killing Legislation.'" *Minnesota Law Review* 42 (May 1958): 969-1042.

Kamm, Frances Myrna. "Killing and Letting Die: Methodological and Substantive Issues." *Pacific Philosophical Quarterly* 64 (1983): 297-312.

Kary, Carla. "A Moral Distinction between Killing and Letting Die." *The Journal of Medicine and Philosophy* 5 (1980): 326-32.

Kass, Leon R. "Death as an Event: A Commentary on Robert Morrison." *Science* (1971): 698-702.

Kelly, G. "The Duty of Using Artificial Means of Preserving Life." *Theological Studies* 11 (1950): 203.

Kelman, Herbert C. "Violence without Moral Restraint: Reflections on the Dehumanization of Victims and Victimizers." *Journal of Social Issues* 29 (1973): 25-61.

Kennedy, Foster. "The Problems of Social Control of the Congenital Defective." *American Journal of Psychiatry* 99 (July 1942): 13-16.

Koessler, Maximilian. "Euthanasia in Hadamar Sanatorium and International Law." *Journal of Criminal Law, Criminology, and Political Science* 43 (1953): 735-55.

Kuhse, Helga, and Gerard Hughes. "Debate: Extraordinary Means and the Sanctity of Life." *Journal of Medical Ethics* 7 (1981): 74-82.

Kushner, Thomasine. "Having a Life versus Being Alive." *Journal of Medical Ethics* 1 (1984): 5-8.

Lachs, John. "Humane Treatment and the Treatment of Humans." *New England Journal of Medicine* 294 (1976): 837-40.

Lamb, David. "Diagnosing Death." *Philosophy and Public Affairs* 7 (1978): 144-53.

Lappe, Marc. "Dying While Living: A Critique of Allowing-to-Die Legislation." *Journal of Medical Ethics* 4 (1978): 195-99.

Lewin, Roger. "Is Your Brain Really Necessary?" *Science* 210 (1980): 1232-34.

Lewis, Gilbert. "The Place of Pain in Human Experience." *Journal of Medical Ethics* 4 (1978): 122-25.

Linehan, Elizabeth A. "Neo-Cortical Tests and Personal Death: A Reply to Robert Veatch." *Omega* 12 (1981-82): 329-37.

Lynn, Joanne, and James F. Childress. "Must Patients Always Be Given Food and Water?" *Hastings Center Report*, Oct. 1983, pp. 17-21.

McCartney, James J. "The Development of the Doctrine of Ordinary and Extraordinary Means of Preserving Life in Catholic Moral Theology before the Karen Quinlan Case." *Linacre Quarterly* 47 (Aug. 1980): 215-24.

McCaughey, J. Davis. "Suicide: Some Theological Considerations." *Theology* 70 (1967): 63-69.

McCormick, Richard A. "To Save or Let Die: The Dilemma of Modern Medicine." *Journal of the American Medical Association* 229 (1974): 172-76.

McKegney, F., and P. Lange. "The Decision to No Longer Live on Chronic Hemodialysis." *American Journal of Psychiatry* 128 (1971): 267-74.

Mannsson, Helge Hilding. "Justifying the Final Solution." *Omega* 3 (1972): 70-87.

Mead, Margaret. "The Right to Die." *Nursing Outlook* 16 (1968): 20-21.

Meilaender, Gilbert. "The Distinction between Killing and Allowing to Die." *Theological Studies* 37 (1976): 467-70.

Micetich, Kenneth; Patricia H. Steinbecker; and David C. Thomasma. "Are Intravenous Fluids Morally Required for a Dying Patient?" *Archives of Internal Medicine* 143 (May 1983): 975-78.

Morrison, Robert S. "Death: Process or Event?" *Science* 173 (1971): 694-98.

Murphy, Jeffrie. "The Killing of the Innocent." *The Monist* 54 (1973): 527-50.

Neale, Robert E. "Call Us Ishmael: Suicide in Contemporary Society." *Christianity and Crisis*, 27 Nov. 1972, pp. 260-63.

Newman, M. "Pulling the Plug." *Theoretical Medicine* 5 (1984): 141-46.

Bibliography

O'Neil, Richard. "Defining 'a Good Death.'" *International Journal of Applied Philosophy* 1 (1983): 9-18.

"Optimum Care for Hopelessly Ill Patients." *New England Journal of Medicine,* 12 Aug. 1976, pp. 362-64.

Pearlman, Robert A.; Thomas S. Inui; and William B. Carter. "Variability in Physician Bioethical Decision-Making: A Case Study of Euthanasia." *Annals of Internal Medicine* 97 (1982): 420-25.

Rabkin, Mitchell T.; Gerald Gillerman; and Nancy R. Rice. "Orders Not to Resuscitate." *New England Journal of Medicine,* 12 Aug. 1976, pp. 364-69.

Rachels, James. "Active and Passive Euthanasia." *New England Journal of Medicine,* 9 Jan. 1975, pp. 78-80.

Richards, Norvin. "Double Effect and Moral Character." *Mind* 93 (1984): 381-97.

Rosner, Fred. "Suicide in Biblical, Talmudic and Rabbinic Writings." *Tradition: A Journal of Orthodox Thought* 11 (1970): 25-40.

Rudikoff, Sonya. "The Problem of Euthanasia." *Commentary* 57 (1974): 62-68.

Schauer, Frederick. "Slippery Slopes." *Harvard Law Review* 99 (Dec. 1985): 361-83.

Siegler, Frederick. "Omissions." *Analysis* 28 (1968): 99-106.

Skillman, J. "Ethical Dilemmas in the Care of the Critically Ill." *Lancet* 7881 (1974): 634-37.

Strong, Carson. "Can Fluids and Electrolytes Be 'Extraordinary' Treatment?" *Journal of Medical Ethics* 7 (1981): 83-85.

Suckiel, Ellen Kappy. "Death and Benefit in the Permanently Unconscious Patient: A Justification." *Journal of Medicine and Philosophy* 3 (1978): 38-52.

"'Terminal Weaning': Discontinuance of Life-Support Therapy in the Terminally Ill Patient." *Critical Care Medicine* 11 (1983): 394-95.

Thomasma, David C. "The Comatose Patient, the Ontology of Death, and the Decision to Stop Treatment." *Theoretical Medicine* 5 (1984): 181-96.

Thomson, Judith Jarvis. "Killing, Letting Die, and the Trolley Problem." *The Monist* 59 (1975): 204-17.

Trammell, Richard L. "Euthanasia and the Law." *Journal of Social Philosophy* 9 (1978): 14-18.

———. "Saving and Taking Life." *Journal of Philosophy* 72 (1975): 131-37.

Twycross, Robert G. "The Assessment of Pain in Advanced Cancer." *Journal of Medical Ethics* 4 (1978): 112-16.

———. "The Use of Narcotic Analgesics in Terminal Illness." *Journal of Medical Ethics* 1 (1975): 10-17.

Van Der Horst, P. W. "A Pagan Platonist and a Christian Platonist on Suicide." *Vigiliae Christianae* 25 (1971): 282-88.

Van Till-D'Aulnis de Bourouill, Adrienne. "Diagnosis of Death in Comatose Patients under Resuscitation Treatment: A Critical Review of the Harvard Report." *American Journal of Law and Medicine* 2 (1976): 1-40.

Veatch, Robert M. "The Whole-Brain-Oriented Concept of Death: An Outmoded Philosophical Formulation." *Journal of Thanatology* 3 (1975): 13-30.

Vickery, K. O. "Euthanasia." *Royal Society of Health Journal* 94 (1974): 118-22.

Vlith, Ilza. "Reflection on the Medical History of Suicide." *Modern Medicine,* 11 Aug. 1969, pp. 116-21.

Walters, Orville S. "A Psychiatrist's Approach to Death." *Christian Medical Society Journal* 6 (Fall 1975): 4-6.

Walton, Douglas N. "Active and Passive Euthanasia." *Ethics* 86 (1976): 269-74.

———. "Death and Dying in Medicine: What Questions Are Still Worth Asking." *Theoretical Medicine* 5 (June 1984): 121-39.

Young, Robert. "Voluntary and Nonvoluntary Euthanasia." *Monist* 59 (1976): 264-83.

———. "What Is So Wrong with Killing People?" *Philosophy* 54 (Oct. 1979): 512-28.

Zerwech, Joyce V.; Judith R. Brown; and Marion B. Dolan. "The Dehydration Question." *Nursing '83,* Jan. 1983, pp. 47-51.

INDEX

243